MW01053525

ATLANTIS

About the Author

A student of magic and the occult for more than thirty years and the author of more than a dozen books on magical traditions, including the award-winning *New Encyclopedia of the Occult* (Llewellyn, 2003), John Michael Greer has earned a reputation as one of the most original writers in the occult field today. His background combines academic study in the history of ideas with training and initiation in several occult and Druid orders, including the Hermetic Order of the Golden Dawn and the Order of Bards, Ovates and Druids, and he currently serves as Grand Archdruid of the Ancient Order of Druids in America. He lives in the mountains of southern Oregon with his wife, Sara.

ATLANTIS

ANCIENT LEGACY, HIDDEN PROPHECY

JOHN MICHAEL GREER

Llewellyn Publications
Woodbury, Minnesota

First Edition
First Printing, 2007

Book design and layout by Joanna Willis
Cover design by Kevin R. Brown
Cover symbol image © John Michael Greer
Cover wave image © Digital Stock

Photo Credits:
Helena Blavatsky (page 42): Reproduced by permission of Quest Books, the imprint of the Theosophical Publishing House.
Aleister Crowley (page 60): © Ordo Templi Orientis, 2007. All rights reserved.
Dion Fortune (page 66): Permission and photos provided by the Society of the Inner Light.
Edgar Cayce (page 68): A.R.E.—Association for Research and Enlightenment, Inc.
Ignatius Donnelly (page 81): Minnesota Historical Society.
The island of Thera/Santorini (page 107): Index Open.
The devastation left behind by a tsunami (page 127): U.S. Geological Survey.
The Bimini Road (page 183): Drs. Lora & Greg Little.

The illustrations of Sundaland (page 104), Paleolithic writing (page 154), and Grand Bahama Bank during the last ice age (page 169) are by the author.
Illustration on page 203 by Llewellyn art department.

Llewellyn is a registered trademark of Llewellyn Worldwide, Ltd.

Library of Congress Cataloging-in-Publication Data
Greer, John Michael.
  Atlantis : ancient legacy, hidden prophecy / John Michael Greer. —1st ed.
    p. cm.
  Includes bibliographical references and index.
  ISBN 978-0-7387-0978-9
  1. Atlantis (Legendary place) I. Title.
  GN751.G74 2007
  001.94—dc22   2007023950

Llewellyn Worldwide does not participate in, endorse, or have any authority or responsibility concerning private business transactions between our authors and the public.
  All mail addressed to the author is forwarded but the publisher cannot, unless specifically instructed by the author, give out an address or phone number.
  Any Internet references contained in this work are current at publication time, but the publisher cannot guarantee that a specific location will continue to be maintained. Please refer to the publisher's website for links to authors' websites and other sources.

Llewellyn Publications
A Division of Llewellyn Worldwide, Ltd.
2143 Wooddale Drive, Dept. 978-0-7387-0978-9
Woodbury, MN 55125-2989, U.S.A.
www.llewellyn.com

Printed in the United States of America

Contents

The Myth of Progress

Every culture has some distant place in space or time where it parks its dreams of a perfect world, and ours is no exception. Devout Christians in the Middle Ages imagined a heaven somewhere off beyond the outermost sphere of the sky, where angels and blessed souls sang in perfect harmony in the presence of God, far from the discord of life in the lowly world of matter. Centuries before, the ancient Greeks sang of a Golden Age somewhere in the distant past when fields sprouted crops without human labor and the world was at peace under the rule of the wise old god Kronos. We have our heaven and our Golden Age too, but unlike most other cultures, we put ours in the future and tell ourselves that we're moving closer to Paradise with each day that passes. Other cultures put their faith in gods or stars or cosmic cycles; we put ours in progress.

It's not going too far to call progress the ruling myth of the modern world. For most people nowadays, the story of progress defines all of human history as a vast upward sweep from the brutal squalor of a primitive past to the Promethean splendor of a science-fiction future out among the stars. Even though human beings just like us have existed for hundreds of thousands of years, the story insists that only in the last five millennia have people begun to build

1

civilizations, and only in the last three centuries—since the dawn of the scientific revolution—have we gained any significant knowledge about the universe.

The intensity of our faith in progress can be measured by the way we play down the achievements of past peoples in order to make ourselves look better and smarter. For example, popular history books still insist that most of Columbus's contemporaries believed the world was flat, even though this fable has been disproved countless times.[1] No less a historian of ideas than Jeffrey Burton Russell demonstrated years ago that this claim is a nineteenth-century invention without a scrap of evidence to support it, and yet it remains fixed firmly in place in the popular imagination and still gets repeated in history books.[2]

The future is still more subject to distortion in the name of the myth. Most people today assume that the future will look like the present, only more refined, with ever more elaborate technologies extending the story of progress out to infinity. Even those people who believe that the story of progress will shortly come to an apocalyptic finale insist that our civilization's end will have brighter fireworks and louder explosions than any before it.

To use the word *myth* for our belief in progress, though, is to court misunderstanding, since most people today think that a myth is a story about the world that isn't true. Other cultures had myths, the modern claim goes, but we don't; we have facts. You can even find books insisting that the modern world suffers from "amythia," a pathological lack of myths.[3]

Our word *myth*, though, comes from *muthos*, a Greek word that originally just meant "story." Early on, it came to be used for the most important stories, the ones people tell to explain who they

1 For example, the *De Sphaera* of John of Sacrobosco—the standard textbook on astronomy for the equivalent of high school students in the Middle Ages—states that the earth is a sphere and provides several solid proofs for that claim. See Thorndyke 1949.

2 Russell 1991.

3 See, for example, Rue 1989, also my source for the word *amythia*.

are, where they come from, where they are going, and what powers guide them on their way and give the journey meaning. The Greek myths did this for the ancient Greeks, Christian theology did this for the Middle Ages, and faith in progress does it for us. The fact that a handful of countries have experienced progress in the last few centuries doesn't prevent progress from filling a mythic role. Far from it, the myth of progress—like all myths—only has power over the human mind because believers can point to examples where it has actually worked.

Every myth encodes its own values and its own agenda, and the myth of progress is no exception. Believers in progress treat historical periods as stages in a process that inevitably leads to us. When we say that hunter-gatherer tribes in the Third World are "still in the Stone Age" and that non-Western cultures are "in the Middle Ages" while modern industrial nations are the only ones that have actually reached the twenty-first century—as so many people do say—we are talking nonsense. The hunter-gatherers and the non-Western cultures are just as much a part of the twenty-first-century world as the industrial cultures are. This figure of speech reflects, though, the common belief that all human societies are headed where today's industrial societies have already arrived.

To believe in progress, in other words, is to believe that whatever trajectory our civilization happens to have followed is the right one, since it is clearly more progressive and therefore better than the paths taken by less progressive societies, and that for the same reason we ought to do even more of whatever we've been doing. Faith in progress thus provides powerful justifications for the status quo, whatever that happens to be, and allows any attempt to choose a different trajectory for our civilization to be dismissed as "going backward," since to believers in progress, this is the one unforgivable sin.

The myth of progress also implies that whatever modern civilization happens to be good at doing is the most important thing human beings can do, and whatever we aren't good at doesn't count.

This belief remains fixed in place even as the details change. In the nineteenth century, for example, many believers in progress pointed to the Western world's literature, philosophy, music, and art as evidence that it was more advanced and therefore better than anyone else. Twentieth-century literature, philosophy, music, and art all slipped well below nineteenth-century standards, but twentieth-century science and technology passed the previous century's mark, so inevitably people today point to our science and technology as proof that we are more advanced and therefore better than anyone else. Like most faiths, in other words, belief in progress chooses its own evidence and provides its own justifications.

Powerful and pervasive as the myth of progress is today, though, there's another story that murmurs through the crawlspaces of modern imagination, challenging our faith in progress at every turn. This second story whispers that progress is a temporary thing, for history moves in a circle, not in a straight line from the caves to the stars. It claims that somewhere in the distant past, another civilization—maybe as advanced as ours, maybe even *more* advanced than ours—collapsed and gave way to a long age of decline and darkness, from which humanity has only just recovered in our own time. It hints that our age may turn out to be not a stepping stone on the way to a glorious future, but rather a temporary summit from which all roads lead down. This alternative story takes many forms, but the oldest and most powerful center on a place out of legend, a drowned country called Atlantis.

The legend of Atlantis exercises a potent fascination on many people—so potent that it often gets in the way of clear thinking and common sense. Since 1882, when the first important modern book on the subject became an overnight bestseller, Atlantis has become the storm center of a hurricane of claims and counterclaims in which clouds of myth, legend, history, occult symbolism, speculation, outright fiction, and sheer delusion conceal far more than they reveal. Ask a question today about Atlantis—almost any question, to almost anyone—and you can expect to get a dozen different answers, few of them backed up by anything like solid evidence or clear reasoning, and half of them contradicting the other half in every detail. Even debunkers who try to disprove the Atlantis story routinely end up using the same kind of shaky logic and dubious evidence as the true believers.

In all this confusion, another book on Atlantis may seem like wasted effort, but there are aspects to the legend that have been neglected by all sides in the current debates. The story of Atlantis is not just about a civilization that may have existed around eleven thousand years ago, after all. It's also about our modern world's fascination with the past and the efforts of several different groups in the reality wars of the late nineteenth century to cast light on their own time by imagining the past in different ways. At the same time, it *is* a story about a civilization that may have existed at the end of the last ice age, when the world underwent profound and traumatic changes that may well be reflected in the Atlantis legend and many other old stories besides. Finally, for reasons discussed in this book's last chapter, it's a story that has at least as much to say about our future as the present and past.

I came to study the Atlantis legend in a roundabout way. When I began my studies of occult philosophy and practice back in the mid-1970s, I could hardly avoid hearing about Atlantis. Much of the traditional occult lore that I learned in those days referred to Atlantis constantly, and the popular occultism of the time—then making the transition from the fading counterculture of the sixties to the dawn of the New Age movement of the eighties—had even more to say about it. At that time, though, I could not have cared less about lost continents and ancient civilizations. Like so many young students of the occult, I wanted to learn the disciplines of magic, not speculate about vanished cultures and weigh alternative visions of history. Debates about whether an advanced civilization existed somewhere in the Atlantic basin thousands of years ago seemed completely irrelevant to me.

Years passed before I learned enough about the history of occultism and the broader cultural history of the Western world to guess at the reasons why the Atlantis legend had explosive relevance to the occultists of the 1870s and 1880s. Only then did I understand how actions taken by members of a handful of occult societies in those days redefined the human past in ways that still echo in popular culture and the collective imagination today, and why the legend remains just as important now as it was then. As I pursued those discoveries, this book became inevitable.

Readers who expect an ordinary book about Atlantis, therefore, may be in for a surprise. The possibility that an ancient civilization like the Atlantis of legend might actually have existed on land now flooded by the Atlantic Ocean provides one theme for the pages that follow, but not the only one. Another theme, at least as important, is where the Atlantis legend came from, how it developed, and how it has been used by various groups for their own purposes. The practices used by occultists to try to reach back through time and learn about Atlantis directly form a third theme of this book, and an appendix presents a complete set of instructions for those who want to try their hand at these practices themselves. Additionally, as I have suggested above, the Atlantis legend has a great deal of relevance to our own future, and this provides a fourth and final theme.

No author works in a vacuum, and this book, like all my projects, has relied at every turn on help provided by others. The staff at Rogue Valley Metaphysical Library, the Hannon Library of Southern Oregon University, and Ashland Public Library were unfailingly helpful in my quests for unlikely lore bearing on the Atlantis legend. Richard Brzustowicz Jr. and Mark Stavish provided valuable references and insights. The infectious enthusiasm of Elysia Gallo at Llewellyn Publications convinced me to set aside several other projects and bring this one to completion much sooner than I had anticipated. As with all my books, finally, this one could not have been written without encouragement, support, and sympathetic criticism from my wife, Sara. A hearty thanks goes out to all.

ONE
Plato's Riddle

Since ancient times, the legend of Atlantis, a great civilization drowned beneath the waves of the Atlantic Ocean, has gripped the human imagination, sparked debates among scholars and ordinary people alike, and inspired countless quests to find traces that would prove or disprove a reality behind the legend. Far from fading out with the passing years, the riddle of Atlantis has become a modern obsession, and in fact more books about Atlantis have been published in the past fifty years than in all of history before that time.

Unfortunately, most of this vast outpouring offers no help at all in the search for answers to the ancient riddle. There has probably been more nonsense written about Atlantis than about any other single subject anywhere. Those who argue for the historical reality of Atlantis as described in the original sources of the legend, those who have tried to link it to some other ancient civilization, and those who have dismissed it as empty myth have all contributed mightily to the fog of confusion and misinformation that surrounds the subject.

The reasons behind this go deep into the murky underpinnings of our modern culture. Like many other riddles of history and nature, Atlantis has been swept up in the running battle between scientific materialists, occultists, and proponents of other alternative visions of reality. In the process, a simple historical question—was there a civilization somewhere in the Atlantic basin that flourished and then drowned in the tenth millennium BCE?[1]—has been turned into a battleground for struggles over cultural politics that have nothing to do with Atlantis at all.

These issues can't be avoided, if only because the claims and counterclaims surrounding the Atlantis legend relate to much larger issues: the nature of history, the reality of spiritual experience, and the meaning of the modern myth of progress, to name just a few. Still, to make sense of Atlantis on its own terms, it's best to start with the oldest and most definitive version of the legend itself.

The Philosopher's Tale

This earliest account of the Atlantis story appears in two philosophical dialogues written by one of the greatest minds in human history: Aristocles of Athens, better known by his boyhood nickname, Plato. Born in the cosmopolitan city of Athens in 428 BCE, he wrestled in the Olympic Games in his youth but became a philosopher and teacher under the guidance of his mentor, Socrates. After Socrates's execution by the Athenian government, Plato traveled to Sicily and Egypt, then returned to found a school in Athens called the Academy. There, before his death in 348 BCE, he created the most influential system of philosophy in the history of the Western world. Most of his surviving writings are quasi-fictional dialogues that pit his old teacher Socrates and an assortment of learned friends against most of the big questions of human existence.

The Atlantis legend appears in two of these dialogues, the *Timaeus* and the unfinished *Critias*. Both are among Plato's very last works, written near the end of a long and eventful life, and Socrates plays only a small role in them. In both dialogues, the material on

---

1 BCE stands for "before the Common Era" and is the secular equivalent of the religious dating system's BC, "before Christ." The secular equivalent of AD ("*Anno Domini*," "year of the Lord") is CE, "Common Era."

Atlantis is put in the mouth of Critias, one of the characters, but Plato has several other characters agree that the story is true, "not a mere legend but an actual fact";[2] Critias claims that he heard the story of Atlantis from his grandfather, also named Critias, who heard it from the great Athenian statesman and lawgiver Solon.

The *Timaeus* sets the story by explaining how Solon traveled to Sais, the capital of the last independent dynasty of ancient Egypt, and spoke with an old priest there. The priest laughed at Solon's ideas of history and told him that the Greek legends commemorated only one of many catastrophes that devastated the earth in past times:

> There have been, and will be again, many destructions of mankind arising out of many causes; the greatest have been brought about by the agencies of fire and water, and other lesser ones by innumerable other causes. There is a story that even you have preserved, that once upon a time, Phaethon, the son of [the sun god] Helios, having yoked the steeds in his father's chariot, because he was not able to drive them in the path of his father, burned up all that was upon the earth, and was himself destroyed by a thunderbolt. Now this has the form of a myth, but really signifies a declination of the bodies moving in the heavens around the earth, and a great conflagration of things upon the earth which recurs after long intervals. [. . .] Just when you and other nations are beginning to be provided with letters and other requisites of civilized life, after the usual interval, the stream from heaven, like a pestilence, comes pouring down and leaves only those of you who are destitute of letters and education, and so you have to begin again like children, and know nothing of what happened in ancient times, either among us [the Egyptians] or among yourselves.[3]

---

2 Plato *Timaeus* 22c. All passages from Plato's works cited here are from Jowett 1892.

3 Plato *Timaeus* 22c and 23b.

The priest went on to tell Solon that the Athenians were descended from the survivors of an earlier Athens, which was founded nine thousand years before Solon's time and destroyed in earthquakes and floods some years later. In the interval, this ancient Athens fought a war with another nation—the empire of Atlantis. This is what the priest had to say:

Many great and wonderful deeds are recorded of your state [Athens] in our histories. But one of them exceeds all the rest in greatness and valor. For these histories tell of a mighty power which unprovoked made an expedition against the whole of Europe and Asia, and to which your city put an end. This power came forth out of the Atlantic Ocean, for in those days the Atlantic was navigable, and there was an island situated in front of the straits which are by you called the Pillars of Heracles [the Strait of Gibraltar]. This island was larger than Libya [that is, North Africa] and Asia [that is, Asia Minor, modern Turkey] put together, and was the way to other islands, and from these you might pass to the whole of the opposite continent which surrounded the true ocean, for this sea which is within the Pillars of Heracles [the Mediterranean Sea] is only a harbor, having a narrow entrance, but that other is a real sea, and the land surrounding it on every side may be most truly called a boundless continent.

Now in this island of Atlantis there was a great and wonderful empire which had rule over the whole island and several others, and over parts of the continent, and furthermore, the men of Atlantis had subjected the parts of Libya within the Pillars of Heracles as far as Egypt, and of Europe as far as Tyrrhenia [northern Italy]. This vast power, gathered into one, endeavored to subdue at a blow our country and yours and the whole of the region within the straits, and then, Solon, your country shone forth, in the excellence of her virtue and strength, among all mankind. She was pre-eminent in courage and military skill, and was the leader of the Hellenes

[Greeks]. And when the rest fell off from her, being compelled to stand alone, after having undergone the very extremity of danger, she defeated and triumphed over the invaders, and preserved from slavery those who were not yet subjugated, and generously liberated all the rest of us who dwell within the Pillars. But afterward there occurred violent earthquakes and floods, and in a single day and night of misfortune all your warlike men in a body sank into the earth, and the island of Atlantis in like manner disappeared in the depths of the sea. For which reason the sea in those parts is impassable and impenetrable, because there is a shoal of mud in the way, and this was caused by the subsidence of the island.[4]

Plato's Atlantis

In the *Timaeus*, the story of Atlantis just given is a small part of a much more complex work that deals with the creation and nature of the universe. After finishing that dialogue, Plato started a sequel, the *Critias*, that put Atlantis at center stage. According to the *Critias*, the gods and goddesses divided up the world in early times, each one taking a country, and Poseidon, god of the sea, took the island of Atlantis as his share. There he mated with a mortal woman named Cleito and fathered five pairs of twin brothers, who became the ten kings of Atlantis.

The place where Poseidon bedded Cleito was a hill near the middle of an oblong plain some 340 miles long and 230 miles wide. Around the plain, Plato says, was a line of mountains, and just beyond the mountains lay the sea, so the entire island could not have been a great deal larger than the dimensions just given. Wild animals, notably elephants, flourished on the island. Fertile soil that yielded two harvests a year and lavish mineral resources, including an unknown metal called orichalcum (which translates to "mountain copper" in Greek), made its inhabitants fabulously wealthy. On

---

4 Plato *Timaeus* 24d–25d.

the basis of this wealth, they built a huge capital city, dug a rectangular gridwork of canals across the island's central plain, and created another canal for shipping that connected the capital's natural moats with the sea.

After recounting the military arrangements of the country and the laws and customs of the ten kings, Plato has Critias explain how Atlantis came to make war on the nations of the Mediterranean basin. For many generations, the Atlanteans were content with their own great wealth, but as the divine blood of Poseidon began to run thin, they became greedy for more wealth and hungry for power. Zeus, the king of the gods, saw this and decided to teach the Atlanteans a lesson. He called the other gods into council and said . . .

There the dialogue ends. No one knows why Plato never finished it.

Critias mentions the important detail that the war between Atlantis and Athens broke out nine thousand years before he told his story to Socrates and his friends. Some scholars claim that this contradicts the *Timaeus* account,[5] which puts the founding of ancient Athens nine thousand years before the priest's conversation with Solon, but they haven't paid enough attention to the details of the text. According to the *Timaeus*, Solon (who lived between 639 and 559 BCE) was a contemporary of Critias's great-grandfather, and the conversation in which Critias told his story took place when Socrates (who lived between 470 and 399 BCE) was an adult. The war with Atlantis thus took place between one and two centuries after the founding of ancient Athens.

The bits of information in these two dialogues make up everything Plato has to say about Atlantis, and they present a picture that differs sharply from most of what has been said in modern books on the subject. To start with, Plato calls Atlantis an island, not a continent, and places it in the Atlantic ocean in front of the Strait of Gibraltar (the Greek phrase is *pro Hêrakleis stêlas*, and *pro*

---

5 For instance, Settegast 1990, 17.

can mean "in front of," "before," or "outside"). Beyond it lay other islands, and beyond those, within easy reach of Atlantis itself, lay a continent on the far side of the Atlantic Ocean. If Plato's words have anything close to their literal meaning, this description puts Atlantis in the western Atlantic not far from North America, and reasonably close to 36° north, the latitude of Gibraltar.

The accounts differ sharply in their reports of the size of the island of Atlantis. The detailed account in the *Critias* gives it very modest dimensions, a few hundred miles in any direction at most. Both dialogues, however, also say that it was "larger than Libya and Asia [Minor] put together," or well over ten times the *Critias* measurement. One of these measurements has to be wrong, but it's impossible to tell which one from Plato's testimony alone.

The island of Atlantis had fertile soil and mineral resources, including a metal unfamiliar to Plato or his sources, and it supported elephants as well as other wild animals. The society that emerged there was a large city-state, with a central city surrounded by an agricultural hinterland, and an empire of subject kingdoms surrounding it. Its architecture and technology were those of Plato's Athens on a bigger scale. Its navy consisted of triremes, the standard warship of ancient Greece, and its army used much the same equipment and organization as an ancient Greek army.

At its peak, the Atlantean empire included the island of Atlantis itself, several other islands, parts of the nearby mainland to the west, and the western parts of southern Europe and North Africa. Sometime around 9400 BCE, the Atlanteans tried to expand into the eastern Mediterranean as well, but like many empires since that time, they overstretched their strength, and their army was defeated by a force from Athens. At some point after this defeat, finally, Atlantis sank suddenly beneath the ocean, and ancient Athens was devastated by floods and earthquakes.

What isn't part of Plato's account is in many ways more interesting than what appears in the dialogues. The crystals, airships, pyramids, and space-age technologies that feature so often in modern accounts of Atlantis are nowhere to be found. Plato's Atlantis is a city-state about as technologically advanced as the Greek city-states of Plato's own time, or a little less so: the Atlantean army used chariots, for example, which had been discarded by civilized armies centuries before Plato's time. The mysterious metal orichalcum is the only thing even slightly unusual about Atlantean technology.

Nothing in this account, it especially bears noting, is impossible. Some of it, as we'll see in later chapters, contradicts certain widely accepted ideas about prehistory, but if those ideas turn out to be false, a few social forms and technological discoveries would simply be dated earlier than they are now; the history of the world would not have to be completely rewritten.

Fact or Fiction?

Plato frequently used fables and stories in his dialogues as a way of getting complicated points across to his readers, and many writers who have tried to debunk the Atlantis legend have argued that the narratives in the *Timaeus* and the *Critias* are simply two more of these stories. There is even a bit of historical fact that might have provided Plato with the seed for his conception of Atlantis. The Greek historian Thucydides, who lived in the generation before Plato, described in his history of the Peloponnesian War how an earthquake and a tsunami destroyed part of an Athenian fort on an island in the Gulf of Corinth near Locris. The name of the island, curiously enough, was Atalante.[6]

The problem with this claim is that Plato consistently labeled his fables and speculations as such, drawing a distinction between them and matters of fact. When the discussion in the *Timaeus* turns from Atlantis to the creation of the world, for instance, the character Timaeus of Locris admits that his account—which takes up most of the dialogue—is simply a speculation, as likely as any other

---

6 The Thucydides quotation is cited in Childress 1996, 147.

account.[7] In the same way, in his dialogue *Phaedo*, Socrates prefaces a strange account of the shape of the world with a cheerful admission that he believes it to be true but does not claim to be able to prove it.[8]

This is not what Plato says about Atlantis, though. Instead, he states three times in the *Timaeus* alone that the story Solon heard from the Egyptian priest is true, "not a mere legend but an actual fact."[9] This is the only place anywhere in Plato's dialogues that he puts this much emphasis on the factual nature of one of his stories. This doesn't guarantee the truth of his account of Atlantis, of course, but it does suggest that he wanted to make sure that his story was not dismissed as "a mere legend."

The question of the story's original source is a vexed one and has been much debated by scholars on all sides of the Atlantis dispute. Plato's dialogues combined fiction and fact; some of the characters were actual people, while others were fictional creations, and the events that surround the dialogues are drawn partly from history and partly from Plato's imagination. The chain of transmission from the Egyptian priest to Solon, from Solon to Critias's grandfather, and from him to Critias may thus be fact, fiction, or a combination of the two.

Some circumstantial evidence supports this aspect of Plato's story. Ancient historians agreed that Solon did in fact travel to the city of Sais in Egypt, as many Greek notables did during his time. Sais was the capital of Egypt during Solon's lifetime, and the pharaohs of the Saite dynasty, the last independent ancient Egyptian ruling house, had a military alliance and important trade connections with the Greek city-states.[10] As for Critias, he was a real person, a gifted historian and poet who also played a part in Athenian politics.

---

7 *Timaeus* 29d.

8 *Phaedo* 108d.

9 *Timaeus* 21a6.

10 The *Timaeus* mentions Amasis (Ahmes-sa-Neith, reigned 570–526 BCE), the next to last pharaoh of the Saite dynasty, but—despite statements made in the

On the other hand, the story may have reached Plato via another route. The philosopher had close connections with Orphic and Pythagorean mystical circles in Sicily and southern Italy, and these circles drew heavily on spiritual and philosophical teachings that came from Egypt.[11] Plato himself visited Egypt during his years of traveling after the execution of his teacher Socrates, so he could certainly have obtained an Egyptian story about a lost civilization from sources other than Solon—even from priests at Sais, which still remained a center of Egyptian religion in Plato's time. Ultimately, we simply don't know where Plato's story comes from.

Plato's contemporaries, and generations of Greek and Roman scholars after his time, disagreed about the reality of Atlantis. Plato's student and rival Aristotle dismissed the story as a work of fiction, but then Aristotle rejected nearly everything his erstwhile teacher taught him. Another of Plato's students, Crantor, treated the Atlantis story as historical fact. Crantor wrote commentaries on each of Plato's dialogues; these did not survive the fall of the Roman Empire, but Proclus—a philosopher of the fourth century CE who had access to Crantor's commentaries—states that Crantor himself went to Sais, asked the priests about Solon's story, and was shown a pillar carved with hieroglyphics that, according to the priests, told of the sinking of Atlantis.[12]

Later authors disagreed just as sharply about the Atlantis story. The Stoic philosopher Posidonius, one of the most brilliant minds of his time, accepted Atlantis as a historical reality, and included it in a book he wrote about earthquakes, as an example of land swallowed by the sea. Posidonius's student Strabo, the greatest of Greek geographers, cites Aristotle and Posidonius and makes a comment suggesting he agrees with the latter. Pliny the Elder, the Roman sci-

---

debunking literature—does not say that this pharaoh was on the throne during Solon's visit. Compare *Timaeus* 21d and de Camp 1970, 5.

11 Kingsley 1989 gives details of the Egyptian connections of these movements.

12 The debates about Atlantis in the ancient world summarized in this and following paragraphs are discussed in de Camp 1970, 10–20, and Ramage 1978b, 20–27.

entist, and Plutarch, the Greek essayist, both suspended judgment, while the Roman historians Marcellus and Ammianus Marcellinus both treated Atlantis as a real place that had suffered the fate described by Plato.

Among the Neoplatonists, the last major school of Pagan philosophers to flourish before the long night of the Dark Ages rolled in, the reality of Atlantis was a point wide open to debate. Neoplatonism developed out of Plato's own philosophy in the third century CE as a school of mystical philosophers who sought to bring spirituality and reason into harmony with each other. Masters of symbolism and esoteric tradition, the Neoplatonists recognized that some of Plato's stories were meant symbolically while others were meant as literal fact, but some prominent Neoplatonists assigned Atlantis to one category, and some to the other. Syrianus, Proclus's teacher, and Iamblichus of Chalcis saw it as history, while Porphyry and Origen considered it an allegory in which Athens represents the powers of virtue while Atlantis stands for the influences of moral decay.

Another leading Neoplatonist, Amelius, argued that the Athens of Plato's story stood for the realm of the stars, while Atlantis represented the realm of the seven planets of ancient Greek astrology, the powers of time and fate. Behind his theory lies a vast body of traditional lore that played a potent role in shaping the legend of Atlantis and traced the outlines of the lost continent among the stars.

The Great Wheel of Time

When people in today's rejected-knowledge movement draw connections between the stars and the Atlantis myth, most of the time they are talking about alien beings from other worlds. This has come to play such a large role in some currents of modern speculation about Atlantis that it can be easy to forget that ancient peoples saw the universe in a very different way. To Amelius and his fellow Greeks, the planets that moved through the night sky were not worlds inhabited by intelligent beings; they *were* intelligent beings.

Even today, we call the planets by the names of gods: Mercury, Venus, Mars, and so on. In ancient times, this was not just a habit of speech. Across the Old World and in at least some parts of the New, religious traditions identified the sun, the moon, and the five visible planets as divine beings who watched over the world. The stars that formed the unchanging backdrop to the dance of the planets were gods as well, less concerned with earthly affairs but still potent in their own realms. Atheists were few and far between at a time when anybody could see the gods by looking up into the night sky. The great religious debates of the time focused instead on whether the gods cared for human beings and whether the gods had any freedom of choice or simply obeyed the inflexible laws of time and fate.

A great deal of ancient mythology, in turn, was actually astronomy and astrology—the two were a single science then, and for many centuries afterward—expressed in memorable images. We know this because the ancient writers themselves said so. After discussing the fate of Atlantis, Plato's *Timaeus* turns to a narrative of the creation of the universe in which the stars are the first generation of gods and the planets the second. Aristotle, whose writings preserved a great deal of ancient lore that might otherwise have perished in the fall of the ancient world, stated as a well-known fact that the planets were gods.[13] The same observation forms a commonplace in dozens of other ancient writers.

The roots of this ancient belief reach back far beyond Greece to Mesopotamia, "the land between the rivers" in what is now Iraq, where some of the world's first known urban cultures—Sumer, Akkad, Babylon, and Assyria—flourished more than three thousand years before Plato was born. There, along the banks of the Tigris and Euphrates rivers, traditions of starlore and divination like those found everywhere else on earth evolved into the world's oldest known system of astrology. From the tops of massive mud-brick

---

13 De Santillana and von Dechend 1977, 4.

pyramids, Mesopotamian astronomer-priests tracked the moving lights of heaven and compared their motions to events on earth.

Thousands of their clay tablet records survived the ages and were excavated by archaeologists in the nineteenth and twentieth centuries. The following passage from a tablet found at Nineveh in the library of the great Assyrian king Ashurbanipal is typical: "When a halo surrounds Sin [the moon], and Nergal [Mars] stands within it, a king will die and his land be diminished; the king of Elam will die."[14] Phrased in the language of prophecy, recent scholarship has pointed out, this was also a historical record: on one occasion, a king of Elam, the country to the east of Mesopotamia, died shortly after a conjunction between the moon and Mars was sighted through a lunar halo, and so this combination of events could be expected to occur again. To the astronomer-priests, data from the past was the key to understanding the future, since all things moved in cycles governed by the turning heavens.

The largest of those cycles was marked out by precession, the slow wobble of the earth's axis that moves the sun's position at the equinoxes and solstices slowly backward through the sky, at a rate traditionally measured as one degree every seventy-two years. (Some ancient writers argued for different estimates, and in fact the actual speed of precession is still debated by astronomers.) Most modern historians of science insist that precession was first discovered by the Greek astronomer Hipparchus in the late second century BCE, but this is simply another distortion imposed on the past by the modern belief in progress. As documented in Giorgio de Santillana and Hertha von Dechend's profound and neglected book *Hamlet's Mill*, precession—like other cycles of the starry heavens—had a central role in the starlore of civilizations far older than the Greece of Hipparchus's time. The astronomer-priests of Mesopotamia in particular, as they pored over their centuries-old records of events in the sky, could hardly have missed it.

---

14 Thompson 1900, 107; see also Campion 1994.

The Great Months	
Aquarius	1880–4040 CE
Pisces	280 BCE–1880 CE
Aries	2440–280 BCE
Taurus	4600–2440 BCE
Gemini	6760–4600 BCE
Cancer	8920–6760 BCE
Leo	11,080–8920 BCE

At a rate of one degree every 72 years, it takes 25,920 years to bring the equinoxes and solstices back around to the same position relative to the stars. This interval was called a Great Year, and ancient astronomers divided it into twelve Great Months, named after the twelve main constellations along the sun's path: Aries, Taurus, Gemini, and the other signs of the zodiac. (It's important to remember that while precession moves through these familiar signs, it reverses their usual order—going from Pisces back into Aquarius, for example, rather than from Aquarius to Pisces.) When the sun's position at the spring equinox precessed from one sign into another every 2,160 years, a new Great Month began. Contemporary talk about the Age of Aquarius comes straight out of this millennia-old tradition.

In *Hamlet's Mill*, de Santillana and von Dechend show that several key themes in ancient mythology refer to precession, thereby using the memorable images of myth to encode what were, by the standards of the time, profound religious teachings. On this basis, they argued that ancient myths of catastrophic fire and flood actually refer to precession: one set of coordinates in the heavens was symbolized by fire, another by water, and as the sun's positions at the solstices and equinoxes shifted, the world was symbolically "burned" or "drowned."

This is a possible interpretation, of course, but the ancient sources on astronomical myth apparently had something different in mind. The Egyptian priest in the *Timaeus* spoke for an ancient consensus when he told Solon there had been "many destructions of mankind . . . brought about by the agencies of fire and water"—real destructions, not symbolic ones. De Santillana and von Dechend apparently did not consider the possibility that over long periods of time, astronomy offers one of the very few effective ways of locating important events in time. Civilizations and calendars come and go, but if tradition records that an event happened at a certain point in the cycle of precession or at the time of some other astronomical event, its date can be worked out even thousands of years after the fact.

The priest in the *Timaeus* showed no signs of doubt about the reality of the catastrophes he described, and he spoke of them as something distinct from the cycles of the heavens. His words are worth repeating: "[The story of Phaethon] has the form of a myth, but really signifies a declination of the bodies moving in the heavens around the earth, and a great conflagration of things upon the earth which recurs after long intervals."[15] Whether the celestial cycles cause the earthly catastrophe is a good question that can't be clearly answered from the priest's comment. Still, one way or the other, movements of the heavens provide the one sure way of tracking the "long intervals" between catastrophes.

Berossus, a Babylonian priest who lived in the early third century BCE, provides a clear account of this same concept. One of the last inheritors of the old Mesopotamian starlore, Berossus wrote a book in Greek, the *Babyloniaca*, outlining the history and wisdom of his people for the Greek rulers of Mesopotamia in the aftermath of Alexander the Great's conquests. His book was lost during the fall of the Roman Empire, but the Roman author Seneca quoted Berossus's words about the cycles of time in a book that still survives. According to Seneca, Berossus taught that when a conjunction of all the planets occurred in the constellation of Cancer, the world was ravaged by fire, and when a similar conjunction occurred in Capricorn, the world was swept by a great flood.[16]

---

15 *Timaeus* 22c–d.
16 Campion 1994, 61–67.

If Seneca reported it correctly—and of course this is anyone's guess, since the original did not survive—Berossus's account of the old starlore, with its focus on planetary conjunctions, took a different tack than the teachings about precession chronicled by de Santillana and von Dechend. Still, the reference to Cancer yields an important clue. Berossus was anything but alone in suggesting that at a certain point in the cycles of time, an earthly catastrophe caused by fire ravaged the world. Many other classical sources, starting with Solon's conversation with the priest in the *Timaeus*, stated the same thing. But Berossus is among the few who give a date for it, and he and the others associate it with the sign of Cancer.

The teaching that the world was fated to undergo destruction at regular intervals set by the stars became widespread in the ancient world after Berossus's time. As it spread, it helped feed a belief that the planet-gods cared nothing for human beings or their sufferings, but simply imposed a harsh fate on the world below. This was the belief that lay behind Amelius's theory that Atlantis was the realm of the planets while the ancient Athens was the realm of the stars. In this symbolic way of thinking, Atlantis represented the power of fate in human life, forcing itself on the individual in the way that Atlantean armies tried to force their domination on the world in Plato's tale. Athens represented the freedom of the human spirit, which had its origin in the timeless world of the stars and was the only force strong enough to overcome fate.

To many people in the last few centuries of the ancient world, the promise of freedom at the core of the human spirit was not enough as they watched their civilization crumbling around them. Many became convinced that the planet-gods were actually hostile to the human race. Many of the Gnostics, a diverse religious movement that started around the beginning of the Common Era, argued that the planet-gods were evil powers who trapped human souls in bodies of matter and kept them from returning to their true home in the world of light among the stars. They believed that knowledge— in Greek, *gnosis*—would allow them to climb through the planetary spheres and escape the world of matter forever. The Neoplatonists argued fiercely against the Gnostic movement and its world-hating tendencies, but with little result. The Gnostics were in tune with their times, and over the next few centuries, most of their ideas were absorbed into the rising faith of Christianity.

After the Neoplatonists, only one ancient writer had anything to say about Atlantis. This was Cosmas Indicopleustes, a merchant turned Christian monk of the sixth century CE who provided the early Christian church with a geography stretched and trimmed to fit the worldview of the Bible. A modern fable, part of the mythology of progress, claims that everyone before Columbus believed that the earth was flat. As mentioned in the foreword, this isn't even remotely true. It takes about fifteen minutes of research to find out that every educated person in ancient Greece and Rome and medieval Europe knew perfectly well that the world was round, but the fable persists, and Cosmas is one of the reasons why. He was the exception to the rule. In his book *Christian Topography*, he claimed that the world was flat because the Bible said it had four corners, and he argued that the Atlantis legend was simply a garbled retelling of events from the Book of Genesis, especially Noah's flood.

By the time Cosmas wrote this, the lights were going out all across the Western world, and after his time no one discussed Atlantis for many centuries. As classical civilization collapsed under the weight of its own unsolved problems, the suggestion that another civilization might also have crashed into oblivion nine thousand years before must have seemed academic at best. The Dark Ages had arrived, and nearly a thousand years passed before the riddle of Atlantis once again caught the curiosity of scholars and explorers.

A World of Flood Legends

One of the traditions that Cosmas and his fellow believers passed on to the future, of course, has been linked to the Atlantis story over and over again by writers ever since. This is the story of Noah's ark, which appears in the ninth chapter of the Book of Genesis in the Bible. From Cosmas's time right up to the present, practically every legend or scrap of geological evidence that could possibly be related to large-scale flooding has been seized on by that subset of Christians who are obsessed with the idea that the Bible must be literally true in every detail. For obvious reasons, the more unlikely incidents from the Bible got the lion's share of attention from the Christian literalists, and the story of Noah and the ark—which claims, among other improbable things, that so much rain fell from the sky that every mountain on the earth was under water, and that two representatives of every species of land animal on the planet somehow fit into a boat 450 feet long, 75 feet wide, and 45 feet high—inevitably took center stage.

The story of Noah, as it turns out, is a copy of an older Babylonian legend in which the survivor of the flood was named Utnapishtim, and this latter was copied from an even older Sumerian myth in which the survivor was named Ziusudra. The role played by Jehovah in the Biblical story belonged earlier to Ea, the Babylonian god of the sea. There's reason to think that a real if more localized flood lies behind the legend, for archaeological digs at a number of the cities of southern Mesopotamia have found layers of flood-deposited silt up to ten feet thick that date from the fourth millennium BCE.[17]

But the story of Ziusudra in its various guises is only one of hundreds of flood legends from around the world. Another very famous example comes from Greek mythology, and here Deucalion and his wife, Pyrrha, were the protagonists. Deucalion, who was the son of the titan Prometheus, received a timely warning from his father that Zeus meant to destroy all humanity for its wickedness by means of a flood. He and Pyrrha prepared a wooden chest and stocked it with nine days' worth of food and water. When the flood came, they drifted safely to shore on the slopes of Mount Parnassus. This flood was considered to be historical fact by nearly

---

17 Vitaliano 1973, 154.

all the ancient Greek scholars, including the arch-skeptic Aristotle, and chronologies from ancient times dated it to around 1430 BCE.

Europe has its share of non-Biblical flood stories, and how many others were absorbed by the Biblical story during the spread of Christianity is anyone's guess. The Celtic countries are particularly rich in them. Welsh mythology includes a tale in which a water monster, the Afanc, caused the lake of Llion to flood its banks and drown the whole island of Britain until the divine hero Hu the Mighty and his even mightier oxen, the Two Calves of the Speckled Cow, dragged the Afanc from the depths. The Irish *Leabhar Gabhala* (*Book of Invasions*), a traditional history lightly overlaid with bits of Bible imagery, describes a series of floods from the sea that annihilated several of the earliest races to settle Ireland.

Another branch of Celtic flood legends detail a set of remarkably precise claims about specific tracts of land overrun by the rising sea in historical times. The city of Ys off the present-day coast of Brittany, the duchy of Lyonesse beneath the waters west of Cornwall, and several cantrefs (provinces) of Wales now under the Irish Sea all belong here, and according to the accounts, all were drowned during the sixth century CE. Calling these accounts "legends" begs a number of points, because solid evidence points to drastic changes in sea level in exactly these areas within the relatively recent past. This evidence is as close as the ancient standing stones and burial mounds of Brittany, many of which—well above the water's edge when they were built—now rise from the surf or can only be seen at all at low tide.[18]

Asia has fewer flood legends, though some of the ones that do exist have dramatic evidence backing them. The city of Dwarka in Gujarat, on the west coast of India, is a fine example. Dwarka, or Dvaraka, as it was once called, was the sacred city of Krishna, one of the incarnations of the great Hindu god Vishnu. According to the *Vishnu Purana*, an important sacred text, the sea rose up the day that Krishna died and drowned the entire city.

---

18 See Burl 1985 for descriptions of several such sites.

It is still there, about a kilometer offshore from the present-day city of Dwarka: a sprawling underwater ruin built of massive stone blocks. It has been examined many times by Indian archaeologists, who currently date it to sometime before 1500 BCE.[19] Traditional Hindu chronologies date it instead to 3100 BCE, the beginning of the Kali Yuga—the last and worst age of the world in Hindu tradition, in which we now live. Not far away, in the Gulf of Cambay, two more underwater cities were found in 2002, making international headlines.

Elsewhere along the coasts of India, especially along the southeast coast facing the Bay of Bengal, references to lost cities are also common in tradition, and their remains are equally common in the shallow waters offshore. The Tamil peoples of southern India recall a great land named Kumari Nadu or Kumarikkandam that once extended well into the Indian Ocean, a rich and thickly populated land. Ancient Tamil writings speak of such lost cities as Kavatapuram, the great port of Pukar, and Old Maturai, where an ancient academy founded much of classical Tamil culture.[20] Chronicles from Sri Lanka, the island off the tip of the Indian subcontinent, record similar drastic floods that swallowed entire cities in the distant past.

The Pacific Islands have a wealth of accounts of islands drowned by vast waves—not surprising in a part of the world where volcanoes are common and big tsunamis are far from rare. A classic example comes from Raiatea, in the Society Islands. A fisherman from that island one day strayed into waters sacred to the sea god Ruahatu. When he cast his line, the hook caught in Ruahatu's hair, and after a long struggle, the fisherman found that he had pulled to the surface not a fish but a very angry god, who declared that he would avenge the insult by destroying the island. The fisherman threw himself down and begged for mercy, and the god told him to go with his family to the little islet of Taomorama to the east of

---

19 The sunken city of Dvaraka is documented in Rao 1999.
20 See Ramaswamy 2004.

Raiatea. The next day, the waters rose up and swept over Raiatea, drowning all its inhabitants except the fisherman and his family, who waited out the flood on Taomorama and then returned to become the progenitors of today's Raiateans.[21]

The world's greatest concentration of flood stories, though, is found in the Americas. Hardly a Native American people whose legends survive at all is without one. The following account from the Duwamish people of the northwest coast of Puget Sound is typical. It happened that Sparrow was married to a woman whose relatives despised and insulted him. Five times he asked them not to do so, and when they did anyway, he went down to the shore of the sound and dipped his beak into the water. When he had done this the fifth time—five is the sacred number of the Duwamish—the waters of Puget Sound began to rise, and they kept rising until all of the land was covered.

Most of the animal people were drowned, but a few managed to stay afloat in a canoe. To keep from drifting into the open ocean, they tied the canoe to the top of Storm King Mountain, a peak in the Olympic range west of the sound, but the top of the mountain broke off and they drifted for many days over featureless water. Finally, the animals decided to dive to the bottom of the sea to bring up some mud and make a new world. Each of them tried, but only Muskrat was able to reach the bottom and return with a pawful of mud. The animals cast this on the waters and sang, and it turned into the land of the Duwamish people.[22]

This colorful story contains more than meets the eye. The breaking off of the top of Storm King Mountain was a real event. It took place near the end of the last ice age, around thirteen thousand years ago. Around that same time, the ice sheet that dug out the Puget Sound basin retreated far enough to allow the ocean in through the Straits of Juan de Fuca, causing a catastrophic flood. Other native tribes from the Puget Sound region have legends of a similar flood,

---

21 Vitaliano 1973, 166–67.

22 Several versions of this story are collected in Ballard 1999.

and the possibility exists that in this case, oral tradition preserves details of an event more than five hundred generations in the past.

Other aspects of the story are harder to read but may contain messages of their own. Does the odd story about Sparrow and his relatives conceal a reference to astronomy, with Sparrow a constellation that "dipped his beak in the water" when the precession of the equinoxes moved its "beak" below the western horizon at sunrise or sunset at a significant date? No one knows enough about the Duwamish people's traditional astronomy nowadays to be sure.

What stands out most strikingly about all these stories, however, is that there is no reason to think they are all talking about the same flood. The rising waters that claimed Cantref Gwaelod, one of the "lost cantrefs" of Wales that drowned in the sixth century, had nothing to do with the filling of Puget Sound in 11,000 BCE, and neither of them has any necessary connection to the flood that Zuisudra/Utnapishtim/Noah may have survived in his ark sometime before 3000 BCE—or the drowning of Atlantis around 9600 BCE. The habit of assuming that all flood legends must be about the same worldwide flood seems to have been started by Cosmas and his fellow Christians, but for some reason it was also adopted enthusiastically into Atlantis studies in the nineteenth century and has played an important role there ever since.

The local reality behind the Duwamish flood legend is a good reminder, though, that this habit misleads. As Dorothy Vitaliano points out in her useful volume *Legends of the Earth* (1973), "The universality of flood traditions can be explained very easily without requiring a widespread flood of cosmic or any other origin, if we bear in mind that *floods, plural, are a universal geological phenomenon.*"[23] Nearly every part of the world, in other words, has suffered catastrophic flooding at one time or another, so it is hardly surprising that legends of catastrophic floods are common around the globe. As we'll see in a later chapter, the time Plato gave for the sinking of Atlantis falls squarely within a period when floods on

---

23 Vitaliano 1973, 144; emphasis in original.

a gargantuan scale swept much of the planet, but there were also floods before then and many afterward. The notion that every flood mentioned in the world's legends must refer to one and the same event has to be set aside if any sense is to be made out of the Atlantis legend.

Antarctica, Antilia, and America

During the Dark Ages, Noah's flood was the only one that mattered to most Europeans, but as scholarship began to revive in the early Middle Ages, a handful of scholars found references to Atlantis in old books and brought Plato's narrative back out of oblivion. The French monk Honorius of Autun, who lived around 1100 CE, included a brief note about Atlantis in his widely read encyclopedia *De Imagine Mundi* (*On the Image of the World*), and a few other authors of the Middle Ages did much the same. Still, at a time when most people never traveled out of sight of the village of their birth and many people in France firmly believed that Englishmen were born with tails, the story of Atlantis was just one more wonder added to the countless mysteries of the world and so attracted little attention.

Nearly everything known about geography in those days came from ancient books. Some of this information was quite accurate—much more so than today's popular culture realizes or today's scientists are willing to admit. Medieval books on astronomy repeated classical Greek proofs that the earth was round, much smaller than the sun, and very, very far away from the nearest stars.[24] Books on geography talked about India, China, and Africa and explained that on the far side of the tropics lay another, southern temperate zone and a frozen realm of ice and snow surrounding the South Pole.

These books also spoke of large islands and a continent on the far side of the Atlantic Ocean as well as another continent at the southern end of the world. These scraps of accurate geographical knowledge have come in for quite a bit of manhandling from defenders of

---

24 The *De Sphaera* of John of Sacrobosco, the standard school textbook of astronomy in the later Middle Ages, includes all these. See Thorndyke 1949.

the myth of progress. One debunker insisted that ancient and medieval geographers stocked the world with additional continents out of a passion for "artistic symmetry"—an interesting claim he neglected to back up with even a single scrap of evidence.[25] Still, some such assumption is the only alternative to admitting that people long before the most recent age of exploration knew quite a bit more about the shape of the earth and its continents than modern theories permit. As far back as the second century BCE, the Greek scientist Crates of Mallos taught that the world contained three more continents besides Europe, Asia, and Africa. If Australia is classed as a large island—as it was for many years after its most recent discovery—he was right, too.

The fact that land existed on the far side of the Atlantic Ocean was actually common knowledge many centuries before Columbus set sail. The classical Greek writer Plutarch, whose works were read throughout the Middle Ages, explained in one of his essays that five days sailing west from the shores of Britain lay a large island where night lasted only for an hour at midsummer. Another five hundred miles farther west, across a sea often blocked with ice, lay a large continent and many islands, some of them wrapped in endless summer. This is not a bad description of the sea route from Britain to Iceland, Greenland, and the North American coast, and Plutarch makes matters much worse for conventional historians by claiming that every thirty years the ancient Britons sailed across to the land on the far side of the ocean.[26]

This was not simply Plutarch's invention, either. Irish and British legends make very similar claims. Irish stories tell of Tír na nÓg, "the land of youth," on the far side of the Atlantic, while old British stories make similar claims about the Summer Country and the island of Avalon across the sea. While most modern writers dismiss all these legends as empty tales, the islands of the Caribbean fit the legends of "islands wrapped in endless summer" very well indeed.

---

25 See de Camp 1970, 26.

26 Ashe 1990, 119–20 and 261–66, provides details of these legends.

Canadian writer Farley Mowat has argued on good evidence that the pre-Celtic inhabitants of Scotland made Atlantic crossings, following the same route Plutarch seems to be describing, and mingled with the Native American peoples of Newfoundland.[27] The Irish saint Brendan may well have made the same voyage,[28] and the Norse certainly did so; the Norse colony in Greenland, a narrow strait away from Canada, survived for more than three centuries in the Middle Ages before climate change finally pushed it over the edge into extinction.[29]

By the late Middle Ages, to make matters worse, some of the world's "unknown" continents were shown on maps with a fair degree of accuracy. More than a dozen maps from the early sixteenth century, for example, show Antarctica, which was not officially discovered until the late eighteenth century and not effectively mapped until the end of the nineteenth.[30] Many of these old maps put it in the right place and give it the right shape, too. Most of them show Antarctica larger than it actually is, to be sure, but getting the dimensions of landmasses right was a constant problem for mapmakers in those days. The same maps often get the size of Scotland completely wrong, for example, but this hardly proves that Scotland got added to the maps out of a passion for artistic symmetry.

The degree of accuracy of these old maps has been overstated by some enthusiastic modern writers. They contain plenty of inaccuracies, and no two of them give exactly the same data. On the whole, though, their portrayal of lands supposedly unknown at the time they were made is as good as their portrayal of Europe and the Mediterranean countries. One very awkward detail, though, is that several of the maps that portray Antarctica show it as it was

27 Mowat 1998.

28 Severin 2000.

29 Diamond 2005, ch. 5, has a good summary of the rise and fall of the Greenland colony.

30 These maps are reproduced and discussed in Hapgood 1969.

before its coasts were covered with ice.[31] According to recent studies, much of the Antarctic coast was ice-free from around 14,000 BCE, when the West Antarctic Ice Sheet collapsed, until around 6000 BCE, when it finished reestablishing itself—but that is still far too long ago to fit within current ideas of history.

Nobody today knows where the information in these maps came from. Geographer Charles Hapgood, one of the few scholars to investigate them, suggested in his *Maps of the Ancient Sea Kings* (1969) that they came from libraries looted when Constantinople fell to the Turks in 1453.[32] The dates are approximately right, and other ancient documents that can be traced to Constantinople are known to have surfaced around the same time, but Hapgood's suggestion remains unproven. Another set of maps full of improbable details, the astonishingly accurate "portolan" sea charts of the Mediterranean and nearby waters, were in circulation well before the sack of Constantinople, and nobody knows where they came from, either.

One of the things that appears frequently on these maps, and other maps from the fourteenth, fifteenth, sixteenth, and seventeenth centuries, is a large rectangular island in the western Atlantic in a place where no island exists today. Its name was Antilia, a word that has been interpreted as garbled Latin for "the opposite island" ("opposite" the Strait of Gibraltar, like Atlantis), and it ended up giving its name to the Antilles, the chain of islands east of the Caribbean Sea that includes Cuba and Santo Domingo.

Antilia first surfaced in a 1367 map, where it was spelled "Atilae" and located close to the Azores, which, according to modern historians, hadn't been discovered yet at that time. In later maps, the island moved farther west. Details varied, but most of the time it was shown as a rectangle of land in the ocean somewhere west of Spain. It was a constant feature on maps for a century or more before the most recent discovery of the New World, and in 1474, when Columbus was still a lone crackpot trying to find a sponsor

---

31 Ibid.
32 Ibid.

for his proposed voyage westward, the astronomer Toscanelli wrote him to suggest that Antilia would make a good place to stop and restock provisions on the way to the Indies.[33]

A number of Renaissance geographers identified Antilia with Atlantis, which is by no means an impossibility, since the shape of Antilia fits Plato's description of the rectangular central plain surrounded by mountains, and even the names are similar. Another scholar of the period, the brilliant polymath Athanasius Kircher, treated Plato's narrative as a matter of plain history and put Atlantis in the central Atlantic halfway between Spain and America. Still, the mainstream opinion after 1492 placed Atlantis the rest of the way across the Atlantic Ocean, in the New World itself.

This theory first appeared in the writings of the poet Girolamo Fracastoro in 1630, and it found a scholarly audience after the Spanish scholar Francesco López de Gómara put it into his *General History of the Indies* (1553), one of the first significant accounts of the Americas to circulate in Europe. Like most of the learned writers of the Renaissance, López de Gómara liked to make connections between his subject and classical Greek and Latin literature, and so Plato's comment in the *Timaeus* about a continent on the far side of the Atlantic was grist for his mill. He made the eminently sensible suggestion that Atlantis was either located in the Americas, if Plato's story was accurate historically, or based on rumors about the continents of the New World, if it was a romantic fiction.

In its heyday, the Atlantis-in-America theory came in several varieties. The most widely accepted version was repeated by English author John Swan in his 1644 textbook of geography, *Speculum Mundi*: "This I think may be supposed, that America was sometime [i.e., at one time] part of that great land which Plato calleth the Atlantick island, and that the Kings of that island had some intercourse between the people of Europe and Africa. . . . Yet that such an island was, and was swallowed by an earthquake, I am verily perswaded; and if America joyned not to the west part of it,

---

33 De Camp 1970, 22–23.

yet surely it could not be farre distant."[34] To Swan and the many other writers who agreed with him, in other words, Atlantis was either part of the North American continent or an island not far east of its shores, which was flooded in a geological catastrophe.

This quite reasonable theory was accepted by serious scholars up to the middle of the nineteenth century. The Comte de Buffon, one of the great naturalists of the eighteenth century, considered it a hypothesis worth exploring, as did the respected nineteenth-century German scientists Jakob Krüger and Alexander von Humboldt. Only with the hardening of scientific orthodoxies in the second half of the nineteenth century was the entire subject of Atlantis ruled off limits to investigation.

As the Spanish gathered more information about the Native American cultures they had destroyed, the Atlantis-in-America theory gained more support. Sixteenth-century savants soon discovered that the Aztecs, rulers of Mexico until the Spanish invasion, traced their origin back to a place called Aztlan, "the place of reeds," which was somewhere across water to the northeast of the Valley of Mexico. For that matter, the Aztec capital Tenochtitlán, surrounded by the waters of Lake Texcoco and divided by canals, seemed to many European scholars to have more than a passing resemblance to the capital of Atlantis as described by Plato.

Nor did it escape the attention of European scholars that Native American traditions included teachings about ages of the world that each ended in catastrophe, very like the lore recorded by Berossus. In versions of the story from Mexico and the Yucatán, four world ages, called "Suns," preceded the present one. Each Sun took its name from the catastrophe that marked its end. The first, the Ocelot Sun, ended when its people were devoured by wild animals; the second, the Wind Sun, ended in a titanic windstorm; the third, the Fire Sun, ended in a rain of fire; the fourth, the Water Sun, ended in a colossal flood; and the fifth, the Movement Sun, in

---

34 Ramsay 1972, 94–97.

which we now live, will end in a great earthquake.[35] The end of the Water Sun sounded enough like the fall of Atlantis to help make the idea that Atlantis had been in or near America plausible.

Not until long after the conquest of the Americas did European scholars realize that the same precessional cycle that governed so many Old World mythologies lay behind these traditions as well. The decipherment of the Mayan calendar was the key. Many centuries in the past, Mayan astronomers calculated the length of the Great Year as 25,625 years—a little different from the Old World figure, but close enough to be within observational error—and divided it into five great ages of 5,125 years each. The current age, equivalent to the Movement Sun of Aztec lore, began in 3113 BCE and will end in 2012 CE. This latter date, at least, has entered into popular culture and become the focus of a flurry of apocalyptic speculations.

Few of those who look forward to 2012 with hope or fear, though, have counted the Mayan calendar cycles back into the past and noticed that the age before ours, equivalent to the Aztec Water Sun, began in 8238 BCE. On that date, the age equivalent to the Fire Sun ended in flames—and 8238 BCE falls in what the precessional lore of the Old World called the Great Month of Cancer, where tradition places the destruction of the world by fire.

Atlantis in Renaissance Occultism

In the sixteenth century, long before any of the Mayan calendar lore surfaced, the connection between Atlantis and America found two influential defenders, one in France and the other in Britain. Their names were Guillaume Postel and John Dee, and both men proposed—Postel in 1561, Dee in 1580—that North America should be named Atlantis after Plato's lost civilization. Their proposal marks the first major contact between Atlantis and the occult traditions of the Western world.

---

35 Waters 1975 presents an evocative account of the Aztec calendar.

So much confusion has been spread about occultism over the last two thousand years, mostly by people who know nothing about it, that a few words of explanation probably need saying here. The word *occult* comes from the Latin term *occultus*, "hidden"; it has nothing to do with the word *cult*. During the late Middle Ages, people who studied the hidden powers of nature and the human mind via traditional crafts such as magic, alchemy, and divination used Latin phrases like *philosophia occulta* ("hidden philosophy") and *scientia occulta* ("hidden science") for their studies. During the Renaissance, the word found its way from this Latin source into most European languages, including English.

Though there has been quite a bit of confusion on this point over the years, occultism is neither a religion nor a science. Rather, it is a system of philosophy and practice that enables people to open up the hidden dimensions of the human mind and work with the subtle linkages between human consciousness and the world around us. All the ornate hardware of occultism—symbols, candles, incense, colored robes and altar cloths, wands, words of power, tarot cards, and the rest of it—are simply tools occultists use to focus hidden aspects of the mind. The goal of occultism is *adeptship*, a state of higher consciousness like that of the enlightened mystics of the Orient. An adept, according to occult tradition, has achieved perfect self-knowledge and can use all the secret powers of the self at will.

Despite the stereotype, these powers aren't "supernatural," and in fact, most occultists deny that anything supernatural exists at all. According to occult teaching, the effects of magic, divination, alchemy, and other occult arts are entirely natural, and they seem supernatural to us only because we don't know as much as we think we do about the laws of nature. No serious occultist claims to be able to shoot lightning bolts from the end of a wooden wand, like the characters in the Harry Potter books, and most occultists today teach that "turning lead into gold" by way of alchemy is a code for subtler forms of transmutation in the mind and spirit. As the old alchemists themselves said, "Our gold is not the common gold."

Guillaume Postel and John Dee were both occultists; in fact, both men were leading figures in the great Renaissance revival of occultism. Postel was a profound scholar of the Qabala, the system of Jewish mystical philosophy then being adopted by mystics and wizards across Europe, and he made the first translation of the *Zohar*, the most influential Qabalistic book of the Middle Ages, into a Western language. For his part, Dee was not only an expert Qabalist but a practicing sorcerer and alchemist, the creator of the Enochian system of magic, and the court astrologer to England's Queen Elizabeth I. Both men lived during the Golden Age of Renaissance occultism, a time when for a few giddy decades it looked as though occult philosophy might establish itself alongside Christian orthodoxy and the newborn movement of scientific materialism as one of the main currents of intellectual culture in the Western world.

Their interest in Atlantis is all the more curious because very few of their fellow occultists cared about the legend at all. Renaissance occultists had no use for the sort of speculative history that many people confuse with occult teachings today. When the occultists of Postel's and Dee's generations talked of lost civilizations, they meant ancient Greece and Egypt, and while their ideas about these cultures seem a little odd by modern standards, those ideas were shared by every educated person in the Renaissance.

Occultists and their opponents disagreed heartily about the value of Greek pagan philosophy and Egyptian magic, to be sure. The pamphlet presses, which served the same social role that web pages and blogs do today, kept busy all through the seventeenth century turning out defenses and denunciations of occultism. Still, all sides in these debates shared a common view of the nature of the world and the shape of human history. The occult teachings of the Renaissance focused on methods of doing things rather than speculative ideas about history and reality, and the debates around occultism centered on whether occult methods were valid ways of perceiving and shaping the world, as the occultists believed, or occultism was nothing more than fraud, delusion, and devil worship, as their opponents insisted.

To most occultists of the sixteenth and seventeenth centuries, then, the tale of Atlantis was just one more passage in Plato. That gave it some relevance to occultism, since Plato's philosophy was a major source of inspiration to the Renaissance occult movement, but most of the occultists who paid attention to it were more interested in mining it for sacred geometry and magical number theory than in speculating about the possible existence of an ancient civilization beneath the waters of the Atlantic. In an age when the shock waves from the discovery of the New World were still echoing throughout European culture, Atlantis just didn't seem that important.

Later occultists would have much more to say about Atlantis, but Postel and Dee were more than two centuries ahead of their time. After them, despite occasional discussions of the Atlantis-in-America theory in scholarly circles, nobody said anything new about Plato's legend for well over two hundred years. It took two of the most colorful figures of the late nineteenth century—an enigmatic Russian occultist and a freewheeling Irish-American politician—to transform Atlantis from a half-forgotten legend to a cultural theme of immense power in today's world.

TWO

The Occult Atlantis

The mythology of progress makes many people think that the present age must be more scientific than any other. If ever a time deserved to be called the Age of Science, though, it was the nineteenth century. Just before that century began, the Montgolfier brothers' triumphant flights in the world's first hot-air balloon and Benjamin Franklin's epochal experiments with electricity launched a tidal wave of scientific and technological breakthroughs that transformed the world. By the middle of the century, telegraph lines and railroads spread over continents and carried news of one astonishing discovery after another to the far corners of the world. In 1859, Charles Darwin's *The Origin of Species* introduced the theory of evolution, breaking the grip of the Bible on the Western world's vision of human history. In its place, the theories of scientific materialism hardened into dogmas just as rigid as the religious creeds they replaced.

Yet the same cultural transformations that launched the Age of Science also allowed occultism to emerge from the twilight realm of secret magical lodges and become, for the first time since the Renaissance, a major social force. In an age of discovery when no truth seemed permanent, the possibility that scientific research might overthrow the materialist doctrines of science itself seemed impossible to rule out. In 1848, eleven years before Darwin's book saw print, the birth of the Spiritualist movement offered the hope that life after death might become a subject of objective research rather than sectarian dogma. In the wake of Spiritualism, older occult traditions came out of hiding and began to challenge the scientific worldview in public.

The occult reaction to the Age of Science was a part of its own time, though, and made use of the same dreams and images as the materialist science it opposed. Many of those dreams and images took shape in a new branch of literature that put science and technology at center stage: science fiction. Some of the greatest works of science fiction ever penned saw print in the late nineteenth century, and of the science-fiction writers of that time, none was more popular than the brilliant French novelist Jules Verne (1828–1905).

One of Verne's greatest bestsellers, *Twenty Thousand Leagues Under the Sea* (1870), featured the *Nautilus*, a submarine powered by atomic energy that pursued a secret crusade beneath the oceans of the world. Somewhere in the depths of the Atlantic, the *Nautilus's* mysterious Captain Nemo took the novel's protagonist, Professor Pierre Arronax, on an excursion in diving suits across the bottom of the sea, where he pointed out an unexpected sight:

> There, indeed, under my eyes, ruined, destroyed, lay a town— its roofs open to the sky, its temples fallen, its arches dislocated, its columns lying on the ground, from which one could still recognize the massive character of Tuscan architecture. Further on, some remains of a gigantic aqueduct; here the high base of an Acropolis, with the floating outline of a Parthenon; there traces of a quay, as if an ancient port had formerly abutted on the borders of the ocean, and disappeared with its merchant vessels and its war-galleys. Further on again, long lines of sunken walls and broad deserted streets—a perfect Pompeii escaped beneath the waters. Such was the sight that Captain Nemo brought before my eyes!

Where was I? Where was I? I must know, at any cost. I tried to speak, but Captain Nemo stopped me by a gesture, and picking up a piece of chalk stone, advanced to a rock of black basalt, and traced the one word—

ATLANTIS.[1]

As he so often did, Verne had his finger on the pulse of the future. In the same decade that *Twenty Thousand Leagues Under the Sea* first saw print, Atlantis surfaced as a powerful new image in the imagination of the Western world. Its emergence began, curiously enough, with the arrival of a middle-aged Russian woman on a New York City pier.

The Advent of Theosophy

In July of 1873, Helena Petrovna Blavatsky disembarked from a steamship in New York Harbor, one of countless immigrants from the Old World to pass through America's busiest port. She rented cheap rooms in a modest New York neighborhood and struggled to find work as a journalist, supporting herself as a seamstress on occasion. Within a few years of her arrival, though, this unlikely revolutionary set the world on fire with a new version of ancient occult traditions—and in the process launched Atlantis back into the collective imagination of the Western world.

Blavatsky was born in 1831 in Ekaterinoslav, in what was then the Russian Empire, to an aristocratic German-Russian family.[2] Occultism was a constant presence in her childhood; her maternal great-grandfather Prince Paul Dolgorouki was a high initiate of an important occult secret society, the Rite of Strict Observance, and the young Helena Hahn spent many hours studying occult traditions in the old wizard's library. At the age of nineteen, her father married her off to an elderly Russian nobleman, Nikifor Blavatsky,

---

1 Verne 1925, 276–77.

2 I have relied for Blavatsky's biography on Godwin 1994, Johnson 1994, and Webb 1974.

Helena Blavatsky

but Helena, a headstrong and spirited young woman, found the marriage intolerable and ran away after a few months.

The next quarter century of her life left few traces, and she did her best to hide most of those later on. According to some accounts, early on in her travels she worked for a time as a bareback rider in a European circus, had a love affair with a Hungarian opera singer named Mitrovich, and bore him a child who died in infancy. These experiences and many others taught her the relevance of the occult traditions she first encountered in her childhood, and launched her on a quest for the secret wisdom her great-grandfather had studied. She became an initiate of an occult secret society—the Brotherhood of Luxor,[3] a magical order active in the European expatriate community of Cairo, Egypt—and plunged into the hidden realms of existence with the passionate energy that marked every stage of her life. By the time she came to America, she was an accomplished

---

3 Confusingly, this was not the same as the Hermetic Brotherhood of Luxor, an occult order of the 1880s. Many magical lodges of the nineteenth century shared similar names, a point that continues to mislead historians. See Godwin 1994, 278–83.

occultist with an encyclopedic knowledge of occult philosophy and practice.

As she struggled to make a living as a freelance journalist in New York, Spiritualism gave her an obvious topic for articles. In 1874, pursuing a potential story, Blavatsky visited the Vermont farm of the Eddy family, then famous figures in the American Spiritualist circuit. There she met Colonel Henry Steele Olcott, a psychic researcher. The two quickly became close, to the extent of sharing an apartment, and Blavatsky began to pass on some of the Brotherhood of Luxor's teachings to Olcott.

By the following year, they decided to attempt to create a public teaching organization to communicate occult wisdom to the wider world. One of Blavatsky's occult associates, the high-ranking Freemason and Rosicrucian Charles Sotheran, suggested the word *theosophy* (literally "divine wisdom," from the Greek words *theos*, "god," and *sophia*, "wisdom") as a label for the new organization.[4] Olcott and Blavatsky liked the term, and their newly founded Theosophical Society had its first meeting on September 7, 1875, in their apartment, where another of Blavatsky's occult associates, George Felt, gave a lecture on ancient Egyptian sacred geometry.

Public organizations passing on occult teachings are so common nowadays that it's easy to forget just how much astonishment the Theosophical Society caused when it first came into being. Nothing of the sort had existed in the Western world for well over fifteen hundred years. The traditions of Western occultism had been passed on in secret since the bitter years of the Middle Ages, when people suspected of occult study and practice risked death at the Inquisition's hands, and in Blavatsky's time, people who wanted to learn them still had to pass stringent examinations and take an oath of secrecy before receiving even the most basic occult teachings. In India, China, and other ancient cultures around the world, similar rules guarded mystical, magical, and spiritual traditions. The idea of sharing occult knowledge in public was nearly unthinkable.

---

4 Godwin 1994, 283–84.

Yet the Theosophical Society set out from the beginning to put the unthinkable into practice. The notion of a public occult organization was so radical that Blavatsky and Olcott themselves had no real idea how to run one. For a while in 1875 and 1876, they even used the standard security methods of occult lodges—passwords, secret handshakes, and the rest—before finally discarding them. After several such false starts, the society found a successful niche running a program of lectures and public education, and Blavatsky went to work on a much more ambitious project: a book that would present the basic ideas of occultism to the public and defend these ideas against orthodox science and religion.

The two hefty volumes of *Isis Unveiled* appeared in 1877 and won immediate acclaim from the occult community and the general reading public alike. In its more than 1,300 pages, Blavatsky leveled an all-out assault on the accepted doctrines of her age. Her goal was to demonstrate that occult philosophy offered a valid alternative to materialist science and Biblical religion. The myth of progress came in for some of her heaviest fire. She argued that occult tradition *"divided the interminable periods of human existence on this planet into cycles, during each of which mankind gradually reached the culminating point of highest civilization and gradually relapsed into abject barbarism."*[5]

Central to her project was a strategy of pointing out gaps in scientific and religious worldviews and then showing how occult teachings filled them in. Atlantis provided the raw material for one of the most important of these gaps. Blavatsky argued that theories of history promoted by scientific historians simply didn't make sense of the evidence. In 1877, most historians held that prehistoric humans had been brutal, ignorant savages until the first literate societies suddenly came into being around 3000 BCE, and nobody had any solid evidence to show a transition from one state to the other. Blavatsky's suggestion was that earlier civilizations thrived on a land that had since vanished beneath the waters: the lost con-

---

5 Blavatsky 1972, vol. 1, 5; italics in original.

tinent of Atlantis. Her comments on the subject cover fewer than a dozen pages and draw heavily from the Atlantis-in-America writers of previous centuries, but several crucial new ideas surface for the first time in this discussion—above all else, the theory that what destroyed Atlantis was a war between two parties of occult initiates, one good, the other evil.[6]

In *Isis Unveiled*, though, Atlantis shared space with another lost continent named Lemuria. While some of today's New Age writers have backdated traditions about Lemuria to ancient times, it was quite a modern idea in Blavatsky's era, and it had its roots in what was then cutting-edge science, not occult tradition. Like most occultists, then and now, Blavatsky had a lively interest in the sciences, and the genesis of Lemuria shows the eclectic roots of the traditions she put into circulation under the banner of occultism.

In the early 1860s, biologists faced major problems trying to make sense of the distribution of lemurs, a type of primate now found only on the island of Madagascar off the east coast of Africa. At that time, lemur fossils had been discovered in southern Africa and southern India, but nowhere else in the world. Several writers suggested that a land bridge might once have connected these two parts of the world, spanning most of the Indian Ocean. In an 1864 article in the *Quarterly Journal of Science*, British zoologist Philip Lutley Sclater gave the land bridge the name of Lemuria, after the primates who had inspired it.[7]

At the time, this was an entirely reasonable theory. Land bridges were an important part of geology back when the modern theory of continental drift had not yet been proposed, much less accepted. Paleontologists could easily show that animals and plants had somehow crossed from the Old World to the New and vice versa; most argued for a Bering Strait land bridge, the most widely accepted theory now, while a minority proposed land bridges over the Atlantic. Given the state of geological knowledge in Sclater's time (and

6 Ibid., 592–93.

7 I have relied on Ramaswamy 2004 for the history of the concept of Lemuria.

Blavatsky's), a land bridge across the western Indian Ocean was as plausible a theory as any of these.

In 1870, not long after Sclater had given Lemuria its name, the popular German science writer Ernst Häckel proposed that the sunken land bridge might have been the place where the first human beings evolved from apes. His logic was straightforward and, in terms of the scientific knowledge of the time, compelling. Lemuria linked the two parts of the world, Africa and southern Asia, where great apes had survived into modern times. It therefore would have been a likely home for other species of apes, possibly including those from which human beings evolved. In Häckel's time, the "missing link" between apes and humans was still very much missing, and the hypothesis of a Lemurian origin offered a plausible explanation: the bones of the "missing link" were at the bottom of the Indian Ocean.

All this was grist for Blavatsky's mill. Sclater's paper and Häckel's hypothesis proved, at least by the standards of the time, that the Atlantis legend could not be dismissed out of hand. Still, her task in *Isis Unveiled* was to challenge old orthodoxies, not to set up new ones in their place, and so her comments on Lemuria moved nimbly from one suggestion to another. At one point, she hinted that Atlantis and Lemuria might have been the same place, but she also moved Lemuria well over a thousand miles east from its original position in the western Indian Ocean, querying whether "[t]he great lost continent might have, perhaps, been situated south of Asia, extending from India to Tasmania?"[8] This curious shift, as we'll see, echoes an unexpected detail of prehistory.

The Secret Doctrine

The years following the publication of *Isis Unveiled* saw Blavatsky rise to the zenith of her career, as the Theosophical Society became the most influential occult organization in the Western world. Bla-

8 Blavatsky 1972, vol. 1, 591.

vatsky and Olcott moved the organization's headquarters from New York to Adyar, a neighborhood of Chennai (Madras), India, in 1879. After a major scandal there in 1884—Blavatsky's housekeeper accused her, possibly with good reason, of faking supernatural happenings using stage magic—Blavatsky relocated to London, reorganized the Theosophical Society to bring it under her personal authority, and began work on an occult manifesto even more gargantuan than *Isis Unveiled*.

That book, *The Secret Doctrine*, was published in 1888. Readers who expected another work like *Isis Unveiled* were in for a surprise. Where the earlier book focused on undercutting accepted ideas in science and religion, *The Secret Doctrine* presented a complete alternative worldview that stood nearly all the assumptions of Victorian science and religion on their heads. Its pages mapped out a vast cosmic history in which souls and worlds alike pass through immense cycles of time and space, moving up the rungs of a cosmic hierarchy that soared far beyond the human level; our own world, the fourth globe of the fourth round of this corner of the cosmos, has been inhabited by five Root-Races so far, with two still to go before the souls of its present inhabitants move off to a new set of experiences on the planet Jupiter.

Lost continents play a major role in the intricate speculative history of *The Secret Doctrine*. Each of the Root-Races before ours evolved on a continent no longer on the map. The Polarian Root-Race, the first, inhabited a land not quite physical, the Imperishable Sacred Land, which still exists above the North Pole but cannot be perceived by present-day humanity. The second, third, and fourth Root-Races, however, emerged on continents that have now vanished beneath the sea. The second Root-Race inhabited the polar continent of Hyperborea—literally "the land beyond the north wind," a place from ancient Greek legend that Blavatsky adapted to her own purposes. The third emerged on Lemuria, while the fourth was born on Atlantis. The homeland of the present or fifth Root-Race in Central Asia is still above water, but *The Secret Doctrine* hints that it, too, will sink beneath the oceans when the sixth Root-Race emerges sometime in the future.

As the homeland of the fourth of the seven Root-Races, Atlantis took center stage in *The Secret Doctrine*, taking up more pages than any other part of Blavatsky's elaborate cosmology.[9] According to Blavatsky, the people of Atlantis traced their descent from the Lemurians, who had been egg-laying hermaphrodites with four arms each. The Atlantean Root-Race was the first fully human race, though they were giants by modern standards. Blavatsky's Atlanteans inhabited a huge continent located where the Atlantic Ocean is now, and many of them—including the ruling caste of the lost continent—belonged to the "red race" (that is, they were related to today's Native Americans).

Three of the central themes of Blavatsky's Atlantis are of special importance to our theme. None of them are found in Plato's narrative, but all three went on to become key elements of later speculations about Atlantis. The first one was the idea of a struggle between two warring factions of Atlantean occultists. This appeared back in *Isis Unveiled* but took on new importance in *The Secret Doctrine*. Early on, according to Blavatsky, the Atlanteans split into two religious sects—one revering the One Spirit of Nature, the other worshipping the demons of matter—and the struggle between these factions shaped most of Atlantean history.

The second theme, unfolding from the first, held that the Atlanteans—specifically, the Lords of the Dark Face, the leaders of the demon-worshipping sect—bore direct responsibility for the destruction of their homeland. Toward the end of Atlantean history, the Lords of the Dark Face seized power in the Atlantean empire, and their misuse of magical powers caused a series of catastrophic floods that eventually left all of Atlantis underwater. The flood described by Plato, Blavatsky claimed, was simply the last of these disasters, the one that sent the final remnants of Atlantis to the bottom of the sea.

9 For the following discussion, see Blavatsky 1972, vol. 2, 277–350.

The Atlantean response to the destruction of their continent formed the third original theme Blavatsky brought to the Atlantis legend. She claimed that the worshippers of the One Spirit of Nature, recognizing what the rule of the Lords of the Dark Face would bring, sent parties of initiates by ship to the four corners of the world to preserve the sacred lore of Atlantis for future generations. The priesthoods of ancient Egypt and many other lands, according to her, derived their mystery teachings from Atlantean exiles, who in this way became the seedbearers of the age of the fifth Root-Race—the age of modern humanity.

These three themes took place in a worldview that was radically new to Blavatsky's readers. While her Atlantis and the rest of her sprawling cosmology drew on most of the popular themes of late-nineteenth-century thought, it reshaped them in ways that left few of the assumptions of the age unchallenged. In place of Darwin's vision of humanity evolving from lower animal forms, *The Secret Doctrine* claimed that animals had devolved from earlier forms of humanity. In place of religious beliefs that portrayed salvation as something granted once and for all by the arbitrary act of a judgmental god, Blavatsky described a spirituality in which souls evolved over countless incarnations, gradually growing in wisdom and power through literally unimaginable cycles of time. In place of the comfortable mythology of steady progress believed by almost everyone in her time, finally, she offered a more challenging vision of history in which nations, cultures, and races emerge, flourish, decline, and collapse against a background of repeated global catastrophes.

Perhaps the most interesting thing about *The Secret Doctrine*, though, is that it was just as different from older occult traditions as it was from the scientific and religious beliefs of the time. Compare the ideas presented in *The Secret Doctrine* with those in *Isis Unveiled* and you'll find huge differences on almost every point of theory and practice.[10] *Isis Unveiled* provided a clear account of

10 Compare Godwin 1994, 305–6 and 328–31.

most of the standard ideas of nineteenth-century occultism, but *The Secret Doctrine* taught something else again.

Nothing remotely like *The Secret Doctrine*, in fact, had ever appeared in the occult traditions of the West before. Much of her inspiration came from the philosophy and cosmology of India, where reincarnation and immense cosmic cycles had played an important part in religious speculation for centuries, but another major source for *The Secret Doctrine* was a new intellectual movement in the Western world itself—a movement that had nothing to do with occultism at all but has been confused with it ever since Blavatsky's time. Even today, it lacks a common name. The term this book will use for it is the *rejected-knowledge movement*.

"Rejected knowledge" is a term used by sociologists for the underworld of ideas that have been dismissed by accepted scientific authorities but have developed a following of their own. Occultism certainly counts as rejected knowledge by this definition, just as it counted as religious heresy back in the days when religion rather than science claimed the final say about what is real. There were plenty of heresies in the Middle Ages that had nothing to do with occultism, though. In the same way, most of the rejected knowledge current in today's world has nothing in common with traditional occult philosophy and practice.

Every society has its fund of rejected knowledge. What makes the rejected-knowledge movement of modern times all but unique is that it embraces nearly every kind of rejected knowledge, just because it is rejected. In the Middle Ages, to continue the example just mentioned, the followers of one religious heresy usually condemned other, competing heresies just as harshly as they did the Christian orthodoxy of the time. For their modern equivalents in the rejected-knowledge movement, though, any evidence that the reigning scientific orthodoxy might be wrong is as good as any other, and attempts to combine every kind of rejected knowledge into a single more or less coherent worldview have been standard practice in the movement for most of its short history.

Blavatsky helped start this last fashion by mining the newborn re-jected-knowledge movement for everything it was worth and packing *The Secret Doctrine*'s two vast volumes with enough lost continents, cosmic catastrophes, and historical speculations to satisfy anyone's taste for intellectual heresy. The result was a heady blend of Eastern mysticism and Western alternative thought, with just enough occult-ism thrown in to confuse the issue. Because the Theosophical Society had taken on a dominant role in the occult community by the time *The Secret Doctrine* saw print, its teachings were mistaken for traditional occult teachings for most of a century after its publica-tion. This case of mistaken identity had an immense impact on the occult traditions of the Western world, as well as the wider culture of the age.

Blavatsky's Mission

At the same time, much more may have been involved in the gen-esis of *The Secret Doctrine* than meets the eye. For that matter, Blavatsky's career seems to have been shaped by factors that have rarely been taken into account, either in mainstream biographies or in works by people associated with the Theosophical Society. Two recent historians, K. Paul Johnson and Joscelyn Godwin, have shown that Blavatsky was in close contact throughout her career with some of the most influential people in the occult community at that time, and the identical message she attempted to communi-cate in *Isis Unveiled* and other early publications of the Theosophi-cal Society was simultaneously being passed on by many other voices linked to the same occult circles.[11]

All this needs to be understood in its own historical context. By 1875, many thoughtful people had become profoundly worried about the future of Western civilization. Between the social im-pact of industrialism, the first stirrings of today's environmental

---

11 See Godwin 1994, 292–306, for the parallels between Blavatsky's early teach-ings and those of other occult fraternities of the time.

concerns, and the growing recognition that scientific advances were making humanity more powerful without making it any wiser or more responsible in the use of its powers, the mythology of progress rang increasingly hollow, and older teachings about history that traced civilizations through a cycle of ebb and flow gained a wide audience. The possibility that the onward march of Western civilization might be headed down the same dead-end road as the extinct civilizations of the past became impossible for many people to ignore.[12]

The occult community of the 1870s was at least as aware of these possibilities as anyone else, and a tradition deriving from the ancient magical lore of precession gave added force to their concerns. At the beginning of the sixteenth century, the great Renaissance sorcerer Johannes Trithemius wrote a strange book titled *De Septem Secundeis* (*On the Seven Secondaries*) that, in effect, put a minute hand on the great clock of precession. He divided each Great Month into smaller periods, each one ruled by an angel, and his figures pointed to November 1879 as the beginning of a new cycle of time. In the eyes of many occultists at the time, this marked nothing less than the end of one Great Month—the Age of Pisces—and the dawn of the Age of Aquarius.

The role this bit of astrological symbolism played in the 1960s counterculture can make it hard for people today to recognize the mingled emotions of hope and dread that affected occultists of the old school as they considered the turning of the great wheel of time. To them, the Age of Aquarius did not predict a time when "peace will guide the planets and love will steer the stars," in the words of the musical *Hair*. In traditional astrology, Aquarius is ruled by Saturn, the planet of limitation, correction, and harsh judgment, and the Age of Aquarius shares in these unwelcome qualities. Aquarius is also the water bearer in traditional astrological symbolism, and the possibility that the Age of Aquarius might bring the "torrent

12 Rather 1979 discusses the spread of these ideas in nineteenth-century culture.

from heaven" mentioned by the priest from Sais in Plato's narrative was on many minds just then.

To many of the occultists of the late nineteenth century, then, they and their world stood at the hinge of two ages, and they knew enough about history to know that such times commonly usher in the fall of civilizations. Given the close interconnections linking the occult groups of the time and the signs of coordinated action in the publication of *Isis Unveiled* and its sister works, the spectacular public resurgence of occultism in the 1870s and 1880s makes most sense as a deliberate effort on the part of occultists to turn Western civilization aside from a path they believed would lead it straight to self-destruction. Many occultists argued that a society that rejected the spiritual side of reality and turned its efforts entirely to the pursuit of material goals was making the same mistake as the legendary enchanter Faust, who bought seven years of power and wealth at the cost of his immortal soul.

Yet the occult community of the late nineteenth century was hardly omnipotent. Whatever its powers on the inner realms of magic and the spirit, in the outer world of everyday affairs it was a relatively small subculture with limited influence and even more limited financial resources. The only hope occultists had of changing the course of history lay in the realm of ideas. If enough people could be brought to a new way of looking at themselves and their world—a way that made spiritual self-development more relevant than the pursuit of material wealth and power—that might, they hoped, turn Western civilization away from the road to collapse.

The two phases of Blavatsky's public career, and the two major books she produced, both make most sense as efforts to pursue this goal. A change in strategy, though, marked the shift from one to the other. In the first phase, the one that centered on *Isis Unveiled*, Blavatsky focused on communicating the basic ideas of the occultism of her time to a wider audience, using her writings and the activities of the Theosophical Society as a medium. A number of her fellow occultists contributed to the same project with books of their own: the American occultist Emma Hardinge Britten published *Art Magic* in 1876, while the extraordinary Scottish occultist Marie, Countess of Caithness, in the same year published her *Old Truths in a New Light*. Both these books drew on the same traditions of occult teaching as *Isis Unveiled* and shared many of its central themes.[13]

By 1885, though, Blavatsky—and the circle of leading occultists who worked with her and supported her mission—apparently became convinced that this approach had failed. Though the Theosophical Society had become the largest occult organization of its time, and indeed one of the largest in recorded history, it remained a small fringe group in terms of the culture around it, and the influence of its occult teachings had failed to spread noticeably beyond its own membership. Meanwhile the world situation grew steadily bleaker as the major powers pursued an arms race every thinking person knew could have only one result. Britain and France blundered to the brink of war over their African colonies in the 1880s, while on the far side of the Rhine the German Empire made no secret of its plans for world power. The times called for drastic measures. The one Blavatsky chose—or her allies chose for her—was a potent but risky method perfected centuries earlier in occult lodges.

Russian occultist G. I. Gurdjieff, himself a master of the method, called it a *legominism*. The term (which comes from the Greek word *legomenon*, "something communicated") means a structure of ideas by which ancient wisdom is passed on in a form apparently intended for some entirely different purpose. The classic example of an occult legominism is the tarot deck, which takes the form of a pack of playing cards but encodes the entire worldview of Renaissance Italian occultism.[14] Created in Milan in the early fifteenth century, the tarot survived only as a card game until the late eighteenth century, when a handful of French occultists figured out

---

13 Godwin 1994, 303–6 details these parallels.
14 Olsen 1994 documents this.

how to unpack its teachings and put them to work. Most modern systems of Western occultism, including some that are completely unaware of its actual origins, still use it as a master key to occult philosophy as well as a tool for divination.

A legominism is always a high-stakes gamble, though, and the tarot itself might have failed to accomplish its purpose if the French occultists who rediscovered it had been a little less perceptive. The chance always exists that people will miss the point of the lego-minism completely and use it for its apparent purpose rather than recognizing the deeper meaning hidden inside it. The risk is not a small one. Many occultists of Blavatsky's time believed that Christianity itself was the product of just such a failed legominism; the gospels, according to this way of thought, were symbolic stories never meant to be taken literally, and the events and people in them were intended to pass on spiritual truths that became totally obscured once literal belief in the invented gospel stories became the basis for a dogmatic religion.

This was the risk Blavatsky's sprawling cosmic history ran. She evidently hoped to draw the rejected-knowledge movement into occultism by presenting a compelling vision of human history and destiny crafted to appeal to everyone troubled by the claims of the materialist science of her day. The goal of this project was twofold. On the one hand, it would inject a set of carefully chosen ideas into the popular culture of the time, in an attempt to counterbalance the influence of materialist thought and encourage alternative ways of thinking that were still easy for nineteenth-century audiences to assimilate. On the other hand, it would lead a certain number of those attracted by the new ideas into circles, such as the Theosophical Society, where they could enter the more challenging world of authentic occult teachings.

Her reorganization of the Theosophical Society during the years she spent writing *The Secret Doctrine* shows the same strategy at work. A new and largely secret branch, the Esoteric Section, formed an inner circle for those Blavatsky judged fit for serious occult training, while the regular membership was encouraged to study *The*

Secret Doctrine and practice simple forms of meditation and self-discipline. This was apparently not just Blavatsky's idea. The same period saw several other groups of occultists launch new organizations devoted to systematic occult training and initiation while circulating a watered-down version of occult teaching among the general public. The Hermetic Brotherhood of Luxor, founded in 1884, and the Hermetic Order of the Golden Dawn, founded in 1887, were two of the most important of these.[15]

These organizations shared more with *The Secret Doctrine* than the decade in which they took shape. All three also embraced a vision of history as a cyclic process, with cultures and civilizations rising and falling over time. The Hermetic Brotherhood of Luxor devoted one of its central teaching documents, *The Key*, to an intricate system of historical cycles partly based on Trithemius's writings.[16] The Hermetic Order of the Golden Dawn put less emphasis on this teaching, but it was certainly present in the minds of the order's founders and adepts.

In one of the Golden Dawn's private instructional papers, for example, cofounder Samuel Mathers commented, "The life of nations is like the life of men; they are born, become intellectual, direct that intellect to black ends, and perish. But every now and then at the end of certain periods, there are greater crises in the world's history than at other periods."[17] The writings of two other Golden Dawn adepts, William Butler Yeats and Aleister Crowley, both include the same concept as a central theme.[18] The same set of ideas pervades *The Secret Doctrine* and was likely among the central concepts Blavatsky hoped her legominism would communicate to the world.

---

15 See Godwin et al. 1995 and Regardie 1971, respectively.
16 Godwin et al. 1995, 140–65.
17 Mathers et al. 1987, 136.
18 Compare Yeats 1990, especially 243–83, with Crowley 1976.

The Theosophical Century

Blavatsky died in London in 1891, and after a power struggle among her lieutenants, her place was taken by Annie Besant, a former political activist who possessed extraordinary energy and enthusiasm but had little talent for diplomacy and not a trace of Blavatsky's occult background. Besant proceeded to turn the Theosophical Society into an ordinary religious sect. The Esoteric Section quietly dissolved, *The Secret Doctrine* took on the role of an infallible work of scripture, and Besant began promoting Theosophy as the world religion of the future.

Eventually, this led Besant and her allies to promote Jiddu Krishnamurti, the son of a servant at the society's Adyar headquarters, as the next World Teacher, a figure on the same level as the Buddha and Christ. From 1911 on, much of the Theosophical Society's resources went into this dubious project. In 1929, however, in an act of uncommon courage, Krishnamurti renounced the role of World Teacher that his handlers had crafted for him and dissolved the organization founded to promote him. The Theosophical Society effectively imploded over the years that followed, losing the vast majority of its members, and fragmented into several factions whose bitter quarrels did nothing to repair the damage of the Besant years. Three of the fragments remain active today, and these still teach the material from Blavatsky's legominism as the essence of the occult tradition.

Ironically, the self-destruction of the Theosophical Society took place at the same time as the triumph of Theosophical ideas in Western culture. By Besant's death in 1935, the teachings of *The Secret Doctrine* defined popular occultism throughout the Western world. The central role played by lost continents in Blavatsky's work guaranteed that Atlantis would become one of the main beneficiaries of the Theosophical triumph. During the Besant years, the society's presses published several books that condensed *The Secret Doctrine* into a form more suited to its new role as religious dogma, and these highlighted Blavatsky's teachings about Atlantis. The Theosophist

William Scott-Elliot completed the process with his popular work *The Story of Atlantis* (1896), which filled in many of the details Blavatsky left out. A few years after its publication, Scott-Elliot combined it with a book on Lemuria to produce *The Story of Atlantis and the Lost Lemuria*, which became the standard account of the two lost continents in popular occult circles all throughout the first half of the twentieth century.

Scott-Elliot, who could have had a very successful career as a science-fiction writer, treated readers to colorful word pictures of twenty-foot-tall Lemurians walking tame plesiosaurs on leashes and red-skinned Atlantean kings ruling much of the world from their capitol, the City of the Golden Gates, now deep under water off the coast of Senegal. Unfortunately, these fancies ended up being treated as fact by a great many people, convincing far too many of them that this sort of wild speculation was what occultism is all about.

Like other organizations that need to attract members, however, occult societies have to adapt their public presence to the demands of the market, and in the wake of Blavatsky's legominism, what the occult market demanded was Atlantis. By the dawn of the twentieth century, as a result, all of the significant occult organizations in the Western world had something to say about Atlantis in their public teachings, and what they had to say was usually based on *The Secret Doctrine*. Thus, Danish-American occultist Carl Grashof, who wrote under the name Max Heindel, titled his 1909 textbook of occult philosophy *The Rosicrucian Cosmo-Conception, or Mystic Christianity*, but readers were treated to a slightly Christianized version of *The Secret Doctrine*'s cosmology, complete with an extensive discussion of Atlantis almost entirely based on Blavatsky's version of the legend.[19]

Even occult orders less dependent on Theosophical sources still found it impossible to do without the basic ideas of Blavatsky's legominism. One of the most creative occult orders of the early twentieth

---

19 Heindel 1909, 291–304.

century, the Societas Rosicruciana in America (SRIA), attempted to bring the occult and scientific mentalities of the time closer together by drawing on contemporary science as well as occult tradition for its teachings; its textbooks include detailed accounts of what were then up-to-date scientific ideas. Even so, the SRIA was unable to get by without Atlantis and Lemuria and struggled to fit the Theosophical versions of these two lost continents into the worldview of early twentieth-century geology.[20]

The Ancient Mystical Order Rosae Crucis (AMORC), another American Rosicrucian order (there were dozens of them at the time) found lost continents equally indispensable; its founder, H. Spencer Lewis, wrote a popular 1923 book on Lemuria under the pseudonym W. S. Cervé and sent expeditions to California's Mount Shasta in search of a Lemurian colony said to be hidden somewhere inside the mountain.[21] Shasta, a snowcapped volcano famous for the complex cloud formations above it, has been the subject of many strange legends from Native American times to the present, and the explosive growth of American popular occultism in the early years of the twentieth century brought a wealth of additional legendry to the enigmatic mountain. To this day, New Age lore in the region repeats old stories of two underground cities, Ilethelme and Yaktavia, where survivors of the drowning of Lemuria preserve secrets older than Atlantis itself.

Even Aleister Crowley, whose efforts to promote himself as the Antichrist enlivened the occult scene all through the first half of the twentieth century, made a contribution to Atlantis literature. Born in 1875, Crowley was raised in the Plymouth Brethren, a fundamentalist sect of Christianity. He rebelled against his upbringing by deciding that he must be the Great Beast 666 described in the Book of Revelation and trying to act the part by way of sex, drugs, and occult practices. After a brief flirtation with Theosophy, he joined the

---

20 Khei 1920, 35–36.

21 See Cervé 1923 for the AMORC view of Lemuria, and Kafton-Minkel 1989 for the Lemurian mythology surrounding Mount Shasta.

Aleister Crowley

Hermetic Order of the Golden Dawn in 1898. After a mystical experience in 1904, however, he became convinced that he had been chosen as the prophet of the new religion of lust for life that would replace Christianity, and he devoted the rest of a long and eccentric life to the pursuit of this goal.

Crowley's version of the Atlantis legend took the form of a short story titled *Liber LI: The Lost Continent*. Like most of his writings, this story combined abstruse magical philosophy with the pursuit of shock value for its own sake. Crowley portrayed the Atlanteans as a race of red-haired sex magicians who extracted sweat from armies of slaves and transformed it through a combination of machinery and orgiastic rituals into a mysterious substance called Zro. Once they achieved the proper transmutation of Zro, the entire island headquarters of the Atlanteans, with all but a few of its people on board, blasted off on a one-way journey to the planet Venus, causing the tsunamis and earthquakes of the legend. Like *The Secret Doctrine*, or for that matter Crowley's other works of fiction, *Liber LI* was a legominism meant to pass on occult teachings, though Crowley's limitations as a writer, occultist, and human being kept him from achieving a fraction of the impact on his time that Blavatsky had on hers.

Still, Crowley could hardly have avoided saying something about Atlantis. Long before he achieved his fifteen minutes of fame, it became *de rigueur* for any significant occultist to talk about the subject. Whether or not Atlantis existed as an actual place around 9600 BCE, it's fair to say that it existed in everything but a physical sense in the occult community during the "Theosophical century," the period between 1875 and 1975 when Theosophical ideas dominated Western occultism and permeated popular culture as well. Even occult traditions with solid historical origins that had nothing to do with Atlantis routinely put on Atlantean garb; for instance, one popular book based on the Emerald Tablet of Hermes, a fundamental text of alchemy dating from the Arab alchemists of the early Middle Ages, redefined its subject as "the Emerald Tablets of Thoth the Atlantean."[22]

A connection between Atlantis and the occult became so widely assumed that, faced with Aleister Crowley's refusal to publish the meaning of the initials of one of his secret societies, the A.A., British newspapers jumped to the conclusion that it must mean "Atlantean Adepts." (It actually meant *Argenteum Astrum*, "Silver Star" in Latin.) Decades later, when Charles Portis (better known as the author of *True Grit*) turned America's alternative spirituality scene into raw material for his wry fiction, the same assumption still permeated the zeitgeist so completely that the novel could have only one possible title. *Masters of Atlantis*, a raucous comedy about the unsteady rise and much-prolonged fall of an American occult society, appeared in 1985. It makes for excellent reading, not least as an antidote to the pompous air of certainty that pervades so much Atlantis literature then and now.

Theosophical ideas even found a foothold in the very different cultural setting of Asia. Among the Tamil peoples of southern India, as

---

22 Doreal 1939.

mentioned in chapter 1, old legends told of a vast land to the south of the Indian subcontinent, called Kumari Nadu, and great cities—Old Matural, Katapuram, and the great port of Pukar—that had been flooded gradually over a period of thousands of years. Theosophical teachings about Lemuria reawakened interest in these tales, and they became a significant theme in Tamil culture in the early twentieth century. To this day, many Tamils believe that their homeland is the last fragment of Lemuria above water.[23]

A similar process made Lemuria a continuing theme in Japanese occultism and popular culture. Beginning in 1868, when the young emperor Meiji seized power from the last of the shoguns and launched Japan into the modern world, the conflict between traditional Japanese folkways and the pressures of a burgeoning industrial system drove an explosion of new religious and occult movements in Japan, a phenomenon the Japanese themselves have labeled with the appealing name *kamigami no rasshu-awa*, "the rush hour of the gods." Buddhism and Shinto, the two major Japanese religions, both contributed mightily to these new movements, but so did Western occult teachings, with Theosophy very much in the forefront. As a result, many Japanese alternative religious groups consider their home islands to be the last fragments of Lemuria above water.

Just as Blavatsky's ideas spilled over into popular culture in the West, Atlantis, Lemuria, and a variety of other lost continents in turn crop up routinely in Japanese popular culture. Fans of *daikaiju*— Japanese movie monsters such as Godzilla and Rodan—will doubtless recall that the movies about Gamera, a giant jet-propelled flying turtle, and Mothra, a gigantic moth, claim that both were created by the scientists of forgotten civilizations on lost continents.

The Doors of Vision

Not all the occultists of the early twentieth century contented themselves with rehashing the ideas of Blavatsky's legominism or presenting their own, however. In some occult orders, the practical methods

---

23 See Ramaswamy 2004.

passed on in lodges soon took center stage in a dramatic new development of the Atlantis legend.

Most people who don't practice occult disciplines think that occultism mostly has to do with power. In fact, its real keynote is knowledge, and the powers that come out of occult study and practice are simply the results of unusual knowledge applied in practical ways, just as the power of technology comes from knowing unexpected details about how matter and energy behave. Much of occult practice thus focuses on learning how to tap into the hidden powers of the human mind in order to get access to information that can't be found by ordinary means.

Occult traditions have many different methods for doing this, and they apply them to a dizzying array of subjects. One of the most important branches of occult practice in the Middle Ages and the Renaissance, for instance, was a system called *Ars Notoria*, or Notory (not "notary") Art, which involved concentrating on complex geometrical diagrams while reciting incantations in Latin.[24] Occultists who wanted to learn some branch of knowledge would use this art to bring themselves information and insights about what they wanted to learn. At a time when information was hard to come by, books were rare and expensive, and students had to rely on their memories, the diagrams and incantations helped key the occultist's mind to gather, retain, and efficiently process information on a chosen subject. Few occultists today use the Notory Art, but those who have done so can testify that its methods reliably do what they are said to do.

When the information an occultist needs isn't to be found in books, other methods apply. The occult traditions of the late nineteenth and early twentieth centuries had plenty of methods for getting such information, including scrying (the old name for remote viewing), a discipline much practiced in occult lodges then and now. The art of scrying can use external tools such as black mirrors

---

24 Very little exists in English on the Notory Art. One very Christian version of the art, lacking the diagrams, was published in English in 1657 and has been reprinted several times since then; see Turner 1998.

or crystals, or it can rely on the trained mind of the practitioner alone. In either case, the occultist focuses intently on some target or theme and then brings his or her mind to perfect stillness and allows images to surface from the deeper levels of consciousness. Like most of the techniques of traditional Western occultism, the art of scrying was formerly secret but has been published many times in the last century or so; a detailed description of the methods involved can be found in the appendix to this book.

Since occultism is a philosophy as well as a set of practices, it also includes explanations for the way this process works. According to the teachings of occult secret societies from Blavatsky's time to the present, a subtle substance called the astral light fills the universe.[25] The word *astral* literally means "of the stars," and the astral light got its name because it provides the medium by which astrological influences affect things here on earth. Its effects aren't limited to astrology, though, for the astral light is also the medium of dreams, visions, psychic phenomena, and the workings of magic. It exists outside of space and time as we know it, embracing the entire universe and uniting past, present, and future. Ways of working with the astral light thus encompass most of what is taught to students in the process of occult training and initiation.

To the occultists of the late nineteenth and early twentieth centuries, the astral light was as much an ordinary part of life as the Internet is today, so the idea of using scrying and other techniques to catch the patterns of the past in the astral light came naturally to them. Atlantis was an obvious target for this sort of work. Since historical and archaeological data about it were nowhere to be found, occultists turned to scrying and other magical methods in an effort to pierce the veil of time and get access to accurate information, especially about Atlantean magical and spiritual traditions. Other occultists, as well as practitioners of certain disciplines outside the occult community, found information about Atlantis surfacing in their visions willy-nilly.

---

25 Eliphas Lévi, the founder of modern occult philosophy, discusses the astral light at length in his major work *Transcendental Magic*; see Lévi 1972.

A thorough survey of the results of this search through time would take up a book much larger than this one, so two examples will have to serve. One comes out of the work of the premier occult lodge in Britain in the early twentieth century, the Fraternity of the Inner Light. The other unfolds from the visions of a solitary American seer, Edgar Cayce, the "Sleeping Prophet."

The Inner Light

The Fraternity (now Society) of the Inner Light was founded by Violet Firth, an English occultist who wrote more than a dozen important books on magic under the pen name Dion Fortune. Fortune, as everyone calls her today, came from a middle-class Yorkshire family and trained in the Theosophical Society and the Hermetic Order of the Golden Dawn before setting up her own occult lodge.[26] She had a strong talent for visionary work and attracted several other gifted visionaries to her fraternity. The secret history of the world was a central interest of many the fraternity's members, and Fortune and her associates used the traditional toolkit of occultism to carry out systematic visionary explorations into the past.

Atlantis took center stage in this project. This came partly from its importance in Theosophy and the occult community in general, but there was another factor: the fraternity shared the Theosophical belief in reincarnation, and many of its key members became convinced that they had lived previous lives on Atlantis. The archives of the fraternity came to include detailed records of their past-life memories. These and other records of the members' visionary work told a consistent story of the rise and fall of Atlantis that differed in important ways from the Theosophical account and Plato's tale alike.[27]

---

26 See Knight 2000 for information on Fortune and the history of the Fraternity of the Inner Light. Now known as the Society of the Inner Light, this order still exists in Britain.

27 See Fortune 1989 and Richardson 1985. Material from the Fraternity of the Inner Light's account of Atlantis was also used by fantasy author Peter Valentine

Dion Fortune

Fortune's early writings occasionally described Atlantis as a continent, but the visionary material in the Inner Light archives portrayed it as a pair of islands, Ruta and Daiteya, located in the Atlantic Ocean close to the eastern shores of the New World. The Atlantean realm also included the coastal lands along the Gulf of Mexico and the northeastern shores of South America, as well as colonies scattered elsewhere around the Atlantic and Mediterranean basins. Still, Atlantis was a moderately sized country by modern standards, not the sprawling empire imagined by some other authors of Fortune's time and ours.

Ruta, the larger of the two islands, was mostly low-lying jungle and marsh, but a solitary volcanic peak, the Sacred Mountain, stood near its eastern shores. On the slopes of the Sacred Mountain stood the City of the Golden Gates, the capital of Atlantis, and the Sun Temple, the center of the national religion. Some distance away was the Sea Temple, where a higher, more secretive order of initiates preserved a wisdom dating back to Lemurian times.

Timlett as raw material for a sword-and-sorcery novel, *The Seedbearers*; see Timlett 1974.

In its early years, Atlantis was governed by the priests of the Sun Temple, who were drawn along with the kings of Atlantis from a Sacred Clan, but later on, the pressures of empire and the moral and spiritual decadence of the priesthood shifted the center of power to the military. Finally, conflict broke out between the Sun Temple's priesthood and the army. When the priests were on the verge of defeat, they invoked elemental powers that awakened the long-dormant volcano, blew the islands of Ruta and Daiteya apart, and left nothing above water where they had been. Before the catastrophe, though, the priests of the Sea Temple sent small groups of initiates to the Atlantean colonies overseas, preserving the ancient wisdom that eventually came down to the Fraternity of the Inner Light.

This belief in an occult lineage descended from Atlantis made the fraternity's adepts focus their work on recovering Atlantean rituals and magical methods rather than trying to sort out the fine details of Atlantean history or arguing for the lost continent's existence. Fortune herself made use of the Atlantean material in a series of legominisms that took the form of occult novels—notably *The Sea Priestess*, her most famous work of fiction—but the references to Atlantean history and culture that cropped up there and elsewhere in the fraternity's work were of minor importance to the main thrust of the its project. Interestingly, the same thing was true of the Atlantean material in the work of Edgar Cayce, the second visionary source we'll examine here.

The Sleeping Prophet

Cayce (pronounced KAY-see) was born in 1877 to a family in the isolated farm town of Hopkinsville, Kentucky. Like most children of his social background, he had limited formal education and left school following eighth grade, but after leaving home he worked in bookstores and read voraciously. By the time he began his career as a psychic, he was by no means the country bumpkin portrayed by some of his biographers.[28] A devout if idiosyncratic Christian,

---

28 I have relied on Frejer 1995 and Johnson 1998 for Cayce's biography.

Edgar Cayce

he read the Bible from cover to cover each year and taught Sunday school for several years.

From early childhood, however, he had visions and other psychic experiences, and these propelled him in directions hard to reconcile with the narrow Protestantism of his upbringing. In 1901, he learned how to hypnotize himself from a traveling entertainer. When he developed a difficult case of laryngitis that same year, a local doctor encouraged him to try self-hypnotism and was startled when Cayce in trance confidently dictated a treatment for the condition that cured it completely. The same form of trance work turned out to be just as effective for diagnosing other people's illnesses and prescribing treatments, and within a short time, Cayce's gift brought him thousands of patients a year.

At first, Cayce concentrated on developing his psychic talents and trying, with little effect, to interest more orthodox medical practitioners in working with him and investigating his cures. By 1911, however, he had become deeply interested in Rosicrucianism, a branch of the occult tradition very popular in America at that time, and in the years that followed, he studied astrology, Theosophy, and other occult teachings.[29] He never seems to have joined an occult lodge or society, and his work shows no sign of the systematic training of the visionary powers a lodge could have given him. Still, he unquestionably knew his way around the occult teachings of his time, including those concerning Atlantis.

Nineteen twenty-three brought a new dimension to his powers and a crisis of faith, as references to reincarnation began to appear in his readings. The clash between this material and his Christian beliefs troubled Cayce, but eventually he came to terms with it and began to give "life readings" to help people untangle patterns from their past lives that were holding them in states of physical or psychological difficulty. Many of his patients, according to his trance readings, had past lives in Atlantis, and a good deal of information about the lost civilization turned up in the form of brief references in the readings.

According to Cayce's trance readings, Atlantis was originally a continent located where eastern North America and the western Atlantic Ocean now lie, centered on the region of the Bahama Islands.[30] At that time, the region was temperate rather than tropical—one of numerous references to drastic climate changes in the Cayce readings—and the Atlanteans were divided into a ruling caste, which considered itself to be truly human, and a laboring class, which the rulers called "things" or "animals." Just as in Blavatsky's early accounts, the Atlanteans early on divided into two sects, which Cayce called the Children of the Law of One and the Children of Belial. The Children of the Law of One were devoted to spirituality and sought to raise the "things" to full intelligence, while the Children of Belial worshipped themselves, pursued power for its own sake, and treated the laboring class as beasts of burden to be used at will.

---

29 See Johnson 1998 for details on Cayce's connections to the occult scene of his time.

30 For Cayce's Atlantis readings, see the collection in Cayce 1968.

The latter party took control of most of Atlantis not long before 50,000 BCE and developed an advanced technology based on crystals. Unable to control the powers they had awakened, though, the Children of Belial brought catastrophe on Atlantis. The First Destruction, as Cayce called it, broke Atlantis apart into the three islands of Poseidia, Og, and Aryan and killed most of its population.

In the aftermath of the First Destruction, the Children of the Law of One retook control of the remnants of Atlantis and turned the crystal technology to more productive ends. During this period of Atlantean history, according to Cayce, the Atlanteans developed aircraft, methods of long-distance communication, and other equivalents of twentieth-century technology. Eventually, though, the Children of Belial returned to power. Many of the Children of the Law of One fled Atlantis at this time, relocating in Atlantean colonies in South and Central America, Spain, Egypt, and a region called Mayra, located in what is now Colorado and Nevada. Around 28,500 BCE, the Children of Belial once again brought catastrophe on Atlantis—the Second Destruction—and all but a fragment of Poseidia sank. The Children of Belial kept their grip on Atlantis after this, however, and around 10,500 BCE, the Third Destruction ended Atlantis forever.

All this had particular relevance to the present, according to the Cayce readings, because hundreds of thousands of Atlanteans, many of them Children of Belial, were reincarnating in twentieth-century America. Cayce predicted that between 1958 and 1998 the modern industrial world would face many of the same opportunities and challenges that Atlantis did. His visions framed these events in cataclysmic terms that, taken literally, have been disproved by the passage of time; for example, Atlantis did not literally resurface in 1968 or 1969, as he predicted it would, and California has yet to follow Cayce's prediction and fall into the sea.

As historian of the occult K. Paul Johnson points out in his valuable 1998 study *Edgar Cayce in Context*, though, many of Cayce's visions make perfect sense when read not as literal descriptions of future events, but as symbolic expressions of spiritual truths and changes in consciousness. Certainly—and for more reasons than one—Cayce was right to point out the second half of the twentieth century as a time when the legend of Atlantis took on reality on the stage of ordinary history.

The New Age Atlantis

The social revolution of the 1960s brought all these disparate visions of Atlantis—Blavatsky's legominism, its countless reworkings, and its visionary offshoots—to a far larger audience than any of them had ever found in their own time. The Theosophical Society, though it was larger than any occult organization had been for centuries before its time, still had fewer members and less influence on its society than most middle-sized American Protestant denominations, and the Fraternity of the Inner Light rarely had as many as a hundred members at any point in its history. As the intellectual tidal wave of the sixties receded, however, ideas that once circulated quietly in occult societies found their way into every corner of the globalized society of the late twentieth century.

Cultural historians a hundred years from now will probably still be busy sorting out the impact this had on spirituality and popular culture. One result that has already caught the attention of scholars, though, is the rise of the New Age phenomenon, a large and influential movement of popular Western spirituality that draws almost all its inspiration from the popular occultism of a century before.

For all that it followed in the footsteps of these older traditions, the New Age movement had its own complex origins. It first began to coalesce in the United States in the 1950s as a series of overlapping subcultures inspired by a diverse mix of influences ranging from old-fashioned spiritualism through Theosophy to the UFO phenomenon that had recently splashed itself across newspaper headlines worldwide. Many members of these subcultures expected Armageddon in the near future—a belief given plenty of justification by the nuclear saber-rattling between the United States and the Soviet Union during the grimmest years of the Cold War—and circulated claims about the enlightened new world that would emerge after the rubble stopped bouncing. After more than a decade of failed predictions, a handful of leaders in the movement began to suggest that instead of waiting for a better world to arrive, it might be worth trying to live as though it already had. By behaving as though the promised Utopia was already in existence, they suggested, an enlightened minority could inspire others to do the same by proving that a living alternative to the status quo was within reach. The idea spread quickly through alternative circles worldwide. By the early 1980s, when actress and New Age believer Shirley MacLaine's bestselling memoirs launched it into the popular imagination, the New Age concept had become the center of a widespread social and spiritual movement with its own distinctive ideology.

The result has been described as "Theosophy plus therapy," and there's truth to the label. Most of the core ideas of the New Age that don't come from nineteenth-century occultism come from twentieth-century alternative health and psychotherapy methods. Still, it would be even more exact to call the New Age movement the grand fulfillment of the project Blavatsky set in motion with *The Secret Doctrine*: the fusion of occultism with the rejected-knowledge movement. Nearly every detail of Blavatsky's legominism plays a major role in New Age thought, but so does nearly every imaginable form of rejected knowledge, from alternative healing and perpetual motion to conspiracy theories and the hollow earth.

In this process, Atlantis inevitably took a central role. If the legend of Atlantis did not exist, in fact, the New Age would probably have had to invent it. The dream of an age of the world free from the limitations of history was easier to uphold if it had already happened at some point in the past, however long ago and far away. Atlantis filled this need perfectly. Since hard evidence concerning it was in short supply, earlier writings on Atlantis provided a basic framework for the New Age Atlantis, and material received in trance by mediums and people undergoing hypnotic regression filled in the remaining blank spots to provide a colorful narrative of the lost continent's rise, glory, and fall.

The Occult Atlantis   73

Shirley Andrews's two popular books *Atlantis* (1997) and *Atlantis and Lemuria* (2004) are perhaps the best introductions to the New Age Atlantis. Unlike many writers in the Atlantean end of the New Age spectrum, Andrews did a great deal of research and drew together nearly all the significant writings on the subject, from Plato on down, to create her vision of the lost continent. Edgar Cayce's trance communications play an important role in her books, along with later, Cayce-influenced psychics such as Ruth Montgomery, but some astonishingly obscure Atlantologists also contributed to her account of Atlantis as a mystical Utopia. True to her New Age faith, however, the focus of Andrews's books is at least as much on the future as the past:

> During most of their long histories, the citizens of Lemuria and Atlantis were enlightened and connected with their source. They remembered their previous lives and understood who they were, why they were on the Earth, and how to serve others. Although this is not the prevailing situation today, it is possible to return to this Golden Age of the distant past. Many people are working hard to make it a reality and each of us may contribute to the effort.[31]

It's a potent image and, in many ways, an appealing one. Like other narratives of the Golden Age, though, it belongs to the world of mythology rather than history. The huge but geologically unstable mid-Atlantic continent that Blavatsky conjured out of thin air and Plato's hints and handed down to generations of occultists and visionaries never existed in the world of everyday life. A century of geological research, in the process of uncovering the secrets of continental drift, proved that beyond a shadow of a doubt. Still, mere physical nonexistence did not keep Blavatsky's Atlantis—in its original form, or in its various occult and New Age revisionings—from having an immense impact on the culture of the twentieth century.

---

31 Andrews 2004, 207.

Atlantis in Popular Culture

That impact began early and ran deep. Within a few decades of *The Secret Doctrine*'s publication, images and ideas drawn from it started to surface in imaginative literature all over the Western world. The sheer scale of Theosophical influence on popular culture has rarely been measured. Few current readers of Robert E. Howard's popular Conan the Barbarian stories, for example, realize that the exploits of Howard's brawny hero are set entirely in the universe of Blavatsky's legominism, in a period (the "Hyborian Age") between the drowning of Atlantis and the dawn of recorded history. Howard was one of the most popular fantasy writers of the 1930s, and two generations of fantasy authors after him followed his lead and gave a recognizably Theosophical Atlantis a major role in their imaginary worlds.

Nor was Arthur Conan Doyle, better known today as the inventor of Sherlock Holmes, immune to the lure of the Theosophical vision. An active Spiritualist and a student of fairy lore, though never quite a practicing occultist himself, Doyle wove Blavatskian themes into many of his adventure stories. His novel *The Maracot Deep* (1929) was apparently the first work of fiction to picture an Atlantean city surviving under a glass dome at the bottom of the ocean, but even this novel twist did not keep his Atlantis from being stocked with what, after Blavatsky, had become the standard Atlantean paraphernalia of occult powers and mystic priests.

Even the devout Catholic J. R. R. Tolkien, who distrusted occultism in all its forms, put a completely Theosophical Atlantis into the massive personal mythology of Middle-Earth that gave rise to his trilogy *The Lord of the Rings*. Tolkien's Atlantis is called Númenor, but he gives it the elvish name Atalantë, "the downfallen," just to make the point clear. Númenor sinks in the traditional fashion after a Blavatskian struggle between the worshippers of the one true god Iluvatar and the servants of Sauron, Tolkien's Lord of the Dark Face. The survivors of Númenor, followers of Iluvatar and friends of the elves, sailed to Middle-Earth to become the seedbearers of the Third Age, again following Blavatsky's story in detail.[32] Tolkien's close friend C. S. Lewis, in turn, brought Númenor (misspelled "Numinor") into his 1943 fantasy novel *That Hideous Strength*, along with much else borrowed from magical lore.[33]

The high fantasy of Tolkien, Lewis, and their many imitators put lost continents on the maps of plenty of imaginary worlds, but Theosophical ideas about Atlantis and Lemuria went into weirder corners of popular culture as well. Perhaps the strangest of these began with a letter, signed "S. Shaver," that arrived in the mailbox of the science-fiction magazine *Amazing Stories* in 1943.[34] It announced the discovery of an ancient language called Mantong that, Shaver thought, gave "definite proof of the Atlantis legend." It was tossed into the trash by one of the office staff, but the editor of *Amazing Stories*, the legendary Raymond Palmer, retrieved it and ran it in the December 1943 issue. Readers responded favorably, so Palmer wrote the author to ask for more information.

The reply came in the form of a semiliterate ten-thousand-word letter titled "A Warning to Future Man," by Richard S. Shaver. Shaver, a Pennsylvania welder, began some years earlier to hear voices in his head while working, and he took down notes on what they said. The result was a lurid account of Lemurians who fled from the destructive radiation of a sun gone mad into tunnels and caverns beneath the surface of the earth. Later still, the Lemurians abandoned the earth altogether, leaving the tunnels to a race of psychotic dwarfs called "deros" ("*de*trimental *ro*bots" in Mantong) who used forgotten Lemurian technologies such as "telaug rays" (*tel*epathic *aug*mentation) and "sex-stim beams" to play havoc with the unsuspecting surface dwellers. Palmer, one of the all-time masters of lowbrow science

---

32 Tolkien 1977, 319–49.

33 Lewis 1996; see especially 320–27 and 367–72. Lewis's position as a defender of Christian orthodoxy has been much exaggerated by his admirers. His work, like that of his close friend Charles Williams, draws heavily on the more Christian wing of the contemporary occult movement.

34 See Childress and Shaver 1999 and Kafton-Minkel 1989 for the next few paragraphs.

fiction, recognized a gold mine when he saw it. He rewrote the letter
into a thirty-one-thousand-word novella, retitled it "I Remember Lemuria!" and ran it in the March 1945 issue of *Amazing Stories*.

The issue promptly sold out, and Palmer quickly arranged with
Shaver to get more stories about the sinister deros. Serious science-fiction readers denounced the "Shaver mystery," but *Amazing
Stories* doubled its circulation in four months, and 2,500 letters a
month poured through Palmer's mail slot from people who believed
they were being tormented by deros. Well before the Shaver mystery was old news in the science-fiction scene, Palmer left *Amazing
Stories* and founded a new magazine of his own. Called *FATE*, it was
dedicated to "true stories of the mysterious and unknown," where
Shaver's material and many other bits of Atlantean and Lemurian
lore shared space with UFOs, sea monsters, the hollow earth, and
nearly everything else of interest to the twentieth-century rejected-
knowledge scene.[35]

Atlantis inevitably found its way onto the silver screen as well.
The first movie about Atlantis was a French silent production of
1921, *L'Atlantide* (*The Atlantean Woman*), set in a surviving Atlantean city hidden away in the Sahara Desert. Dozens of others have
followed, most of them utterly forgettable and nearly all based on
the Theosophical version of Atlantis. The recent Disney offering *Atlantis: The Lost Empire* is a typical example, touching on nearly every cliché of post-Blavatsky Atlantis lore in the course of a submarine voyage to Atlantis inspired by Doyle's *The Maracot Deep*.

The classic in the genre, however, is certainly the 1961 MGM production *Atlantis: The Lost Continent*, produced by the famous science-fiction producer George Pal. Pal was unable to convince the
higher-ups at MGM to pay for the lavish special effects and high
production values that made his versions of *War of the Worlds* and
The Time Machine among the most successful science-fiction movies
of their time, and the result very nearly defines the term "B movie."

---

35 *FATE* magazine still exists today, and it continues to provide a forum for "true
stories of the mysterious and unknown." See www.fatemag.com.

Most critics consider *Atlantis* to be Pal's worst film. Still, all the usual themes of twentieth-century occult Atlantis lore provided most of the background for the awful acting and preposterous plot that make *Atlantis* an enduring favorite of bad-movie fans.

Even popular music has its Atlantis ballads. The most successful of them, "Atlantis," by sixties pop music icon Donovan, hit the airwaves in 1969 and immediately soared onto the charts. The lyrics of the song present a vision of an ancient mystic culture having nothing at all in common with Plato's narrative and everything in common with Blavatsky's legominism and its reworkings in the rejected-knowledge movement. Most of the millions who listened to Donovan singing about Atlantis, though, knew only the Atlantis he described, which was Blavatsky's Atlantis, the Atlantis of the occult tradition, complete with its seedbearers voyaging to new lands with gifts for the future.

This latter image, the vision of seedbearers bridging the gap between one age and another, would prove to be one of Blavatsky's most enduring creations, and its importance—as the last chapter of this book will show—has not lapsed today.

THREE

The Speculative Atlantis

Occultists often like to think that their traditions have been handed down unchanged since the beginning of time. In reality, though, the occult community has always taken in influences from the wider world around it and adapted its teachings to the needs and interests of each passing age. During the Renaissance, as Europeans struggled to make sense of the rediscovered cultural treasures of Greece and Rome, occultists paid a great deal of attention the ancient Neoplatonists and other classical sources of occult philosophy. During the Age of Science, occultists renamed many of their basic concepts to fit the scientific fashions of the day—you can still find old-fashioned occultists today, for example, who refer to the magical energies of the cosmos as "magnetism."

In the same way, as we've seen, the Atlantis of the occult traditions drew heavily on the ideas of the contemporary rejected-knowledge movement, and a good deal of what passed for ancient occult wisdom about Atlantis in popular occult writings during the "Theosophical century" from 1875 to 1975 actually came from books published in the first great surge of Atlantis speculation in the late nineteenth and early twentieth centuries. In the second half of the twentieth century, the circle completed itself as material from Theosophically influenced occult traditions flowed back into the rejected-knowledge movement and the New Age community to create modern Atlantology. In the process, though, what started out as a legominism meant to communicate profound metaphysical truths ended up being taken as literal history and then jumbled and misinterpreted by people who had no idea of the occult meanings of the traditions they reworked and marketed.

Still, the first great wave of speculation about the Atlantis legend in the late nineteenth century swept over the Western world several years before Blavatsky's great legominism saw print. It came from America, and its creator was one of the most colorful figures in American public life at that time: the Irish-American lawyer, politician, and writer Ignatius Donnelly (1831–1901).

Enter Ignatius Donnelly

Donnelly was born to a working-class family of Irish immigrants in Philadelphia, but he moved west as a young man and settled in Minnesota. He became a lawyer there, then went into politics and won election as lieutenant governor in 1859. In 1872, he was elected to the first of four terms in the House of Representatives, where he soon became known as a fiery radical on the Democratic Party's extreme left wing. Despite being mostly self-educated, he earned a reputation as one of the most learned men in the political scene and spent much of his free time reading voraciously in the Library of Congress. After losing a campaign for reelection in 1880, he returned to Minnesota and plunged into a new career as a writer, choosing the Atlantis legend as the theme of his first book.

The result was *Atlantis: The Antediluvian World*, which saw print in 1882 and quickly ran through the first of more than fifty printings.[1] For most of a century thereafter, almost everything written on Atlantis drew ideas directly or indirectly from its pages. In his book, Donnelly proposed and claimed to prove these thirteen theses:

---

1 I. Donnelly 1976, and the acerbic commentary on Donnelly's work in de Camp 1970, provide the raw material for the following paragraphs.

Ignatius Donnelly

1. That there once existed in the Atlantic Ocean, opposite the mouth of the Mediterranean Sea, a large island, which was the remnant of an Atlantic continent, and known to the ancient world as Atlantis.

2. That the description of this island given by Plato is not, as has long been supposed, fable, but veritable history.

3. That Atlantis was the region where man first rose from a state of barbarism to civilization.

4. That it became, in the course of ages, a populous and mighty nation, from whose overflowings the shores of the Gulf of Mexico, the Mississippi River, the Amazon, the Pacific coast of South America, the Mediterranean, the west coast of Europe and Africa, the Baltic, the Black Sea, and the Caspian were populated by civilized nations.

5. That it was the true Antediluvian world; the Garden of Eden; the Gardens of the Hesperides; the Elysian Fields; the Gardens of Alcinous; the Mesomphalos; the Olympos; the Asgard of the traditions of the ancient nations; representing a

universal memory of a great land, where early mankind dwelt for ages in peace and happiness.

6 That the gods and goddesses of the ancient Greeks, the Phoenicians, the Hindoos, and the Scandinavians were simply the kings, queens, and heroes of Atlantis; and the acts attributed to them in mythology are a confused recollection of actual historical events.

7. That the mythology of Egypt and Peru represented the original religion of Atlantis, which was sun-worship.

8. That the oldest colony formed by the Atlanteans was probably in Egypt, whose civilization was a reproduction of that of the Atlantic island.

9. That the implements of the "Bronze Age" of Europe were derived from Atlantis. The Atlanteans were also the first manufacturers of iron.

10. That the Phoenician alphabet, parent of all the European alphabets, was derived from an Atlantis alphabet, which was also conveyed from Atlantis to the Mayas of Central America.

11. That Atlantis was the original seat of the Aryan or Indo-European family of nations, as well as of the Semitic peoples, and possibly also of the Turanian races.

12. That Atlantis perished in a terrible convulsion of nature, in which the whole island sunk into the ocean, with nearly all its inhabitants.

13. That a few persons escaped in ships and on rafts, and carried to the nations east and west tidings of the appalling catastrophe, which has survived to our own time in the Flood and Deluge legends of the different nations of the old and new worlds.[2]

As if this was not enough, Donnelly also claimed to have located the exact position of lost Atlantis. In the middle of the Atlantic Ocean due west of southern Europe, an undersea mountain range—the

2 I. Donnelly 1976, 1–3.

Dolphin Rise, part of the Mid-Atlantic Ridge—had been discovered not long before Donnelly's time. The Dolphin Rise is surrounded by deep water to the east and west, and its highest peaks form the island chain of the Azores. This, Donnelly argued, was none other than Atlantis, the original home of human civilization.

Donnelly's theory, and the mass of arguments he marshalled to defend them, mark a turning point in the history of the Atlantis legend easily as significant as the one Blavatsky brought about. *The Secret Doctrine* described Atlantis as the homeland of the fourth Root-Race and the source of several ancient cultures, but neither Blavatsky nor any earlier writer claimed Atlantis as the source of all civilization. Moreover, Donnelly's enthusiastic claim that the drowning of Atlantis was the origin of all flood myths contradicts the words of the Egyptian priest quoted in the *Timaeus*, who told Solon that there had been many destructions by water in the past. Of Donnelly's thirteen theses, in fact, only the first, second, and twelfth have any common ground with Plato at all. Most of the other theses came from a different source: the huge popular literature of nineteenth-century euhemerism.

Euhemerus was a Greek philosopher who lived in the third century BCE. He became notorious in his own time for suggesting that the traditional myths of Greece were dim memories of the historical events of an earlier age—that the Greek gods, for example, were ancient kings and queens magnified by legend to superhuman scale. The theory named after him, euhemerism, found few takers in ancient times, but the Christian scholars, artists, and writers of the Middle Ages and Renaissance borrowed it eagerly. If the old gods were simply human beings of the past, after all, good Christians—or heretics and Pagans who wanted to pass as good Christians—could put them and their legends into paintings, sculptures, poems, and stories without being suspected of harboring Pagan religious beliefs.

The first proponents of the myth of progress in the late Renaissance took this concept to a new level, arguing that Zeus and the other Pagan gods were simply early inventors whose discoveries caused them to be revered by their descendants. This version of euhemerism even appears in occult writings of the time. Consider this passage from Trithemius's *On the Seven Secondaries*, the book on historical cycles that played so important a role in nineteenth-century occult teachings about the great wheel of time:

> Verily in these times, as it evidently appears in the histories of the ancients, men more earnestly applied themselves to the study of wisdom, among whom the last learned and most eminent men, were Mercurius, Bacchus, Omogyius, Isis, Inachus, Argus, Apollo, Cecrops, and many more, who by their admirable inventions, both profited the world then, and posterity since. . . . About these times Janus ruled first in Italy, and after him Saturnus, who instructed his people to fat their grounds [that is, compost their fields] with soil or dung, and was accounted or esteemed for a god.[3]

All the people Trithemius named, of course, were Pagan deities or mythic heroes (except Omogyius, who is probably a misprint; the name that belongs at that point in the list is Osiris). The idea of redefining Saturnus, Roman god of agriculture and Lord of the Golden Age, as the human inventor of compost will doubtless seem strange to many modern Pagans, but it follows the same logic Donnelly used, and euhemerism itself still attracts a lively following today. Retellings of ancient mythology that turn the gods and goddesses into astronauts from other planets, after all, simply launch euhemerist ideas out into interplanetary space.

Alternative theorists in the nineteenth century found euhemerism just as useful as today's ancient-astronaut theorists, because it allowed them to force-fit the old gods and myths into a cosmos where they did not belong—in this case, the cosmos of Victorian scientific materialism. Euhemerists like Donnelly's contemporary

---

3 Trithemius 1647, 45–46.

Louis Jacolliot (1837–90), a colonial official in Chandernagore, India, won immense audiences with books claiming to decipher the prehistory of the world by reading myths as historical events. Jacolliot's bestseller *Le Fils de Dieu* (*The Son of God*, 1873), for example, claimed to reveal the hidden history of the Indo-European peoples. This narrative centered on a forgotten Rama Empire based in the capital city of Asgartha, which was simply *Asgarth*—an alternative spelling of Asgard, the heaven of the Norse gods—with an extra *a* stuck on the end to make it look like a Sanskrit word.

The romantic history Jacolliot concocted for his prehistoric Rama Empire was mostly based on Norse mythology, then wildly popular among his European audience, and had nothing to do with the traditional history of India recorded in the *Mahabharata* and other Sanskrit sources. You can still find references to the Rama Empire in a few works of alternative history these days,[4] but Asgartha had a much brighter career ahead of it in the rejected-knowledge movement. It shed the *s* and became Agartha, Agharta, or Agharti, a mysterious underground city supposedly located somewhere in central Asia. In that form, it appeared in the pages of *FATE* during Raymond Palmer's editorship, and it still has many believers today.[5]

Euhemerism's great popularity with the nineteenth-century reading public made Donnelly's job easy, and the generations of euhemerists that came before him gave Donnelly many of his ideas. Donnelly's great innovation was simply to claim that Atlantis, rather than some other corner of the globe, had been the place where myths had taken place as history. Since nobody could bring up alternative evidence about Atlantean history to counter his arguments, he was on much safer ground than Jacolliot, whose speculations about Indo-European history ran headlong into a wall of inconvenient facts about the history of India.

Donnelly's borrowings from the euhemerists also included one of their most common bits of bad logic. Whenever he encountered

---

4 See, for example, Childress 1996, 27.
5 Godwin 1993, 79–94, offers an entertaining guide to the origins of Agharta.

a fact that could be explained by Atlantis, he assumed that Atlantis was the only possible explanation. Thus, he spent much of his book pointing out cultural parallels between the cultures of the ancient Mediterranean and those of ancient Mexico and Peru, on the assumption that only an older civilization halfway between them could account for the similarities. These parallels are real, and some of them cry out for explanation, but Atlantis is far from the only possible reason for them. To Donnelly, however, any parallel that *could* have had an Atlantean source *must* have had an Atlantean source.

This was not the only weakness in Donnelly's book, but many of the others criticized by today's debunkers happened, ironically, because Donnelly paid too much attention to the science of his time. Much of the material that went into his book came straight out of cutting-edge nineteenth-century science, especially geology and biology, and he combed scientific literature for facts that could be used to bolster his theories about Atlantis. When he argued that the Mid-Atlantic Ridge could have been above water ten thousand years ago, for example, he was well within the mainstream of nineteenth-century geology. Unfortunately for him, nineteenth-century geology was wrong far more often than it was right, and critics in the late twentieth century have unfairly pilloried Donnelly for beliefs that the best geologists in the world also held in the 1880s.[6]

Because Donnelly's proposed location for Atlantis and many of the arguments he used to support the claim are still quoted as fact by too many of today's books on the lost continent, it's probably worth explaining why he was wrong. During Donnelly's lifetime, geologists all over the world believed that the continents had always been where they are today. To explain how animals and plants that can't swim crossed from one continent to another, they came up with a series of hypothetical land bridges that rose and sank, connecting the continents in various ways. Lemuria, the land bridge discussed in chapter 2, was one of many such bridges in the geo-

---

6 See, for example, de Camp 1970 and Vitaliano 1978.

logical literature of the time. In a few cases, they were right—the Bering Land Bridge between Siberia and Alaska, for example, did exist during the last ice age—but in most cases, the connections between continents turned out to have been caused by continental drift, a concept that didn't even exist yet when Donnelly wrote his book.

The theory of land bridges lay at the foundation of Donnelly's entire work. To justify the idea that land bridges had risen from the sea late enough in time to allow animals and plants to cross over and then vanished again beneath the waves before the beginning of human history, geologists had to admit that large land areas could rise and sink dramatically over fairly short geological time spans. That was all Donnelly's Atlantis theory needed, and in fact his Atlantis was simply one of the land bridges—the one proposed by many geologists of the time to account for connections between Europe and North America.

Once a series of discoveries in the 1960s proved continental drift, on the other hand, the only evidence for most of the hypothetical land bridges vanished. There is a profound irony in this, because for many years—since it was first proposed by Alfred Wegener in 1923, in fact—the theory of continental drift had been dismissed by mainstream geologists as crackpot pseudoscience, just like Donnelly's theories about Atlantis.[7] Only a series of discoveries along the Mid-Atlantic Ridge that could only be explained by drifting continents finally forced the scientific community to pay attention to all the other evidence pointing the same way. Those same discoveries, however, made it clear that the whole Mid-Atlantic Ridge—including the Dolphin Rise—had been deep underwater for millions of years.

Despite its weaknesses, however, Donnelly's work became the foundation for nearly all later Atlantis theories. *Atlantis: The Antediluvian World* easily ranks as the most influential book ever written about Atlantis—far more so than Plato's original writings on

---

7 See Oreskes 1999 for a good summary of the history of continental drift's rejection by mainstream science.

the subject, which have been stretched and cropped in a dizzying number of ways to fit the Procrustean bed of Donnelly's theories. Blavatsky set the fashion by borrowing freely from Donnelly's work in creating *The Secret Doctrine*, and nearly every other writer on Atlantis since Donnelly's time has done the same.

Donnelly, for his part, refused to rest on his laurels: he went on to write two other best-selling books. The first, *Ragnarok: The Age of Fire and Gravel* (1886), argued that a giant comet collided with the earth just before the beginning of recorded history, leaving traces in the world's geology as well as in the myths and legends of many lands. The second, *The Great Cryptogram* (1888), claimed that the plays and poetry attributed to William Shakespeare were actually written by Sir Francis Bacon, who sprinkled coded references to himself in the "Shakespeare" writings to let cognoscenti in on the secret of their authorship. Both books used the same mix of cutting-edge scholarship and shaky logic as Donnelly's book on Atlantis, and both introduced ideas that still have a substantial following today.

If any one person can be credited with inventing the rejected-knowledge movement, in fact, it would have to be Ignatius Donnelly. Raymond Palmer, who popularized the movement in the pages of *FATE*, and Charles Fort (1874–1932), the indefatigable collector of unacceptable facts who gave his name to the concept of "Fortean phenomena"—a common term nowadays for events that violate the accepted rules of science—also made major contributions to the movement, as did Blavatsky herself. Still, Donnelly's three books set the movement on the course it has followed right up to the present.

In much the same way, the version of the Atlantis legend presented in *Atlantis: The Antediluvian World* remains the standard account in alternative circles to this day. Turn the pages of modern Atlantology books such as Charles Berlitz's *Atlantis: The Eighth Continent* (1994) or Murry Hope's *Atlantis: Myth or Reality* (1992) and you'll find Donnelly's conclusions and much of his evidence cited in detail. Since his conclusions are problematic and most of his evidence is either flawed or outdated, this hasn't helped the case for Atlantis, and it has given the entire field of Atlantis studies a reputation for sloppy scholarship, which not all of it deserves.

A Stone Age Atlantis

Not every book on Atlantis that followed Donnelly's footsteps fell into the same pitfalls, though. Among the very best attempts to follow his lead came from the pen of the brilliant Scottish poet, anthropologist, and Theosophist Lewis Spence (1874–1955). Spence had a solid background in occultism, but he was also a capable and respected scholar, a fellow of the Royal Anthropological Institute, and the vice president of the Scottish Anthropological and Folklore Society. His 1908 translation of the *Popol Vuh*, the sacred book of the Quiché Maya, won praise in scholarly journals, and his *Dictionary of Mythology* (1910) and collections of Native American myths from Mexico remained standard reference works for many years.

Like almost everyone in the occult field in Britain in his time, Spence had Theosophical connections and studied Blavatsky's writings. His background in mythology, however, made it easy for him to see Blavatsky's legominism for what it was, and unlike most people in the rejected-knowledge movement, he knew the difference between occult symbolism and history. The weirder end of occult Atlantis lore—the four-armed hermaphrodites and tame plesiosaurs of Scott-Elliott's fantasies, for example—never managed to find a foothold in his work.

Instead, in a series of five books beginning with *The Problem of Atlantis* (1924), Spence developed an Atlantis theory solidly based on contemporary science and comparative mythology. Donnelly's identification of Atlantis with the Mid-Atlantic Ridge, which was still respectable geology in Spence's time, formed the foundation of his theory. He accepted Blavatsky's claim that Atlantis sank gradually, with the catastrophe chronicled by Plato being only the last of many floods. Combined with the archaeology of his time, these

themes gave him the basis for one of the best of the older generation of Atlantis theories.

According to Spence, Atlantis was a large island in the eastern
Atlantic, far enough south that it escaped the glaciers of the ice
age, but still linked to the European mainland by a land bridge or
a chain of islands.[8] Farther west was another island, Antilia, which
remained above water long after Atlantis itself vanished and survives to this day in fragmentary form as the West Indies.

Sometime well before 23,000 BCE, both islands were settled by
human beings, and their warm climate and rich environment gave
rise to a Stone Age society well in advance of the European cultures of the time. Around 22,000 BCE, earthquakes caused parts of
Atlantis to sink beneath the waves, and some of the survivors fled
to the colder but more geologically stable lands of Europe, where
they appear in archaeological sources as the Aurignacian culture,
the creators of the first cave art in France and Spain. Around 14,000
BCE, another cataclysm drove more refugees across the remnants
of the land bridge to Europe, where they became the Magdalenian
culture, the painters of the great ice age cave paintings of France
and Spain.

In 10,500 BCE, though, the tables turned as a wave of invaders
from Spain, belonging to the Azilian culture, made their way to Atlantis and conquered it, founding the kingship dimly remembered
by Plato. The canals and city of Atlantis described in the *Critias*
date from this period. Once firmly established in Atlantis, the Azil-
ians united their Atlantean possessions with their old homelands in
Spain, southern France, and North Africa and launched a campaign
of expansion eastward along the shores of the Mediterranean.

The struggle with prehistoric Athens marked the high point of
this imperial overreach, which was followed around 9600 BCE with
another series of earthquakes, more severe than the earlier ones,
which put most of the island underwater. The rest of Atlantis sank

---

8 Spence 1968 is my source for the following paragraphs.

gradually over the centuries that followed, leaving only its highest mountaintops as the Canary, Azores, and Cape Verde islands today.

Except for his reliance on geological theories that were only disproved after his death, there is nothing impossible about Spence's Atlantis theory, and he handled the occult dimension with a light touch. The main occult theme in his Atlantis writings was the claim—universal in the occult tradition by that time—that the sinking of Atlantis was a result of the Atlanteans' own mishandling of their powers over nature. His final book on the Atlantis theme, *Will Europe Follow Atlantis?* (1942), suggested that the fate of Atlantis could overtake modern industrial civilization—a theory that, as we'll see in this book's last chapter, may not be as strange as it sounds.

Spence's attempt to make sense of Atlantis by comparing Plato's legend to the known realities of the prehistoric past has immense promise, but very few writers on Atlantis have followed up on it. One who has, though she makes no reference to Spence in her book, is Mary Settegast. Her brilliant 1990 book *Plato Prehistorian* went back to Plato's dialogues and built a strong case that several of the Greek philosopher's accounts of prehistory—including his Atlantis narrative—were rooted in fact.[9]

Settegast's approach to the Atlantis legend was as unconventional as it was clever. Instead of attempting to locate Atlantis or argue for its existence, she left Atlantis itself out of the picture and turned her attention to the rest of the Atlantis narrative: the story of Atlantean colonization of the western Mediterranean basin, followed by war with ancient Athens, Atlantean defeat, and a series of natural disasters that devastated the survivors of both sides. Like Spence, she identified the Atlanteans with the Magdalenian culture of prehistoric France and Spain, but she had the benefit of the half a century of intensive archaeological work done since Spence's time.

---

9 See Settegast 1990 for the following paragraphs.

The picture she developed on the basis of the archaeological evidence is intriguing. By the time Plato gives for the founding of ancient Athens and the glory years of Atlantis, she showed, the peoples of the ancient Mediterranean basin had developed highly sophisticated cultures. Far from the fur-clad cave dwellers most modern people imagine living in prehistoric times—an image that, as we'll see, has much more to do with the modern myth of progress than with the actual evidence of the prehistoric past—the Mediterranean cultures of the time of Atlantis were artistically and technologically gifted, and the evidence suggests that they had already domesticated several animals, including the horse. Complex societies existed already in Egypt and on the eastern Mediterranean coast, though the sparse evidence from Greece does not yield a clear answer to whether an ancient Athens could have existed there.

After the time Plato gives for the fall of Atlantis, in turn, all these cultures went into decline, and evidence for widespread warfare shows up all over the Mediterranean world. In Spain, for the first time in human history, paintings on rock walls show people killing one another; in sites in Egypt and Syria, cemeteries of the time show the unmistakable signs of death by violence in a large fraction of the burials; in Jericho, the first stone fortification in history rose above the plains; all over the Mediterranean world and in Europe as well, distinctive tanged arrowheads appear in large numbers. Settegast identified all these as signs of the war between Atlantis and the Mediterranean nations. Her chronology faces some challenges and requires a war extended over centuries or millennia, but the basic picture—a period of relative prosperity and cultural flowering followed by an age of war and radical decline—fits Plato's narrative well.

Lost Continents Galore

The reasoned approach pioneered by Spence and followed up by Settegast found few takers, though, as Theosophical ideas refurbished by the rejected-knowledge movement put lost continents on the map all through twentieth-century popular culture. Atlantis was not the only beneficiary of this explosion of interest. Lemuria also got a good deal of attention, because of the support given to it by scientists such as Philip Sclater and Ernst Häckel, but other lost continents were quick to find a following too.

Several of these came out of a dubious offshoot of Theosophy called Ariosophy—a movement that took shape in central Europe right after the beginning of the twentieth century as a reaction against some of the more positive aspects of Theosophical teaching.[10] From its beginning, and very much to its credit, Theosophy took a strong stand in favor of racial and gender equality, and this did not sit well with many right-wing German and Austrian occultists, who wanted to combine their occultism with the racist and anti-Semitic beliefs all too common in the Europe of the time.

The major theorists of Ariosophy, Guido von List and Jörg Lanz von Liebenfels, borrowed the basic ideas of Blavatsky's legominism but completely rewrote it so that the so-called "Aryan race" (that is, Germans, Austrians, and people who looked like them) became the only true human beings. In keeping with their beliefs, they defined all other ethnic groups as subhuman beast-men under the control of the Jews, who they described as evil entities from another evolution. This repellent mythology has nothing to do with authentic occult tradition, but it became popular in some corners of the European occult scene in the early twentieth century and still has followers today.[11]

Nearly everything in Ariosophy was a distorted copy of teachings from Blavatsky's Theosophy, and since Theosophy had plenty of lost continents, Ariosophy had to have some of its own. The most important of them was Thule, a drowned continent located either in the North Sea or the Arctic Ocean, supposedly the homeland of the "Aryan race." Its name came from *ultima Thule* ("furthest Thule"), the old Roman name for Iceland, and the history they concocted for

---

10 See Goodrick-Clarke 1992 for a detailed discussion of Ariosophy.

11 Goodrick-Clarke 2002 is the best guide to this movement.

it came out of thin air. Nevertheless, it played a major role in the occult symbolism of some of the groups that laid the foundations for the Nazi movement after World War I. The secret society that originally launched the Nazi Party as its political action wing, in fact, was called *Thule-gesellschaft*, the Thule Society.

Other versions of Ariosophy used different names for their lost continent of the far north. Some called it Arktogäa, a name based on the Greek words for "northern earth," while others borrowed the name Hyperborea either from Blavatsky or the classical Greek sources she used. Under any name, it served as the mythic anchoring point for a debased legominism of its own, designed to justify the poisonous racism and anti-Semitism underlying the Nazi movement and its close equivalents in other European countries.

Less toxic but not much more honest was the invented lost continent of Mu, which had a brief period of popularity in the 1920s and 1930s. Mu was not quite created from whole cloth, as Thule was, and its origins cast an intriguing light on the way that yesterday's misunderstandings often become today's rejected knowledge.[12] Its history goes back to a Spanish Dominican monk named Diego de Landa, who went to the Yucatán Peninsula after the Spanish conquest. He played a central and despicable role in the Spanish campaign to destroy the surviving heritage of classic Maya culture, but in the process he copied down a few notes on Mayan writing. These proved almost completely useless to later scholars, since he thought Mayan writing was an alphabet, which it wasn't, rather than a complex and elegant system of hieroglyphics in which each character stood for an entire word, which it was. Until Mayan writing was finally translated in the 1980s, though, de Landa's notes comprised nearly the only surviving information on the subject at all, and it led generations of scholars down a succession of blind alleys.

One of them was French archaeologist Charles-Étienne Brasseur de Bourbourg (1814–74), who set out in 1864 to use de Landa's

---

12 De Camp 1970 remains the best source for the origins of Mu. See also Churchward 1925.

notes to decipher a Mayan manuscript, one of only four to survive the Spanish purges. Once Mayan writing could finally be read, this manuscript turned out to be an astronomical treatise on the movements of the planet Venus, but Brasseur de Bourbourg didn't know that, and his attempted translation turned into one of the world's great monuments of misplaced scholarly effort. Read through the filter of de Landa's garbled notes, the manuscript seemed to give a confused description of a volcanic catastrophe in a place called "Mu, Land of Mud," and Brasseur de Bourbourg came to the conclusion that he had found an unexpected piece of evidence confirming the Atlantis legend.

Nearly all contemporary scholars rejected this interpretation, and for good reason; even with de Landa's notes to support him, Brasseur de Bourbourg's linguistic interpretations were far-fetched at best. Donnelly borrowed extensively from his work, though, and Atlantologists who followed Donnelly—that is, nearly everyone who wrote on the subject from 1882 on—did the same, citing Brasseur de Bourbourg as another proof of their theories and giving Mu as the ancient Mayan name for Atlantis.

This was how American writer James Churchward came across Mu. Churchward's only previous publication was a guide to hunting and fishing spots in Maine, but in 1925 his book *The Lost Continent of Mu* became an immediate bestseller. Churchward claimed he had studied secret tablets in India and Central America written in Naacal, the language of Mu, and described Mu as a huge continent in the central Pacific. Churchward borrowed heavily from Donnelly and other Atlantis theorists, and so inevitably he claimed Mu as both the original home of humanity and the cradle of civilization. The 64 million Muvians, according to him, were divided into ten tribes and ruled by a priest-king known as the Ra. Around thirteen thousand years ago, a series of underground gas belts beneath the Pacific suddenly deflated, and the Land of Mud sank below the sea, leaving Easter Island and a few other sites in the Pacific as echoes of its lost glory.

Mu had a brief vogue in American alternative circles, but it never really caught on. By the middle years of the twentieth century, most people in the occult community considered Mu an alternate name for Lemuria.[13] The fusion between these two lost continents completed the process of literary "continental drift" that had moved Lemuria thousands of miles eastward since its invention in the nineteenth century; the combined Lemuria-Mu reached from the eastern Indian Ocean to the far southwestern Pacific, with its central region south and east of Southeast Asia. The curious thing about this process, as we'll see, is that it placed the lost continent exactly where a major landmass actually did vanish some sixteen thousand years ago.

Comets and Meteors

As Atlantis speculations flowed into popular culture, they became a magnet for other forms of rejected knowledge, and Donnelly's other writings offered tempting targets to theorists interested in the big picture. As far as I know, only a handful of people on the furthest shores of Atlantology suggested a connection between Atlantis and the authorship of the Shakespeare plays, but Donnelly's theory of a comet collision was another matter entirely. The idea that a comet or asteroid impact destroyed the Atlanteans was a natural result of the fusion, and it remains one of the most pervasive themes in Atlantology today.

The earliest versions of the impact theory were at least as weird as any of Scott-Elliot's leashed plesiosaurs, and they ended up tangled with the same repellent underworld of racist ideas that gave rise to Thule and the other northern lost continents. In early-twentieth-century Germany, an influential figure in the rejected-knowledge scene named Hans Hörbiger created a strange system of thought called the

---

13 Interestingly, this interpretation also appears in Richard Ellis's popular but poorly researched 1998 debunking effort *Imagining Atlantis*. See Ellis 1998, 68–69.

Welteislehre ("World Ice Theory").[14] According to Hörbiger, the earth's moon is made of ice, and it's only the latest of a series of moons that have been captured by the earth's gravity over the course of ages. In Hörbiger's theory, each successive moon orbits in a spiral path, drawing gradually closer to the earth until eventually it breaks apart and showers the earth with huge masses of ice, causing a global catastrophe and an ice age.

The moon before ours, according to Hörbiger and his followers, caused most of the dramatic events recorded in mythology, including the sinking of Atlantis. As the old moon spiraled closer to the earth, its gravity began to affect terrestrial life forms by pulling them upward, so that many of them became giants; as the Bible says, "there were giants in the earth in those days."[15] Finally, the old moon broke apart and its fragments fell to the earth, becoming the ice sheets of the last ice age and exterminating nearly all life on the planet. Strange as all this may sound, it was widely discussed in popular circles in the 1920s and 1930s, and Hörbiger achieved his fifteen minutes of fame in the late 1930s when his theories were adopted as the semi-official cosmology of the Nazi party.

German scientist Otto Muck presented a less giddy version of the impact theory in his 1978 book *The Secret of Atlantis*. Muck was quite literally a rocket scientist; he worked on the team that designed the V-2, the first successful guided missile, and he had more than two thousand patents to his name by the time of his death. He argued that a huge asteroid hit the western Atlantic Ocean in 8498 BCE, punching holes in the sea floor and unleashing catastrophe on the whole Atlantic basin.[16] Like Donnelly and Spence, Muck argued that the Azores were the remnant of Atlantis, and he proposed that the impact of the asteroid and the huge volcanic eruptions unleashed by it caused Atlantis to sink beneath the waves.

---

14 See Bellamy 1936 for a detailed presentation of Hörbiger's theories.

15 Genesis 6:4.

16 Muck 1978.

This catastrophe, he suggests, became the starting date of the Maya calendar, recalled by the distant descendants of Atlantean refugees in America. This last detail runs into one difficulty: the Mayan calendar didn't begin in 8489 BCE. The starting date for the current Mayan age of the world is August 11, 3113 BCE, and 8489 BCE isn't a significant date in the Mayan calendar at all—it's an ordinary year about 250 years short of the end of the second age before the current one.[17]

The unexpected discovery in the 1980s that the age of dinosaurs may have been ended by a collision between the earth and a large asteroid 65 million years ago made impact theories of all kinds very popular, and well over a dozen books arguing that Atlantis was destroyed by a meteor or comet accordingly saw print in the 1990s. No two of them proposed exactly the same version of the theory, and many of them combined this theory with the relocation of Atlantis to some other corner of the world, a theme we'll consider shortly.

The impact theory has thus become a central element of many recent Atlantis theories, as well as other alternative visions of history. Something about the idea of worldwide destruction by a comet or meteor seems to have a powerful appeal to the modern collective imagination. Perhaps the appeal comes from the fact that, unlike global warming and the other disasters that industrial society seems intent on bringing down on its own head, a meteor from outer space is nobody's responsibility, and avoiding it doesn't require us to give up our unsustainable lifestyles.

Atlantis Anywhere

Popular as impact theories were, the main stage of the twentieth-century Atlantology market was occupied by arguments that Atlantis had been somewhere besides the place where Plato put it,

---

17　See Edmundson 1988 and Schele and Freidel 1993 for details on the Mayan calendar, a subject that—like Atlantis itself—has become a focus of rejected-knowledge theories in recent years.

in the Atlantic Ocean west of the Strait of Gibraltar. Most of these theories share a common and curious feature: they offer evidence that an ancient city, civilization, or landmass was overtaken by a catastrophe and then leap to the conclusion that this must have been Atlantis, whether or not any scrap of evidence connects it to Plato's narrative. The cautionary words of Plato's Egyptian priest about the many catastrophes in the past have been completely forgotten by today's Atlantologists, while Donnelly's insistence that all the world's flood legends tell the story of Atlantis and Atlantis alone has been taken to its logical extreme.

Attempts to relocate Atlantis along these lines, it's only fair to say, go back a very long way. In a sprawling book published in sections between 1657 and 1698, the Swedish scholar Olof Rudbeck (1630–72) proclaimed that he had located Atlantis, along with nearly all the other locations of classical mythology, in Sweden.[18] A century later, the French savant Jean-Sylvain Bailly (1736–93) moved it east into the Arctic Ocean, near Novaya Zemyla, and the *Oera Linda Chronicle*, a nineteenth-century forgery that claimed to reveal the true history of northern Europe, put "Atland" in the North Sea. These speculations are modest, however, compared to the ones that have surfaced in recent decades.

A handful of recent books about Atlantis do take Plato's location seriously, to be sure. Andrew Collins's *Gateway to Atlantis* (2000), one of the few to find a sizeable audience, located Atlantis in what is now the Bay of Batabanó, southwest of Cuba. Collins quite sensibly pointed out that Plato presumably meant to say what he said about the location of Atlantis, and he went looking for it in the Atlantic basin not far from the eastern shores of the Americas. He argued that the western plain of Cuba is about the size of the central plain of Atlantis as described in the *Critias* and noted that large sections of the Cuban coastline would have been flooded at the end of the last ice age, though he also dragged in a meteor impact to explain

---

18 Rudbeck's obsessive quest to put all of ancient history inside the borders of Sweden has been entertainingly chronicled in King 2005.

the sinking of Atlantis. Cuba remains well above water, which is one strike against Collins's theory, and extensive archaeological digs in Cuba have turned up no evidence for an ancient civilization there, which is another. Still, Collins's theory is a good deal more reasonable than most of the competition, and it deserves more attention than it has received so far.

Another book that places Atlantis somewhere near where Plato located it is Henriette Mertz's *Atlantis: Dwelling Place of the Gods* (1976), which resurrects the early modern theory that Atlantis was located in America. Mertz bases much of her argument on one of the puzzling maps mentioned back in chapter 1, the Andrea Bianco map from 1436. This map shows the island of Antilia, in the Atlantic Ocean west of Europe, as a large rectangle that shows certain similarities to Plato's Atlantis and to the part of North America east of the Ohio and Mississippi rivers as well. This and a scattering of other facts lead her to suggest that Atlantis was in fact the east coast of America. It's an interesting theory, and one John Dee and Guillaume Postel would have heartily applauded.

Farther from Plato's location, but still in the Atlantic basin, are theories that place Atlantis somewhere on the Atlantic coast of Europe. A French writer, François Gidon, proposed in 1934 that the legend of Atlantis was based on the flooding of coastal plains off what are now the northwestern shores of France at the end of the last ice age. In her 1951 classic *The Sea Around Us*, Rachel Carson, the famous ecologist and author of *Silent Spring*, proposed that the Dogger Bank—an area of shallow water in the North Sea that was well above water during the last ice age but drowned beneath rising waters around six thousand years ago—might have been the source of the Atlantis legend.

More recently still, Paul Dunbavin proposed in *The Atlantis Researches* (1995) and *Atlantis of the West* (2003) that Atlantis was located in the eastern Irish Sea and was drowned by the aftereffects of yet another comet impact around 3000 BCE. This theory has more evidence behind it than most, since the area in question was above water until relatively recent times—Welsh folklore still recalls the drowning of the "lost cantrefs" in the sixth century CE. The possibility that a sizeable community might have been flooded by the sea, with or without the involvement of a comet, around the time he suggests cannot be dismissed without further research. His attempts to connect this disaster to Plato's Atlantis, however, are a good deal less convincing, since the location and date are wrong and so are many other details.

Another northern European Atlantis surfaced in 1953 when Jurgen Spanuth, a German minister, published *Atlantis: The Mystery Unraveled*. According to Spanuth, Atlantis was located in the North Sea, and its capital was an underwater ruin about six miles northeast of the island of Heligoland. This ruin actually exists, a fact that puts it ahead of most other contenders, though archaeologists have failed to find any sign that it was more than a modest Bronze Age town drowned in the slow reshaping of the northern European coastline.

Like so many other Atlantis theorists, Spanuth proposed an impact theory to give his Atlantis a rousing end. His version sent a comet named Phaethon plunging into the mouth of the Eider River, setting off volcanic eruptions all over Europe and drowning the North Sea Atlantis beneath a series of colossal tsunamis. Refugees from the disaster streamed south across Europe to become the Sea Peoples, who devastated most of the eastern Mediterranean around 1220 BCE.

Northern Europe was far from the only alternative location for Atlantis, though, and other prospects were quick to enter the fray. Eberhard Zangger's 1992 book *The Flood from Heaven*, for example, argued that the Atlantis legend was based on a garbled account of an ancient Egyptian record of the Trojan War. He made this claim even while admitting that Troy is nowhere near Plato's location for Atlantis, was destroyed at the wrong date, didn't sink beneath the sea, and isn't even on an island in the first place. It's hard to find any point in common between Atlantis and Troy except that both places fought a legendary war with the Greeks, and this latter is essentially the only evidence Zangger presents for his claim.

Along the same lines, Peter James's *The Sunken Kingdom: The Atlantis Mystery Solved* (1995) argued that Atlantis was located in what is now western Turkey, where a later Greek legend claims that the city of Sipylus was drowned beneath the waters of a lake. It's entirely possible that a city was submerged there, but only the most tortured logic allows James to link that city with Atlantis. Robert Sarmast's *Discovery of Atlantis* (2003), which places the lost civilization in the Mediterranean southeast of Cyprus, suffers from the same problem; there are certainly drowned cities off the present-day coast of Cyprus, but nothing makes them better candidates for Atlantis than the dozens of other drowned cities in the Mediterranean.

North Africa has been another common site for relocated Atlantises, and for once a piece of old if ambiguous evidence backs up the claims. Herodotus, an ancient Greek historian whom later Greeks called both "the father of history" and "the father of lies," describes in the fourth book of his *Histories* a people called Atarantes or Atlantes who live in western North Africa, close to Mount Atlas. A number of other historians, ancient and modern, have identified these Atlantes with Plato's Atlanteans and have tried to find some way to make the descriptions of the *Timaeus* and *Critias* fit various places in and around the Sahara Desert. Locating Atlantis in one of the driest places on the planet may seem almost perversely improbable, but the Saharan Atlantis theory attracted a great deal of attention in its time and still has followers today.

Two popular books between the two world wars, François Butavand's *Veritable Histoire de l'Atlantide* (*The True History of Atlantis*, 1925) and Otto Silbermann's *Un Continent Perdu: L'Atlantide* (*A Lost Continent: Atlantis*) both placed Atlantis in Tunisia: Butavand just off the coast and Silbermann in the Shott el-Jerid, a region of swamps near Tunis. Leo Frobenius, the famous German explorer and anthropologist, thought he had found it in the Yoruba kingdom of Nigeria, whose people seemed to him to have all the cultural features Plato assigned to his Atlanteans.

Atlantis surfaced much farther afield in Jim Allen's 1998 book *Atlantis: The Andes Solution*. Allen argues that Plato's lost city was located in the Bolivian altiplano, high up in the Andes Mountains. While Bolivia remains well above water—most of the country is more than a mile above sea level—Allen argues that an ancient Bolivian city, like Sipylus in Turkey, sank "in a single day and night" beneath the waters of a shallow inland sea, the remnants of which now form present-day Lake Poopo. The possibility that a lost pre-Columbian city might exist near Lake Poopo is certainly worth investigating, but Allen never manages to present any evidence that this city has any relationship to Plato's account of Atlantis.

Another set of theories about Atlantis have fastened onto one of the more intriguing discoveries of recent geography. Back in 1964, a biologist named D. S. Johnson coined the name "Sundaland" for the sprawling realm of islands spreading across the tropical seas east and south of Southeast Asia, borrowing the name of the Sunda Strait, which runs through the middle of it. As one of the richest and most diverse ecological regions on the planet, it has been carefully studied by generations of scientists. The seas that divide its countless islands are very shallow, and researchers realized early on that the whole region was above water during the last ice age.

Ice age Sundaland was a huge landmass—twice the size of India—that reached from the shores of present-day Indochina most of the way to New Guinea. During the last ice age, its jungles comprised the single largest area of tropical rain forest in the world. Before it perished, it had been settled by humans and humanlike beings for countless thousands of years, since long before the rise of *Homo sapiens*, and at least one major language family seems to have evolved there and spread outward across coastal Asia and the Pacific.

As lost continents go, Sundaland is a prize specimen; it was huge, inhabited, and solidly documented by respected scientists. If the rejected-knowledge movement had identified it as the Lemuria of occult tradition, the debunkers might have been seriously discomfited, since it's in the right place and much of it was submerged well

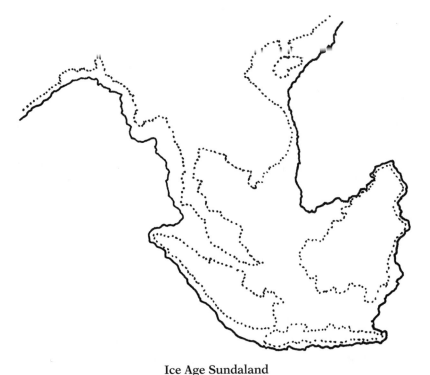

Ice Age Sundaland

Twice the size of India, the landmass of Sundaland was located precisely where occult theorists in the nineteenth and twentieth centuries placed the lost continent of Lemuria.

before Plato's date for the drowning of Atlantis, as the occult traditions say Lemuria was. Instead, for reasons never really spelled out, those writers who connected Sundaland to the lost continent theme identified it as Atlantis. Sundaland is in the wrong ocean and sank at the wrong time, and there are dozens of other coastal regions closer to Plato's site that were also drowned by rising waters at the last ice age. Other than that, it would make an excellent candidate.

Toward the outer edges of modern Atlantis speculation, finally, lies the theory advanced by Rand and Rose Flem-Ath in their book *When The Sky Fell* (1995), expanded by Graham Hancock in *Fingerprints of the Gods* (1995), and further elaborated by Rand Flem-Ath and the veteran rejected-knowledge author Colin Wilson in *The Atlantis Blueprint* (2000). Their theory proposes that Atlantis was located in Antarctica. They suggest that it was destroyed when the earth's crust suddenly slid some 1,500 miles in 9600 BCE and moved the South Pole from the Indian Ocean to its present position, dooming the continent to a slow death under spreading ice.

This notion is not quite as weird as it sounds. The earth's crust does shift over the mantle, the layer of hot semiliquid rock below it, though current evidence suggests that this takes place at a tiny fraction of the speed that the Antarctica-as-Atlantis theory requires. Evidence from paleomagnetism—traces of the earth's magnetic field in rock and sediment laid down in the past—also argues strongly against the crustal-slippage theory, since there are no signs of the sudden massive shifts of magnetic orientation required by the theory in question.

Some sort of exotic crustal slippage isn't essential to the Antarctica-as-Atlantis theory, though. Parts of Antarctica were ice-free during the "Atlantis window," the period from 9600 BCE to sometime after 9400 BCE, when Plato's narrative places Atlantis. The West Antarctic Ice Sheet destabilized and collapsed during one of the warming phases at the end of the last ice age, and it took the ice thousands of years to reestablish itself. During the interval, large parts of Antarctica—including Marie Byrd Land, Ellsworth Land, and the Antarctic Peninsula—were wholly or partly ice-free.

Still, this is about all that can be said for the Antarctica-as-Atlantis theory. Even if the theory of crustal slippage is correct, Antarctica 11,600 years ago would have been at the same latitude as Tierra del Fuego is now, and just as bleak and inhospitable. It might just have supported a sparse population eking out a bare living from fishing and foraging, but it could not have been home to anything like Plato's Atlantean empire. Nor does Antarctica fit anything else in the classical accounts of Atlantis. No stretch of the imagination can make Antarctica fit Plato's description of its location, though it must be said that the Flem-Aths make heroic efforts to bend Plato to fit their theory. Finally, like most of the other offbeat contenders for the site of Atlantis, Antarctica suffers from one other serious drawback: it isn't underwater, as Plato says Atlantis is, and it hasn't been for at least 60 million years.

The Destruction of Santorini

Proposals of the sort considered so far in this chapter have evoked furious and scornful responses from orthodox scientists. There's a long and ugly history behind this attitude and its mirror image, the contempt many Atlantologists have for conventional science. Many of the founders of modern Atlantology, starting with Blavatsky and Donnelly and including most of their early followers, engaged in vitriolic attacks on what they saw as the failings and blind spots of contemporary scientific ideas. Scientists, being human, responded in kind and dismissed Atlantology as crackpot pseudoscience by definition. Some of these latter attacks were well deserved—like most branches of the rejected-knowledge movement, Atlantology has more than its share of faulty logic and dubious evidence—but not all.

By the early decades of the twentieth century, as the rejected-knowledge movement found a cultural niche and following, the mutual hostility between Atlantologists and the scientific establishment spiraled into open warfare. This helped push partisans of rejected knowledge into believing anything rejected by modern science simply because it had been rejected by modern science. It also helped push the movement's opposite number, the debunking movement, into believing that anything affirmed by the rejected-knowledge movement must be false simply because it was believed by the rejected-knowledge movement. Just as Donnelly and many of his followers argued that any evidence that might be explained by Atlantis had to be explained by Atlantis, debunkers who have taken on the Atlantis legend have argued that any evidence that might have another explanation must have the other explanation. All this brought further confusion to a subject that was already murky enough.

The Island of Thera, Remnant of Santorini

During the second half of the twentieth century, though, a significant faction among scientists and Atlantis debunkers alike embraced a new theory arguing that Plato's narrative was actually based on real events. This theory has two major advantages over most others. First, a civilization somewhat like the one Plato describes can be solidly documented in the place and time required. Second, so can a catastrophe dramatic enough to fit Plato's narrative.

Sometime around 1450 BCE, one of the greatest volcanic eruptions ever witnessed by human beings tore apart the island of Santorini, in the Aegean Sea south of Greece.[19] The eruption blasted huge amounts of volcanic ash into the atmosphere, leaving a layer that can still be traced in core samples over 770,000 square miles of ocean floor. At the peak of the eruption, the lava chambers far beneath the volcano gave way, and Santorini collapsed, sending immense tidal waves across the eastern Mediterranean. What remains of Santorini today is a set of three shattered islands—Thera, Therasia, and Aspronisi—surrounding a huge volcanic crater thirty-two

---

19 Galanopoulos and Bacon 1969 and Vitaliano 1973 are my sources for the following account of the Santorini eruption.

square miles in area, with two new lava cones rising from the blue water at its center.

Some eighty miles south of Santorini lies the large island of Crete. During the Bronze Age (2100–1300 BCE), Crete was home to one of the great civilizations of the eastern Mediterranean world—the Minoan civilization, as it's called by modern archaeologists. Excavations at the palaces of Minoan rulers have turned up elegant pottery and frescoes, splendid metalwork, and documents written in a script, called Linear A, that remains undeciphered to this day. Minoan merchants controlled trade routes across the eastern Mediterranean, trading with Egypt, the thriving city-states along the coast of Palestine, and the Hittite Empire in what is now Turkey. At home, the Minoans seem to have been ruled by a confederacy of priest-kings headquartered at the great palace at Knossos, in north-central Crete.

Living in one of the world's most active earthquake belts, the Minoans were familiar with natural disasters, and many of the great palaces show signs of being damaged by earthquakes several times in their history. Sometime during the fifteenth century BCE, though, a far more drastic change overtook Minoan society. Every one of the great palaces except Knossos itself was burned and abandoned, and most of the towns of central and eastern Crete suffered severe damage. Knossos remained standing but was a shadow of its former greatness until around 1300 BCE, when it was finally abandoned forever. By this time, Knossos's rulers did not even come from Crete: its records in its later years were written in Linear B, an archaic form of Greek, showing that invaders from the mainland had taken control of the island.

The approximate fit between the dates of the Santorini eruption and the sudden decline of the Minoan civilization caught the attention of scholars early on. In 1939, the Greek archaeologist Spyridon Marinatos published a paper titled "The Volcanic Destruction of Minoan Crete," arguing that the effects of the Santorini eruption sent the Minoan culture into a decline from which it never recovered.

Matters took an unexpected twist in 1950 when Marinatos proposed that the Santorini eruption was not only the cause of the Minoan collapse but the source of Plato's story of Atlantis. His suggestion was taken up enthusiastically by another Greek archaeologist, Angelos Galanopoulos, who published a series of books attempting to prove that Plato's narrative came from an Egyptian account of the end of Minoan Crete. Over the last few decades, this speculation has become the one theory about Atlantis that orthodox scientists have been willing to accept, and more than a dozen recent books present it as the solution to the riddle of Atlantis.

Galanopoulos, whose version of the theory remains the most popular, argues that the story Solon received from the Egyptian priest was a lightly garbled account of the destruction of Minoan civilization.[20] The most important error, he suggests, is that the Egyptian character for "hundred" was accidentally replaced with the one for "thousand," causing all large numbers to be off by a factor of ten. Thus, for example, the fall of Atlantis had occurred nine hundred years before Solon's time rather than nine thousand. This would make many of the details of the story fit Minoan Crete tolerably enough; nine hundred years before Solon's time would put the fall of Atlantis somewhere around 1500 BCE, near the eruption of Santorini. The figures given for the size of Atlantis's central plain, the number of soldiers in its army, and the like also can be made to fit Minoan Crete tolerably well if all of them are divided by ten. The only problem with this ingenious theory is that the ancient Egyptian characters for "hundred" and "thousand" differ so visibly that not even Solon, much less his Egyptian informant, could have mixed them up.

Minoan culture had some notable things in common with Atlantis as Plato describes it. Like Plato's Atlanteans, the Minoans were great sailors, worked in bronze and other metals, and had a written language. They may even have fought a war with Athens, which

---

20 See Galanopoulos and Bacon 1969 for the details cited in the following paragraphs.

was a city already in Mycenean times. The bull, finally, was a cult animal in Crete and Atlantis alike.

Other details don't fit so well. Nothing like the Atlantean capital described in the *Critias* with its natural moats connected to the sea by a canal, can be found in the remains of Minoan Crete. Galanopoulos argues that the *Critias* description actually includes two cities: an "Ancient Metropolis" with natural moats and a "Royal City" without them. He goes on to claim that the "Ancient Metropolis" was on Santorini itself. Two cities can be extracted from the *Critias* account only by doing violence to the text, though, and the circular moats connected by a canal to the sea could only have existed on a relatively flat island. Santorini was anything but flat; the island was a tall volcanic cone before it blew itself apart in Minoan times.

Equally, Plato's description of the location of Atlantis—in front of the Strait of Gibraltar and not far from the continent on the other side of the ocean—cannot be applied to Minoan Crete by any stretch of the imagination. Defenders of the Santorini theory have done their best to grapple with this last difficulty. They have proposed a variety of reasons why "the Pillars of Hercules," a term that in Plato's time meant the Strait of Gibraltar and nothing else, could have meant something else in this one case, though it must be said that none of these reasons are particularly convincing and no ancient Greek document supports them.

Nor, of course, are Crete or its Minoan palaces under water, and scientists remain fiercely divided on the question of whether the eruption of Santorini caused the collapse of the Minoan civilization or was just one more natural disaster in a region used to turmoil. Like many of the other theories discussed in this section, the Minoan theory identifies a lost civilization, and it has the advantage of identifying one that certainly existed and has been excavated in detail. Still, it deserves repeating that not every lost civilization is Atlantis.

Atlantis Everywhere

A final approach proposed by several Atlantologists is the claim that Atlantis was not a specific place, but rather a dim memory of a worldwide civilization destroyed long before the beginning of recorded history. Some sections of Blavatsky's legominism can be read in this way, and so can the Edgar Cayce readings, whose influence on recent Atlantis theories has been immense. Placing Atlantis on a worldwide scale may seem counterintuitive, but it actually simplifies the process of making sense of Plato. If Atlantis was everywhere, the question of how to interpret Plato's geographical clues can be finessed with relative ease. The challenge that remains is explaining why no unequivocal signs of this lost global civilization have yet been found by archaeologists. At least two Atlantologists in recent years have proposed their own solutions to this challenge.

The first is Graham Hancock, one of the most popular and influential writers in the rejected-knowledge field today. In a series of best-selling books starting with *Fingerprints of the Gods* (1995), Hancock has argued that an ancient technological civilization as advanced as ours—or possibly even more advanced—inhabited the earth until a vast natural disaster obliterated it sometime around 10,450 BCE. Survivors of the cataclysm built a new homeland in prehistoric Egypt, only to be overwhelmed by a second round of catastrophes. Thereafter, only fragmentary traces remained of the ancient civilization in the form of legends and a handful of stupendous ancient structures such as the Sphinx and the Great Pyramid.

All this may seem very familiar to those of my readers who paid attention to the last chapter. Hancock rarely mentions the occult sources of his ideas, but nearly every element of Blavatsky's legominism plays a central role in his theories. The theme of the seed-bearers, the keystone of the Blavatskian Atlantis theory, is particularly important in his work. Nearly the only element of the occult Atlantis not found in Hancock's writings to date is the theme of conflict between the worshippers of the One and the Lords of the Dark Face. It may not be accidental that Hancock's way of presenting his theories parallels the one Blavatsky used in *Isis Unveiled*. The strategy of pointing out holes in conventional scientific ideas and then showing that an alternative hypothesis fills those holes is common to both books.

Just as with Blavatsky's works, too, the details of Hancock's theories shift ground slightly with each of his books. He has pursued an ambitious program of research in search of the lost civilization he believes he has detected, and his findings have guided the development of his ideas. (This is a good sign; the writer who can find only one meaning endlessly repeated in varying data is usually a crackpot.) In *Fingerprints of the Gods*, he accepted the Flem-Aths' Antarctica-as-Atlantis theory and suggested that relics of the lost civilization had not been found because the two-mile-thick Antarctic ice cap covers them. "Here and there around the globe," he suggests, ". . . the *fingerprints* of a lost civilization remain faintly visible. The *body* is out of sight, buried under two miles of Antarctic ice and almost as inaccessible to archaeologists as if it were located on the dark side of the moon."[21]

More recently, his 2002 work *Underworld* shifted focus from Antarctica to the huge areas of coastal land swallowed by rising sea levels at the end of the last ice age. Here he is on firmer ground, since the flooding that followed the melting of the great continental glaciers has been documented in great detail by recent geological research, and discoveries of drowned cities off the coasts of India and elsewhere provide a degree of solid evidence that most theories about Atlantis have rarely been able to muster.

Both theories, though, suffer from a common flaw. If an advanced technological civilization like ours actually existed in the distant past—in Antarctica, the world's continental shelves, or anywhere else—it's hard to believe that conclusive traces of its existence would have been restricted to just those areas that happen to be out of reach of archaeologists. Imagine for a moment that a similar catastrophe overwhelmed today's industrial civilization—a

---

21 Hancock 1995, 473; emphasis in original.

crustal slippage that put western Europe and eastern North America into a polar deep freeze, for example, or another round of global warming that melted the remaining ice caps and took sea levels up another three hundred feet. Ten thousand years from now, scholars trying to piece together the shape of the past might be in the same situation our historians face now, with five thousand years or so of recorded history to work with and, before that, a series of riddles.

Still, those future scholars would have a resource that today's Atlantologists have never been able to uncover. Even if the legendary lost cities of London and New York remained buried under an ice cap or a hundred feet of sea-floor mud, our civilization would have left remains all over the world, and it would take only a few solid finds—a dozen suburban houses buried in a landslide in Canada, the bleached ruins of an airport amid the desert sands of ancient Nebraska, the crumbling remains of a hydroelectric dam in what was once Russia, or what have you—to reveal the existence of our civilization. This is how archaeology works, and plenty of other lost civilizations have been revealed by evidence of this same sort. If a worldwide technological civilization like ours existed in 9600 BCE, why didn't it leave the same traces behind that ours certainly will?

The only Atlantis theorist to have proposed a workable answer to this question so far is the English occultist John Michell. In his bestselling *The View Over Atlantis* (1969), Michell, like Hancock, suggested that the Atlantis legend and its many equivalents are echoes of a worldwide civilization of the distant past, destroyed by its own mishandling of the technology that gave it its power.[22] The reason why this ancient civilization has left no traces of its advanced technology, he suggested, is that it relied on a science so different from ours that modern archaeologists fail to recognize it as a technology at all.

An occultist with a rare grasp of esoteric tradition, Michell constructed an image of a lost natural magic that drew on subtle forces within the earth to create balance between humanity and nature

---

22 Michell 1969, 169–70 and throughout.

and accomplish miracles that went far beyond the ones our modern technology can manage. If this sounds like a legominism rather than a work of speculative history, it should. *The View Over Atlantis*, in fact, is among the most successful legominisms of recent years and has had notable effects in many corners of today's popular culture. Many of its historical claims are doubtful at best. Still, Michell's vision of a civilization built on entirely different principles from ours is a useful reminder that our particular kind of advanced society may not be the only one researchers into the past need to look for.

FOUR

Destruction by Water

The sheer profusion of rival theories about Atlantis is one of the most curious things about the whole phenomenon. At this point, practically every corner of the world has been identified by someone as the site of Atlantis, whether or not it has anything in common with the place described in Plato's dialogues. L. Sprague de Camp's acerbic comment in *Lost Continents*, his skeptical survey of the Atlantis legend, remains just as relevant today as when he wrote it: "You cannot change all the details of Plato's story and still claim to have Plato's story. That is like saying the legendary King Arthur is 'really' Queen Cleopatra; all you have to do is to change Cleopatra's sex, nationality, period, temperament, moral character, and other details, and the resemblance becomes obvious."[1]

What makes these speculative approaches problematic, ultimately, is that they're interchangeable; none of them makes a better case than any of the others. The same logic that puts Atlantis in Anatolia, the Aegean, the Andes Mountains, or Antarctica and scatters potential dates for its sinking across the centuries can be used just as effectively to put it anywhere else in the world at any time in history. The same kind of reasoning could probably be used to

---

1 De Camp 1970, 221.

argue that the Roman Empire was located in India in the Stone Age, the Declaration of Independence was signed in Timbuktu just before the birth of Jesus of Nazareth, and the First World War will be fought on Mars a thousand years from now! One of the weirder productions of the early-twentieth-century Druid movement, a book by one Captain George Cooper titled *The Druid Bible,* used essentially the same logic outlined in the last chapter to "prove" that Atlantis was on the west coast of England near Bristol, the Trojan War was fought near Southampton, and the Garden of Eden was on Salisbury Plain.

The essential flaw in this thinking was explained long in advance by the Egyptian priest who spoke to Solon in Plato's narrative. The priest pointed out that the world had seen many different destructions by fire, water, and other causes. Treat this claim as a hypothesis about prehistory, and it provides a coherent explanation for the dozens of lost cities and civilizations turned up all over the world by Atlantologists. The drowned ruins that dot the world's continental shelves and the scraps of impossible knowledge found in old maps and records from around the world, after all, need not come from a single source in the past. The fall of Atlantis could have been only one of many catastrophes that swallowed civilizations at different places and times over the millennia since human beings first emerged on our world.

Thus it's not enough to find an ancient city that no longer exists, even if it happens to be under the sea, and claim that this city must be Atlantis. There has to be some reason to think that the city in question is the one Plato happened to be talking about in the *Timaeus* and *Critias*. The assumption that there could have been only one significant civilization destroyed in prehistory—an assumption made by far too many Atlantologists in the rejected-knowledge movement—is just as much a product of the myth of progress as the claim that the civilizations of the last five thousand years or so are the only ones that have ever been.

Fortunately, Plato himself provides two crucial pieces of information that allow us to sort through the possibilities: the general location of Atlantis and the approximate date of its destruction. These details make it possible to ask three questions:

- First, is it geologically possible for a large area of land to be suddenly submerged beneath the sea?

- Second, does evidence suggest that this could have happened at some point in recent prehistory—specifically, not long after 9400 BCE?

- Third, was there a large island in the western Atlantic at that time that could have been drowned by such a flood?

We'll examine these questions one at a time.

Uniformitarians and Catastrophists

The first question is the easiest to answer. In the second half of the twentieth century, the earth sciences underwent a revolution, as new evidence showed that spectacular catastrophes of many kinds have ravaged the earth in relatively recent times. Yet deeply ingrained habits of thought stand in the way of taking these catastrophes seriously as a factor in human prehistory. It's worth taking the time here to see where these habits came from, and why.

If you're like most people nowadays, you learned in school that modern science was invented in seventeenth-century Europe and, after a few tussles with organized religion, was quickly accepted by everyone but fanatics and occultists because it did a better job of explaining the world than any other system of thought. This way of thinking about the history of science plays a large role in our modern faith in progress, but it has little to do with what actually happened. In reality, the road that brought science to its present place in society had many more twists and turns, because most of the founders of the scientific revolution were occultists who practiced astrology, magic, and alchemy as well as science.[2]

An unspoken agreement shaped scientific research in those days. Because so many early scientists were involved in the occult, they had to step carefully around religious issues, and so these early scientists avoided any line of research that might call Christian doctrine into question. In return, the Christian churches drew a sharp distinction between science, which was permitted, and magic, which still suffered under ancient prohibitions.

This comfortable arrangement broke apart in the nineteenth century when geologists began to struggle with massive problems fitting the evidence of earth's long history with the myth of the world's creation given in the Book of Genesis.[3] One of the major battlegrounds of this struggle was the story of Noah's ark. According to the Bible story, the entire earth was covered around 2349 BCE by a titanic flood that rose above the tops of the highest mountains on earth. As geologists studied the known effects of floods and sorted out layers of rock and sediment around the world, though, it became clear that no worldwide flood had happened then or at any other time. All through the first half of the nineteenth century, as evidence piled up, scientists and clergymen alike tried to find some middle ground that would allow the old truce to stay intact, but they failed.

In 1859, when Charles Darwin's book *The Origin of Species* introduced the theory of evolution, the fraying truce between science and religion dissolved into open war. Those who refused to give up belief in the literal truth of the Biblical story ended up trying to force the geological evidence to fit the Book of Genesis. To back up their arguments, they turned to an old geological theory called *catastrophism*.

---

2 See Jacobs 1988 and Yates 1969 for good general surveys of the relation between magic and the early phases of the scientific revolution.

3 Huggett 1989 and Palmer 2003 provide good summaries of the catastrophist-uniformitarian conflict in geology.

When it first emerged in the eighteenth century, catastrophism was a scientific theory like any other. It argued that large geological features such as mountains and valleys had come into being in sudden, catastrophic events such as earthquakes and floods. The opposing theory, called *uniformitarianism*, argued that the earth's surface had been shaped entirely by gradual processes such as erosion and uplift. By the early nineteenth century, uniformitarianism was more popular than catastrophism, but only the most extreme uniformitarians insisted that catastrophes had played no role in shaping the earth's surface, and both views had a place in the exchange of ideas that filled the earth sciences in those days.

The struggle over Noah's flood put an end to this relative tolerance. As intellectual positions hardened, conservative Christians denounced those who questioned the literal truth of the Bible as atheists, while scientists blacklisted dissenters from the uniformitarian theory as religious fanatics. Scientific catastrophists came under fire from both sides. By 1900, the uniformitarian theory had hardened into dogma, and it remained the only acceptable way to think about the earth sciences well into the 1970s. Even today, uniformitarian ideas remain almost universal in the scientific world—at least outside the handful of sciences that deal directly with the earth and its history.

In the earth sciences themselves, by contrast, a new form of catastrophism has staged a powerful comeback during the last few decades. To make sense of the evidence that drove the emergence of the "New Catastrophism," we need to take another look at the seemingly familiar planet on which we all live.

Planetary Catastrophes

Imagine for a moment that, instead of a book on Atlantis, you hold in your hands a science-fiction novel about a strange planet wheeling about a faraway star in some distant galaxy. Beneath a brittle outer skin of rock, this planet is literally a ball of molten lava sloshing back and forth as it spins through space. The churning lava tears the thin crust into chunks that jar and shudder against one another as they drift, sending shock waves around the planet and crumpling the skin of rock into jagged peaks and valleys. Here and there, lava bursts through onto the surface, sometimes forming towering volcanic peaks, sometimes blasting out huge calderas or covering thousands of square miles in bubbling liquid rock.

Gases venting out from the planet's molten interior give it an atmosphere of highly reactive, chemically unstable gases, and oceans swept by immense, destructive storms cover much of its brittle surface. When undersea volcanoes erupt or crustal plates ram one another beneath the oceans, huge waves race across the oceans in all directions and crash into continents with killing force. Making matters worse, this alien world has a wildly unstable climate: sometimes the whole planet is covered by tropical jungle from pole to pole, sometimes ice sprawls across the continents, and at still other times the planet has some of each.

Yet the most terrifying dangers come from space. A natural magnetic field and a high layer of toxic gases keep at bay the most lethal radiation from the star the planet circles, but every so often the magnetic field collapses, the gases clear away, and the surface of the planet bears the full brunt of the star's blazing ultraviolet rays. More dangerous still, the planet orbits through a vast cloud of millions of chunks of shattered rock, ranging in size from sand grains to masses the size of mountains, all hurtling around the same star at speeds of thousands of miles an hour. Small ones pelt the planet constantly, and every now and then one of the big ones plunges through the atmosphere and hammers the planet, causing immense devastation.

Improbably, life has emerged on this perilous world, crawling out of protected pockets on the margins of the oceans and struggling with other life forms and the elements to exploit every ecological niche. Tough as the planet they inhabit, the life forms of this distant world have evolved ways to survive everything their harsh environment can throw at them, and many of them have savage defensive or offensive weapons—fangs, claws, poison spines, and much more. Even so, a glance over the weathered rocks of the planet's surface shows the bleached fossil bones of countless other species that drew the wrong number in the lottery of survival.

Sounds like a great setting for a science-fiction adventure, doesn't it?

Welcome to Earth.

The picture just sketched out is a summary of our own world, as shown by the latest research in the earth sciences. Far from the stable arena for slow geological processes once imagined by strict uniformitarians, our planet now stands revealed as an unstable, dynamic system racked by catastrophic changes of many kinds. The shift in worldviews had many causes, but the most important was an unexpected answer to one of the greatest riddles in our planet's long history: the death of the dinosaurs.

Every child today knows what dinosaurs were, and many children—I was one of them—can rattle off the jawbreaking names of the more famous species with ease. Behind the stereotype of vast, hulking creatures lumbering down the road to extinction through sheer stupidity, though, lies a different and much more fascinating reality. The dinosaurs rank as one of the most successful life forms in the history of the planet.

For more than 150 million years, from their gradual emergence in the Triassic Period to their sudden disappearance at the end of the Cretaceous, dinosaurs and their close relatives dominated ecosystems across the planet. By contrast, mammals—the branch of the animal kingdom to which human beings belong—have had the top spot on land for only around 50 million years and have never ruled the seas or the skies the way the great reptiles did. The dinosaurs still hold the all-time world record for biggest flying creature (*Ornithocheirus*, a pterodactyl with a forty-foot wingspan), longest (the ninety-foot-long *Diplodocus*) and heaviest (the one-hundred-ton *Argentinosaurus*) land animal, biggest land predator (*Giganotosaurus*, an oversized tyrannosaur that weighed in at seven tons), and biggest predator anywhere (*Liopleurodon*, a seagoing horror more than eighty feet long with teeth the size of human legs).[4]

Then, 65 million years ago, the last of the dinosaurs vanished forever. Dozens of theories have been floated over the years to explain their disappearance, ranging from the plausible (climate changes that made huge reptiles less successful than smaller, warm-blooded competitors) to the preposterous (the decline of a widespread plant family with strong laxative properties, causing all the dinosaurs to die of constipation).[5] In the late 1970s, however, a smoking gun turned up: a thin layer of clay, laid down right at the end of the Cretaceous Period, that turned out to be full of iridium.

Rare on earth, iridium is common in meteors, and in 1980 physicist Luis Alvarez and his geologist son, Walter Alvarez, proposed in a famous paper that the clay layer represented fallout from a catastrophic collision between the earth and a large meteor.[6] Other geologists found the same iridium trace in sediments all over the world dating from exactly the same time, along with many other traces of a meteor impact. Eventually, the search for the impact site turned up a huge, long-buried crater near Chicxulub (pronounced "chick-SHOO-loob"), on the northwest corner of the Yucatán Peninsula in Mexico. Bit by bit, research pieced together a terrifying story.

One otherwise ordinary day 65 million years ago, a six-mile-wide mass of rock came hurtling out of deep space at hypersonic speed and slammed into the earth's crust at Chicxulub. Milliseconds after the impact, a fireball hotter than the surface of the sun shot outward for more than a hundred miles in all directions, blasting out a huge crater and vaporizing everything in its path. A fraction of a second later came a shock wave that obliterated every living thing across a region the size of Europe. As the fireball faded, white-hot fragments of rock blown clear out of the atmosphere into space

---

4 Figures on dinosaur sizes are from Haines and Chambers 2006.

5 Yes, this was actually proposed; see Hallam 2004, 3–5.

6 See Alvarez 1997 for an account of the discovery of the Chicxulub impact.

rained back down all over the planet, igniting fires that torched every forest on earth. After the fires died, heat gave way to cold as dust and smoke in the upper atmosphere blotted out the sun and sent the earth into a planetwide winter. Starved of sunlight, the few surviving plants died, food chains came apart, and the vast majority of animals starved to death. By the time the skies cleared and conditions returned to normal, months or years later, two-thirds of the species on earth, including all the dinosaurs, had gone extinct.

By the early 1990s, overwhelmed by the evidence for a catastrophic meteor impact at the end of the Cretaceous, the strict uniformitarian theory had gone the way of the dinosaurs themselves. The era of the "New Catastrophism" had arrived.[7] If any additional inspiration was needed, it arrived courtesy of Comet Shoemaker-Levy. This comet made a close approach to Jupiter in 1993, tore itself apart in the giant planet's gravitational field, and swung into a new orbit with a fatal destination. Over a few days in the summer of 1994, the fragments slammed into Jupiter one after another. The largest piece, fragment G, unleashed a 100-million-megaton blast— that is, an explosion equal to about eight *billion* Hiroshima bombs.[8] If it had struck our world on that summer day, the fate of the dinosaurs would probably have been ours.

With these examples of planetary devastation in front of them, scientists looked at old evidence with new eyes and discovered that traces of many other catastrophes could readily be found in the earth. At least three such catastrophes could have set enough water in motion to drown a land area the size of Plato's Atlantis: an oceanic meteor impact, a massive underwater landslide, or a sudden sea level rise caused by melting ice sheets—and all three of them have occurred in the recent geological past.

7 Ager 1993 provides a good overview.
8 McGuire 2002, 138.

The Torrent from Heaven

The discovery of the Chicxulub impact and its devastating results made meteors and comets an obvious first place to start looking for potential causes of catastrophe. The rejected-knowledge movement got there first—Ignatius Donnelly's 1886 book *Ragnarok: The Age of Fire and Gravel* first popularized the idea of a collision between the earth and a comet almost a century before the concept became acceptable among scientists—but rejected-knowledge writers use outdated and inaccurate data often enough to make current scientific research a better resource for understanding the ways that catastrophe can sweep our planet.

The Chicxulub impact, fortunately, also launched major research programs dedicated to finding traces of meteor and comet impacts on the earth. Weathering on land and the buildup of mud undersea make craters difficult to find on our world, but more than 165 impact craters have now been identified on the earth's surface, and more are being found every year.

The relevance of these discoveries to the Atlantis legend is easy to trace. Seventy percent of the earth's surface is covered by ocean, so on average, seven out of every ten meteor impacts fall into the sea. Drop a pebble into a pond and ripples spread to its far edges; the bigger the pebble and the faster it moves when it hits the water, the bigger the ripples. Make the pebble a meteor a quarter mile across and fling it into the ocean at thousands of miles an hour, and the "ripples" become what scientists call a megatsunami.

Consider the catastrophe that hit the Indian Ocean sometime around 2800 BCE, according to scientists of the Holocene Impact Working Group, one of the scientific teams researching meteor impacts in the recent geological past.[9] Four huge wedge-shaped deposits of sediment near the southern tip of the island of Madagascar provide the smoking gun in this case. They contain the remains of animals from the bottom of the ocean mixed with droplets of

---

9 Blakeslee 2006.

melted iron, nickel, and chromium—a mix rare in earthly sediment but common where meteors strike.

About nine hundred miles southeast of the deposits, a recently discovered crater eighteen miles across lies at the bottom of the ocean, dating from the same time as the deposits themselves. When a meteor slammed into the Indian Ocean 4,800 years ago and made the crater, a megatsunami at least six hundred feet high swept out in all directions, loaded with deepwater sediment stirred up by the blast. When it crashed into shorelines all around the Indian Ocean, it destroyed everything in its path and flooded many miles inland, dumping its burden of sediment in some places and ripping away soil from the land in others.

The impact of such a megatsunami on a coastal civilization is terrifying to contemplate. There would have been almost no warning, only a sudden streak of fire across the sky followed by an immense fireball. Then, maybe a few hours later, the sea would have drawn back many miles, exposing huge stretches of continental shelf. When the sea returned, it would have come as a wall of water six hundred feet high—about thirteen times as big as the Aceh tsunami that devastated Indonesia in the last days of 2004. Anyone and anything within many miles of the shore would have been caught in the wave and drowned.

Could such an impact-driven megatsunami have washed away an entire human culture, if that culture was close enough to the impact site? In all probability, yes. Would such an event have left traces in legend? Again, almost certainly yes. Dr. Bruce Masse, an archaeologist with the Los Alamos National Laboratory, has pointed out that fourteen flood legends from different cultures mention a total eclipse of the sun at the same time as a worldwide flood, and a total solar eclipse happened on the morning of May 10, 2807 BCE, right in the middle of the time window for the Madagascar tsunami. The legends from southern India of land swallowed by the sea, mentioned back in chapter 1, take on a very different meaning when read in the light of the Holocene Impact Working Group's discoveries.

Still, two details make impact megatsunamis less than perfect as explanations for Plato's account of Atlantis. First, researchers have not found the signs of an impact in the Atlantic basin dating from the end of the Atlantis window in the centuries immediately after 9400 BCE. Second, as a cause for an Atlantis-style disaster, meteor impacts have a serious drawback. When the megatsunami of 2800 BCE crashed over Madagascar, everyone within miles of the shore would have perished, but Madagascar itself did not vanish beneath the sea; the great deposits of sediment cast up by the wave stand on dry land. If Atlantis had been destroyed by an impact-caused megatsunami alone, then, Plato's island would still be above water, and foundations of Atlantean buildings would give archaeologists far more to work with than the riddles and equivocal traces that point to Atlantis today.

Some impact theorists in the rejected-knowledge movement have done their level best to tackle this difficulty. Otto Muck argued that the meteor impact that destroyed his version of Atlantis triggered volcanic eruptions and the collapse of a hypothetical caldera supporting the Azores, while Paul Dunbavin, who placed Atlantis in the Irish Sea, proposed that a meteor impact literally knocked the earth askew and shifted Atlantis into deeper waters. Neither of these theories have been supported by geological evidence, and most other impact theories about Atlantis simply ignore the issue. This will not do. If Plato is our guide, a cause for the drowning of Atlantis must be sought elsewhere.

Terra Non Firma

Impacts from space, however, are far from the only cause of megatsunamis. As I write these words, a catastrophe as devastating as the one in the Atlantis legend waits for its moment in the eastern Atlantic. The trigger is a huge mass of rock that makes up the entire western side of Cumbre Vieja, a big volcano on the island of La Palma in the Canary Islands. Separated by huge cracks from the rest of the volcano, it stands perched unsteadily on the edge of the

The Devastation Left Behind by a Tsunami

ocean.[10] In 1949, during a volcanic eruption, the entire mass—more than a hundred cubic *miles* of rock—slid thirteen feet toward the sea and then stopped. At some point in the future, many scientists agree, it will finish the trip and go crashing down into the Atlantic.

One hundred cubic miles of rock displace a lot of water, and the result will be a disaster like nothing in recorded history. Imagine a wall of water a hundred feet high crashing into the east coast of North America, going right across the Florida peninsula into the Gulf of Mexico, pounding New York and Washington, D.C., into rubble, and pouring inland all the way to the foothills of the Appalachians. Now imagine a dozen or more such waves coming one after another, hitting at fifteen- or twenty-minute intervals like blows from Poseidon's own hammer. This is what the latest computer models predict will happen when the west wall of Cumbre Vieja finally breaks loose and falls into the sea. North America will have only nine hours' warning before the waves arrive, nothing like enough time to evacuate the tens of millions of people at risk from the catastrophe. At that,

---

10 The following paragraphs are based on McGuire 2002, 115–19.

America is lucky: Brazil will have only six hours, Spain a little more than two, and the coast of northwest Africa just over one hour.

When will this happen? Nobody knows. It might happen tomorrow, or ten thousand years from now. The one thing oceanographers know for certain is that slides and tsunamis on the same vast scale have happened many times in the last million years or so. Submarine surveys of the ocean bottom around the Canary Islands have found huge undersea landslides of broken rock sprawling for more than a hundred miles across the sea floor, the remnants of previous slides on the same scale as the one that will be unleashed when the west wall of Cumbre Vieja finally goes crashing into the sea. Could these have caused some of the great floods chronicled in old legends from the Atlantic basin—for example, the floods from the sea mentioned in the old Irish *Book of Invasions*? The possibility is hard to dismiss.

These terrifying events are by no means restricted to the Atlantic. Around the Hawaiian Islands, submarine surveys have found the tracks of more than sixty gigantic underwater landslides, some of them containing more than 250 cubic miles of rubble. The most recent of these slides went cascading down the undersea slopes of the island of Hawaii just over a hundred thousand years ago. The resulting tsunami tossed chunks of coral reef one thousand feet above sea level on the neighboring island of Lanai and put debris almost fifty feet above sea level seven thousand miles away on the southwestern shores of Australia. When something like this happens in the future—and once again, geologists agree that the question is when, not if—catastrophic tsunamis will sweep outward in all directions and smash into every landmass bordering the Pacific Ocean. Does the thought of a series of fifty-foot tsunamis crashing into Tokyo, Shanghai, and Los Angeles all on the same day seem impossible to you? Get used to the idea. Recent research has shown that such things have happened in the recent past and can be expected to occur again in the future.

As a potential source for an Atlantis-style disaster, though, megatsunamis caused by massive undersea landslides are once again not enough by themselves. Once the waves have come and gone, the land struck by them remains above the water's surface, and any traces of human activity that survived the floods—foundations, underground structures, settlements in highland areas, and wreckage left behind by the waves themselves—would be within reach of archaeologists today. To cause the disaster Plato described, one of two things had to happen: either a large area of land dropped suddenly below sea level and stayed there for some 9,400 years, or sea level itself rose suddenly and stayed risen for a similar time.

So far, at least, nobody has proposed a scientifically plausible force that could sink an island as large as the one Plato portrayed. A sudden surge in sea level, on the other hand, is quite another matter. Not only is such an event possible, but consistent evidence, universally accepted in today's earth sciences, shows that it has happened many times—and the time Plato gives for the rise and fall of Atlantis falls squarely in the middle of one of the most drastic periods of sea level rise in the history of our planet.

The Coming of the Ice

According to Plato's narrative, the civilization of Atlantis emerged sometime before 9600 BCE on an island near the western shores of the Atlantic Ocean and sank beneath the waves sometime after 9400 BCE. Those dates are crucial, because the world of the tenth millennium BCE was in many ways a totally different world from the one we know today. During the time Plato gives for the heyday of Atlantis, the earth was emerging from the immense planetary trauma of the last ice age.

Most accounts of ice ages in the popular media still rely on outdated geological theories more than a century old. Picturesque images of glaciers, woolly mammoths, and grunting cavemen in bearskin kilts provide decoration for a story of immensely slow change, as ice sheets took thousands of years to creep southward from the poles and retreated just as gradually. New discoveries in the earth sciences disproved every detail of that account many years ago—

yes, even the bearskin kilts—but it can take generations for new ideas to find their way out of the laboratories and into popular culture. That lag time blinds most people today to the terrifying reality of an event not all that far in our world's past.

As ecologists have been telling us for more than a century now, the natural world is full of complex cycles and feedback loops that allow very small changes to have huge effects. About two and a half million years ago, driven by small cyclic changes in the earth's orbit, one of the feedback loops that shapes the world's climate spun out of control. Temperatures worldwide plummeted, especially in the Arctic regions. In northern North America and northwestern Europe, cool summers left patches of winter snow unmelted, and these areas of permanent snow reflected more sunlight back to outer space, cooling the world further. As each year's snowfall piled atop the last, ice sheets began to spread across the northern half of the world.

This was not the first round of ice ages to hit our planet.[11] Some 800 million years ago, in the Precambrian Period, when the sun was younger and gave the earth around 6 percent less radiation than it does today, the entire earth cooled past the point of no return and all its water froze. For close to 200 million years, the entire planet from pole to pole was a single vast sheet of ice—the "Snowball Earth," today's geologists call it. Finally, around 600 million years ago, a series of cataclysmic volcanic eruptions pumped so much carbon dioxide into the atmosphere that the greenhouse effect took over and the ice sheets melted away, clearing the way for the distant ancestors of today's life forms.[12]

Around 280 million years ago, in the Permian Period, another round of severe ice ages helped bring about the worst mass extinction in the history of the planet, an age of die-off that erased more than 95 percent of all species then living. The causes of this harrowing event remain a subject of lively scientific debate, but at a time when all the world's landmasses formed the single continent

---

11 Macdougall 2004 gives a good summary of the earth's ice ages.
12 McGuire 2002, 68–70.

of Pangaea, having much of that continent covered by a two-mile-thick sheet of ice cannot have helped. The impact of the most recent period of ice ages—the Pleistocene Epoch, in geologist's jargon—was not quite as drastic as these, but it was severe enough.

Plunging temperatures and spreading ice sheets made up only one part of the ice age's impact. The water that froze into the great continental glaciers had to come from somewhere, and so as the ice spread, seas shrank, jungles turned into grasslands, and grass yielded to desert. The oceans sank up to five hundred feet below today's sea level. Millions of square miles of shallow seas and continental shelves became dry land. These changes drove tens of thousands of species into extinction, and the pressure of a radically changed environment forced extreme changes on the survivors—including our own ancestors.

Many students of human evolution now believe that the ice ages of the Pleistocene Epoch, more than any other factor, made us what we are.[13] For millions of years before the ice came, apes of various kinds spread throughout the Old World. During the slow cooling of the world's climate in the Pliocene, the epoch before the ice ages, some of them learned to walk upright and spread into grassland ecosystems where other apes rarely went. Their descendants became the australopithecines, our distant ancestors.

Only after the beginning of the Pleistocene ice ages, though, did a new kind of ape evolve out of australopithecine stock. These first members of our own genus, *Homo*, were tougher and more muscular than the graceful, lightly built australopithecines. In the harsh world of the Pleistocene, they had to be. They mastered the crucial skills of making stone tools and controlling fire, spread out of Africa across the Middle Eastern land bridge, and found homes everywhere from green Sundaland to the cold tundras of southern Europe. Later on, around 100,000 BCE, a population of these upright apes in the African grasslands evolved into members of our

---

13 Calvin 2002 and Fagan 2004 discuss the role of climate in human evolution.

own species—*Homo sapiens*—and followed the same track out of Africa to face the challenges of the ice age.

The world they encountered was radically different from the one we know today.[14] At the peak of the last ice age, ice sheets two miles thick covered much of the Northern Hemisphere, reaching thousands of miles south from the permanently frozen Arctic Ocean. The Atlantic was hundreds of miles narrower; where the English Channel is today, wide plains spread westward from France, and Ireland and Britain were both part of Europe. Where shallow seas separate the islands and peninsulas of Southeast Asia today, the huge landmass of Sundaland thrust into the southwestern Pacific. The Gulf of Mexico and the Caribbean Sea were a fraction of their present size, full of islands big and small that are underwater shoals today.

North America and Europe, where the ice lay thickest, would have been unrecognizable to modern eyes. Ice sheets covered all of present-day Canada and the northern tier of American states and buried Scandinavia, northwestern Russia, and all but the southernmost edges of the peninsula that today is the British Isles. South of the ice sheets, frozen tundra reached away for hundreds of miles, swept by a constant, freezing north wind generated by the ice itself. Reindeer herds wandered the snowy hills of southern France, walruses basked on Virginia's beaches, and icebergs dotted the ocean off the coast of Spain and Florida.

This is the way our world looked at the end of the Last Glacial Maximum (LGM) sixteen thousand years ago. Sixteen thousand years may seem like a long time at first glance, but compared with the four-billion-year history of the earth, it's barely an eye blink. Even in human terms it's not actually that long. The oldest forms of writing that can be read today date from about five thousand years ago, and the oldest city yet found by archaeologists, located at Jericho in the Middle East, was built around eleven thousand years ago.

---

14 See Gamble and Soffer 1990, Pielou 1991, and Soffer and Gamble 1990 for the sources of this picture of the last ice age.

Only six hundred generations or so separate us from people—human beings just like us—who saw the world of the last ice age with their own eyes.

The End of the Ice Age

Arnold Toynbee's monumental work *A Study of History*, one of the twentieth century's most influential historical studies, offers a crucial insight into the riddle of Atlantis. Toynbee proposed that civilizations are born when a society encounters a major challenge and, in the process of meeting it, breaks through to a new level of social integration. If Toynbee is right, the birth of civilizations at the end of the last ice age would make perfect sense, because the human societies of the Pleistocene faced massive challenges worldwide as the great continental ice sheets began to melt.

Scientific advances in recent decades make it possible to take the earth's temperature far back into the past. The thermometer scientists use is as elegant as it is simple. Water, H_2O, contains two kinds of oxygen, the lighter O_{16} and the heavier O_{18}. The warmer the global temperature, the more O_{18}-containing water evaporates from the world's oceans and ends up falling as snow on the ice caps of Antarctica and Greenland, the last remnants of the vast ice sheets of the LGM. Ice cores extracted from thousands of feet down and painstakingly sorted into layers representing each year's snowfall yield a clear record of the earth's temperature from the depths of the last ice age up to modern times.

Guided by the old uniformitarian dogma, scientists up until the 1980s insisted that temperatures rose and ice melted gradually over thousands of years, but the results of ice-core analysis threw these long-established claims out the window. Instead of centuries of slow warming, the end of the last ice age saw wild swings in global temperature that snapped many regions back and forth from polar cold to semitropical warmth within time spans of a few decades or less. The table below shows the most important stages in this process.[15]

The End of the Last Ice Age		
Atlantic	Cool	6200–3500 BCE
Boreal	Warm	9600–6200 BCE
Preboreal	Cool	10,200–9600 BCE
Younger Dryas (Dryas III)	Cold	10,800–10,200 BCE
Alleröd	Warm	11,800–10,800 BCE
Older Dryas (Dryas II)	Cool	12,400–11,800 BCE
Bölling	Warm	12,700–12,400 BCE
Oldest Dryas (Dryas I)	Cool	14,000–12,700 BCE
Last Glacial Maximum	Cold	20,000–14,000 BCE

The end of the last ice age started around sixteen thousand years ago with the beginning of the Oldest Dryas phase. Not as cold as the LGM, the Oldest Dryas was still harsh by today's standards, but the increasing warmth sent the ice sheets into slow retreat. Around 12,700 BCE, temperatures soared with the beginning of the Bölling phase. The ice sheets retreated hundreds of miles, forming huge lakes of meltwater that spilled into the rising oceans, while at least one major continental glacier, the West Antarctic Ice Sheet, collapsed completely and sent sea levels surging upward. Birch and pine forests spread northward into the European and American tundra as the reindeer herds left southern France.

After six hundred years, the warming trend of the Bölling phase halted, and a cool phase, the Older Dryas, began. After another six centuries, starting around 11,800 BCE, the Alleröd phase brought another warming pulse to the world. For a thousand years, the Alleröd warming sent the glaciers reeling back worldwide.

Around 10,800 BCE, the long warming trend came to another stop. A new cold phase, the frigid Younger Dryas, had arrived.

---

15 The following summary is largely based on Pielou 1991 and Straus et al. 1996.

The West Antarctic Ice Sheet began to reestablish itself, and forest yielded to tundra over much of the Northern Hemisphere as temperatures plunged back to lows that had not been seen since the LGM. The record of the ice cores shows that the change happened very suddenly, taking no more than a few decades and possibly only a few years. By 10,200 BCE, though, the Younger Dryas phase was over and a transitional period, the Preboreal, brought the first stirrings of a new warming trend.

The end of the Preboreal and the coming of a new phase, the Boreal, brought the most dramatic changes of all. Sometime not long after 9600 BCE, the earth's average temperature shot up between thirteen and fifteen degrees Fahrenheit in less than a decade.[16] This planetary heat wave pushed the great continental glaciers into swift collapse. Less than a thousand years after the start of the Boreal phase, the ice sheets were gone everywhere except Antarctica and Greenland. Weather patterns took radically new shapes as the Boreal heat pulse made the world warmer than it had been for hundreds of thousands of years, causing severe droughts that stressed ecosystems worldwide. It is interesting, and may not be accidental, that astrologers in the Old and New World alike put a destruction of the world by heat during the middle of the Boreal phase, during the age of Cancer (8920–6760 BCE) in the Old World system and at the end of the Fire Sun in 8238 BCE in the New World one.

Later in the Boreal, the droughts yielded to a more humid climate over most of the world. Rain fell in the Sahara, turning the desert into an immense grassland where giraffes and gazelles roamed. Finally, around 6200 BCE, the warm Boreal gave way to the cooler Atlantic phase, which lasted up to the beginning of recorded history around 3500 BCE. In the Atlantic phase, the Sahara grasslands dried out and turned back into desert, lands and seas took on their modern shapes, and the world's climate patterns settled into something like today's range. The high temperatures of the Boreal phase

---

16 The lower figure is from Mithen 2003, 54, the higher from Alley 2000, 113.

have never repeated since, though global warming unleashed by modern pollution promises to change that over the next century.

Map these changes onto today's debates about global warming, in fact, and the meaning of the climate changes at the end of the last ice age becomes clearer. Scientists warn now that global warming could cause drastic changes to rainfall and weather patterns, sharply increase the number and severity of hurricanes, give tropical diseases footholds in temperate regions, and send sea levels rising uncontrollably as the Greenland and Antarctic ice sheets destabilize and melt. Changes on the same scale would have happened as temperatures spiked upward in the Bölling, Alleröd, and Boreal period—especially in the last of these.

The world of 9600 BCE, at the beginning of the Atlantis window, was thus a world on the brink of ecological catastrophe. The spike in global temperatures that heralded the dawn of the Boreal phase had drastic consequences worldwide, and several regions in the Atlantic basin took the brunt of those consequences in a way that could well have left echoes in Plato's time nine thousand years later. The people who lived through that time endured natural disasters on a scale that the modern world has never witnessed. Yet the uniformitarian biases of the recent past still stand solidly in the way of a clear assessment of one of the most traumatic periods our species has ever experienced.

Attempts to debunk the Atlantis legend still invoke the old uniformitarian theory in its most extreme early-twentieth-century forms, even though the earth sciences abandoned that stance many decades ago. In a widely cited 1978 essay, for example, geologist Herbert Wright insisted that the end of the ice age could not have caused an Atlantis-style disaster, because sea levels rose only fractions of an inch a year. "So at this point," Wright claimed, "we are left with a picture of a slowly retreating ice sheet and a slowly rising sea level over many thousands of years. . . . Correlating a catastrophic event in cultural history that lasted at most a few decades—whether fact or legend—with the entire period of sea-level rise, or even with a single fluctuation, therefore has no basis because the time scale of the natural events is too long."[17]

Despite his air of certainty, Wright was quite simply wrong. His figures assumed that temperatures rose and ice sheets melted at a steady pace straight through the waning of the last ice age. We now know that this isn't even remotely accurate. The end of the ice age saw dramatic upward and downward shifts in temperature, and these drove equally drastic changes in the rate at which glacial melt-waters poured into the sea. These discoveries had not yet been made when Wright wrote his article, but half a century before then, geologists had already uncovered evidence of catastrophic floods at the end of the last ice age.

An Age of Floods

Some two hundred miles east of Seattle, the rolling plains of central Washington State give way to a barren moonscape of basalt canyons and mesas, called *channeled scablands* by geologists, that covers more than four thousand square miles. Until J. Harlan Bretz, a University of Chicago geologist, began taking students there for research trips in 1913, it was simply one more desolate corner of the American West, of no interest to anyone except a few sheepherders who scratched out a meager living from the land.[18]

Bretz and his students quickly realized, however, that something amazing had happened in the scablands. Sometime in the very recent geological past, some immense force had ripped away up to two hundred feet of soil, gouged deep channels in solid rock, broken through the ridges between watersheds, thrown up gargantuan gravel bars, and tossed boulders three hundred feet up valley walls. All the evidence pointed to fantastic amounts of water. Guessing that the water came from melting glaciers, Bretz published a scientific

---

17 Wright 1978, 167.

18 The account of J. Harlan Bretz and his discoveries is based on V. Baker 1981 and Huggett 1989. See V. Baker 1981 for a collection of Bretz's papers on the subject.

paper in 1923 suggesting that the region had been scoured by a huge flood around 11,000 BCE.

Then and for more than a decade afterward, most geologists rejected Bretz's theory out of hand, because nobody could identify a source for the water. The turning point came in 1940, when another geologist, Joseph Pardee, showed where the water came from: Lake Missoula, a huge lake of glacial meltwater that covered much of western Montana until the bursting of an ice dam sent it pouring westward.

The resulting flood staggers the imagination. Lake Missoula contained around 1,200 cubic *miles* of water.[19] In the space of a few days, that water surged across the plateau country of eastern Washington, crashed through the Columbia River gorge, and poured out into the Pacific Ocean. At the flood's peak, 30 million cubic feet of water per second—ten times as much as all the world's rivers pour into the sea today—went rushing south and west across the land, leaving the channeled scablands to mark their passing.

One such flood is mind-bending enough. Bretz discovered in the last years of his career, though, that Lake Missoula filled and drained many times, causing a catastrophic flood each time. Studies by other geologists confirmed this staggering discovery and found the cause of the floods. Starting around 13,000 BCE, meltwater pooled behind an arm of the Cordilleran Ice Sheet at the site of Lake Pend Oreille in modern Idaho, forming Lake Missoula. Ice is lighter than water, though. When the lake rose high enough, the ice dam began to float, and the lake water lifted the dam up, tore it apart, and poured southwest across the countryside toward the Columbia River Valley and the sea. Once the lake drained, the ice pushed forward again, replacing the dam and allowing a new lake of meltwater to build up behind it. This cycle repeated more than forty times over a period of some 1,500 years, from just before the Bölling phase to about midway through the Alleröd.[20]

---

19 Pielou 1991, 186.
20 Ibid.

Even the most conservative theories about the peopling of the Americas admit that the Columbia basin, with its rich salmon fisheries and abundant plant and animal resources, would have been inhabited by 11,000 BCE. This fact casts an entirely new light on the wealth of flood legends to be found among Native American peoples in the Northwest. Nearly everyone and everything caught in the path of any of the Lake Missoula floods would have been obliterated, but those who happened to be on high ground or live just past the edges of the flood zone would have lived to tell a tale of unimaginable catastrophe. People remember such tales, especially when the event that caused them happened many times.

As study after study confirmed Bretz's theory, furthermore, geologists began to realize that the floods that drained Lake Missoula were far from unique. As the great ice sheets melted, meltwater pooled in huge proglacial lakes all around the Northern Hemisphere and then drained into the seas in a series of immense floods.

During the end of the ice age, dozens of these lakes lay scattered across North America and Eurasia.[21] The basin that now holds the Baltic Sea contained one of the largest, the Baltic Ice Lake. Its waters stood more than eighty-five feet above sea level before it overflowed into the North Sea around 10,200 BCE, at the start of the Preboreal phase, causing what one archaeologist describes as "a major ecological disaster."[22] Another lake formed near the Altai Mountains in Siberia, draining northward during the Alleröd phase in what some geologists claim was the biggest single meltwater flood of the late Pleistocene. Still another, Lake Iroquois, covered much of New York State and reached well up into the province of Ontario until it burst south through the Hudson Valley in three massive floods, the largest around 11,400 BCE.[23]

---

21 The following paragraphs are based on Macdougall 2004 and Eriksen 1996.

22 Huggett 1989, 158.

23 J. Donnelly et al. 2005.

The biggest of all the proglacial lakes was Lake Agassiz, a colossal inland sea that reached from South Dakota to Saskatchewan.[24] As the largest reservoir for meltwater from the huge Laurentide Ice Sheet—the biggest continental glacier on the planet at that time—Lake Agassiz filled and emptied many times before its remnants finally formed what are now the Great Lakes. Many geologists now believe that its largest outpouring, around 10,800 BCE, cut the St. Lawrence Valley and dumped enough fresh water into the sea to disrupt the currents of the Atlantic Ocean, shut down the Gulf Stream, and launch the Younger Dryas phase.[25] Another huge flood around 8200 BCE poured into Hudson Bay as the ice sheets finally loosed their grip on eastern Canada.

Nor were the great proglacial lakes the only source of meltwater floods at the end of the last ice age. The torrents that poured out of Lake Agassiz and its equivalents were matched or exceeded by floods unleashed by the direct collapse of ice sheets bordering on open ocean. One of these events has been documented in the last few years by cutting-edge scientific research.

Back in 1989, marine geologists discovered that ice age coral reefs as far apart as Hawaii, Barbados, and the South China Sea suddenly drowned at the same time, right around the beginning of the Bölling phase. Coral reefs "drown" when sea level rises so far that sunlight no longer reaches them and the ecosystem that supports the coral polyps breaks apart. Something, the researchers realized, caused sea level to jump sharply upward around seventy feet at the same time all around the world. Because the melting of glacial ice sheets was the most likely cause, the event was labeled Global Meltwater Pulse 1A.

More evidence piled up as research continued, and in 2003 a team of scientists finally put the pieces of the puzzle together.[26] Near the beginning of the Bölling phase, the West Antarctic Ice Sheet—at

---

24 Eriksen 1996, 108.
25 See Huggett 1989, 150–53.
26 Weaver 2003.

that time one of the world's largest, sprawling across a third of Antarctica and spreading via sea ice across what is now the Strait of Magellan to join with the ice sheet capping the southern Andes— destabilized and collapsed, sending meltwater pouring into the southern oceans and drowning coral reefs over much of the world. It took some five hundred years in all for Global Meltwater Pulse 1A to complete, but the rate of sea level rise varied sharply during that time; at some points in the process, the waters rose by as much as sixteen inches a year.

The human scale of this age of floods has been mapped out with convincing detail in one corner of the world by researchers at the University of Birmingham in England. Using the same technologies geologists use to search for undersea oil reserves, the Birmingham team has explored a "lost world" off the eastern coasts of Britain—a vast coastal plain that reached from the British Isles east to Scandinavia and north as far as the Shetland Islands. In 10,000 BCE, this plain was above water. Over the next few thousand years, as floodwaters poured into the oceans, the entire plain vanished beneath the waves.[27]

The most striking finding of the Birmingham researchers, though, is that these vanished lands beneath the North Sea were inhabited by human beings. Those of the inhabitants who lived through the flooding would have experienced the trauma of watching their world slip away beneath the waves. "At times this change would have been insidious and slow—but at times, it could have been terrifyingly fast," comments Professor Vince Gaffney of the University of Birmingham. "It would be a mistake to think that these people were unsophisticated or without culture . . . they would have had names for the rivers and hills and spiritual associations—it would have been a catastrophic loss."[28]

The meltwater floods at the end of the ice age, in other words, provide a mechanism for exactly the sort of catastrophic permanent

---

27 Coughlan 2007.
28 Ibid.

flooding Plato's narrative requires. These floods started in earnest just before the beginning of the Bölling phase, a little after 13,500 BCE, and ended in the late Boreal phase, around 6000 BCE or a little earlier. The early Boreal phase, as temperatures soared upward from the frigid Younger Dryas phase and the ice sheets began their final collapse, saw some of the most severe floods. The Atlantis window around 9600–9400 BCE, in other words, came in the middle of one of the most drastic periods of sea level change in the earth's history, when torrents of meltwater poured into the world's oceans and tens of thousands of square miles of dry land sank beneath the rising seas.

Thus, Herbert Wright's comforting image of "slowly rising sea level over many thousands of years"[29] is a uniformitarian fantasy. During the end of the last ice age, as ice sheets collapsed and proglacial lakes drained into the sea, sudden upward jolts in sea level were the rule, not the exception. All this increases the possibility that Plato's narrative might have been built on a foundation of fact.

The Tectonic Factor

The meltwater floods of the early Boreal period, then, clearly could have accounted for the legend of Atlantis—and many other flood legends besides. Still, the same period saw another source of catastrophic flooding shift into high gear. Plato once again points straight to the crucial detail: "But afterward," he wrote in the *Timaeus*, "there occurred violent earthquakes and floods." The floods were certainly real. What about the earthquakes?

Earthquakes happen when sections of the earth's crust slip along fault lines, releasing built-up pressure. Ordinarily, most of that pressure—tectonic stress, as geologists call it—comes from the inexorable push of the deep movements in the earth's molten mantle that power continental drift. California is famous for its earthquakes, for example, because a portion of its coast is part of the

---

29 Wright 1978, 167.

Pacific Plate and is drifting northward across the edge of the North American Plate at about the speed that fingernails grow. The San Andreas Fault is only one of hundreds of fault lines that absorb the strain of this movement and release it in earthquakes.

Other forces can have the same effect, though. The Taipei 101 skyscraper in Taipei, Taiwan, is the world's tallest building as of this writing, standing 1,776 feet tall and weighing more than 770,000 tons. Since its completion, the area of Taipei where it stands—an area that had been geologically stable until construction began—has become the epicenter of several earthquakes, and geologists who have investigated the site have suggested that the sheer weight of the skyscraper opened an ancient, formerly inactive fault.[30] In the same way, a massive earthquake in Maharashtra, India, in 1967 is widely thought by geologists to have been caused by the weight of water in the reservoir behind a newly finished dam, which pressed down on a fault in the rocks far below.

These effects are tiny, though, compared to the tectonic impact of continental ice sheets. As they formed during the ice age, the glaciers loaded sections of the earth's surface with up to two miles of ice, pushing the crust beneath them far down into the mantle below, while seas shrank and lightened the load on the ocean floor. As the earth's climate warmed, the same process ran in reverse, but much faster. Ice sheets that took a hundred thousand years to form melted away in only five thousand, and most of that melting took place in two brief surges: the Alleröd phase, between 11,800 and 10,800 BCE, and the Boreal phase, from 9600 BCE to 6200 BCE. In response, continents rose upward in a process called "isostatic rebound" while sea floors sank, placing huge stresses on the faults between tectonic plates.

The filling and draining of the great ice lakes threw this process into overdrive. A cubic mile of water weighs around 4 billion tons. When a thousand cubic miles of water drained from a glacial lake and poured into the sea in a matter of days, the sudden movement of

---

30 Ravilious 2005.

trillions of tons of water off a continent and into the nearby sea put immense stresses on the earth's crust. Those stresses could only be relieved by earthquakes at plate boundaries. Thus the phases when glacial melting was swiftest must also have been times of vastly increased earthquake activity.

The relevance of this detail to the Atlantis legend was pointed up with tragic intensity by the Southeast Asian tsunami of December 26, 2004. The wall of water that crashed into coastlines around the Indian Ocean, killing hundreds of thousands of people and causing many billions of dollars in damage, happened because tectonic stresses along an undersea fault broke loose in a large earthquake. The fault that caused this particular tsunami is in what geologists call a *subduction zone*—an area where one of the plates that make up earth's crust is forced under another plate. Subduction zones tend to be "sticky," so tectonic stresses build up there longer before releasing, and release more explosively. This is why subduction zone quakes are responsible for nearly all of the largest tsunamis in historical times.

In the aftermath of the last ice age, in other words, rising sea levels and the draining of proglacial lakes were not the only forces that could cause cataclysmic flooding. As ice sheets retreated and trillions of tons of water shifted from the proglacial lakes to the oceans, huge tectonic stresses built up in the earth's crust, and where those stresses found release at undersea subduction zones—as some inevitably did—the "violent earthquakes and floods" of Plato's narrative would have been impossible to avoid. Unlike megatsunamis caused by meteor impacts or undersea landslides, furthermore, tsunamis powered by the tectonic stress of glacial meltwater floods would not have left the land they drowned high and dry after they passed; the steady rise of sea level meant that in many cases, land swallowed by tsunamis during periods of intense melting would never have surfaced again.

Methane Hydrates

As if this were not enough, a third factor also unleashed immense floods on coastal regions around the world at the end of the last ice age. This third factor was not even suspected until the 1990s, and its role remains a subject of lively controversy and ongoing research in the scientific community today. Papers published in the last few years, however, suggest that this factor was a major piece of the puzzle and may also have provided the driving force behind the sudden temperature spike that launched the Boreal phase itself.

Down below the oceans of the world, mostly buried in undersea mud, are trillions of tons of methane hydrates—chunks of ice filled with methane (CH_4), also known as swamp gas, a carbon compound produced by rotting organic matter. The ice and methane aren't chemically combined; the methane is simply trapped in the ice, forming a type of compound chemists call a *clathrate*. Like other clathrates, methane hydrates are very unstable and break down quickly with changes in temperature or pressure. Oceanographers who work with methane hydrates like to impress novices on shipboard by bringing a chunk of hydrate up from the sea bottom and holding a lit match to what looks like a block of ice. The methane fizzing out of the hydrate ignites readily, and the result looks for all the world like ice on fire.

Rising ocean temperatures during each of the warm phases of the Pleistocene-Holocene transition would have destabilized methane hydrates all by themselves, but the tectonic factor we've just discussed adds a wild card with drastic effects. Slow changes in temperature and pressure can make the methane leak out gradually, but a sudden shock of the sort caused by an earthquake can release huge amounts all at once. Where enough methane hydrates have become unstable due to rising deepwater temperatures, an undersea earthquake can cause the sudden, explosive blowout of huge quantities of methane. The results include vast undersea mudslides. Areas of continental slope the size of the island of Jamaica, up to two or three thousand cubic miles of sediment, went crashing down into the deep ocean in the largest of these events.[31]

Two consequences of these catastrophic underwater mudslides bear directly on the Atlantis legend. First, the sudden injection of huge amounts of methane into the atmosphere from the sea bottom amplifies the warming trend that makes methane hydrates unstable in the first place. Methane is twenty times as effective a greenhouse gas as carbon dioxide, the gas at the center of today's global warming crisis, and thousands or even millions of tons of it can be dumped into the air from a single large undersea mudslide under the right conditions. Climatologist James Kennett has recently proposed what he calls the "clathrate gun" hypothesis, arguing that sudden blowouts from methane hydrates at the bottom of the sea were the main driving force behind the temperature spikes that appear in the Greenland ice cores.[32]

The second consequence bears even more directly on the Atlantis legend than the first. Drop a piece of sea bottom the size of Jamaica off the edge of the continental shelf, and one thing you can count on is a megatsunami that is big even by prehistoric standards.[33] Oceanographer Mark Maslin, whose studies of undersea mudslides helped to confirm Kennett's "clathrate gun" hypothesis, has examined the dates of known undersea mudslides in the Atlantic basin. He found that at least seven very large events of this kind took place in the Preboreal and Boreal phases, and his paper on the subject stresses that every one these undersea disturbances triggered a megatsunami. There may have been many more that haven't been found yet. So little of the ocean floor has been explored so far that the traces of dozens more undersea landslides dating from the same period could easily lie hidden on the bottom of the sea.

---

31 Maslin 2004 discusses these huge undersea landslides in detail.

32 See Kennett et al. 2002 for details of the "clathrate gun" hypothesis, and Maslin 2004 for additional evidence supporting it.

33 Maslin 2004, 56.

So far, the only known undersea mudslide dating from around the time Plato gives for the sinking of Atlantis is in the western Mediterranean off the east coast of Spain, tentatively dated around 9500 BCE.[34] This slide sent between five and six cubic miles of sediment careening into the deep waters of the Mediterranean Sea, which would have produced a massive tsunami. It's tempting to identify this with the catastrophe that, according to Plato, swallowed up the army of Athens after its victory over the Atlanteans, but that is a guess at most.

Plato's broader narrative, however, passes the test of current scientific knowledge with flying colors. No fewer than three different factors—glacial floods, tsunamis caused by the tectonic stress of melting ice sheets and the emptying of proglacial lakes, and megatsunamis caused by undersea landslides amplified by methane hydrate blowouts—could easily have caused the catastrophe he describes at the date he gives for it, and no other date in the last 120,000 years would have been a more likely setting for such a disaster. If this is a coincidence, it surely must be one of the most remarkable in history.

---

34 Maslin 2004, 54.

FIVE
Atlantis Found?

A t this point, a summing-up may be in order. Plato, whose account of Atlantis is the earliest known source for the legend, gives a general date and location for the lost civilization, along with a great deal of circumstantial detail. Some parts of his account are contradictory—Atlantis cannot have been both as large as North Africa and Asia Minor put together and as small as the description in the *Critias*—and other parts have probably been influenced by his own cultural background. A civilization in 9600 BCE, for example, probably didn't equip its soldiers in Greek armor and its navy with Greek warships.

Still, the general outlines of Plato's narrative can stand as a working hypothesis. In its simplest terms, this hypothesis claims that a powerful seafaring culture existed around 9600 BCE on an island somewhere in the Atlantic, within easy reach of the shores of the Americas. Since geological evidence rules out a location in the central Atlantic and other locations are not close enough to the New World to fit Plato's description, the most likely location for that culture is in the western Atlantic close to the North American coast. The Atlantean culture had watercraft capable of making the crossing between the Old World and the New, and for a time it exercised some sort of political control over societies in the western

Mediterranean basin. Sometime after 9400 BCE, after losing its Mediterranean empire, the homeland of that culture sank beneath the ocean in a catastrophic flood and the culture itself collapsed.

A certain amount of evidence supports these claims, though none of it is conclusive. Strong similarities between ancient cultures in the Middle East and Mexico might be explained by the existence of Atlantis, though other explanations are possible. The fact that both Babylonian and Mayan astrological lore have the world experiencing a catastrophe caused by heat at the same point in the precessional cycle—the age of Cancer (8920–6760 BCE) is the Old World figure, the end of the Fire Sun in 8238 BCE the New World one—is another curious parallel, though it could be explained by the shared experience of the Boreal phase just as well as by some form of transatlantic contact.

More compelling are the ancient maps collected by Charles Hapgood in his *Maps of the Ancient Sea Kings* and discussed by many of the current writers in the rejected-knowledge field. These maps show the coastlines of Antarctica and a variety of other geographical features centuries before those features were first visited by Europeans, and in some cases show them as they were thousands of years before the maps were drawn. The geographical knowledge of the ancient and medieval world likewise extended much farther than ancient and medieval explorers ever went. All this makes sense if Europe inherited some of the knowledge of an older maritime culture located in the Atlantic basin. To that extent, it supports Plato's claim.

Most current discussions of Atlantis, though, veer far from Plato's ideas. The occult traditions, under Blavatsky's influence, made use of the Atlantis legend as raw material for a legominism, a teaching story intended to be taken as symbolically rather than literally true. Some later occult groups continued to promote the legominism, while others used it as a launching point for visionary experiences that provide an intriguing image of what Atlantis might have been. The rejected-knowledge movement, for its part, mistook the legominism for history and then started ringing changes on it, producing a dense fog of confusion around the whole subject. At the same time, attempts to locate Atlantis in many corners of the world have turned up evidence for many lost cities and civilizations, raising the uncomfortable possibility that the fall of Atlantis may have been only one of many civilization-wrecking catastrophes in the history of our species.

Meanwhile, recent discoveries in the earth sciences provide a remarkable body of evidence that supports Plato's basic scenario. At the exact date he gave for the flowering and fall of Atlantis, we now know, the earth went through drastic changes, including rapidly rising sea levels, glacial floods, tectonic stresses capable of causing massive tsunamis, and the collapse of undersea methane hydrates combining with earthquakes to amplify both the warming and the tsunamis. Such periods are rare in the long history of the earth, and it's remarkable that Plato, who knew nothing at all about modern geology or oceanography, chose a date that mirrors scientific fact so exactly.

Plato's date, in other words, checks out. What about the rest of his story?

The "Caveman" Myth

Uniformitarian arguments against a sudden catastrophe of the sort Plato describes are a constant presence in attempts to debunk the Atlantis legend, but they do not stand alone. Another theme, just as important in debunkers' arguments, insists that human beings in 9600 BCE could not possibly have reached a level of culture like the one Plato describes. When it comes to prehistory, the myth of progress still maintains its tight grip on the modern imagination, and any attempt to make sense of Atlantis has to deal with that fact.

Think of the words "prehistoric man" and what comes to mind? If you're like most modern people, your imagination will instantly present you with the image of a filthy, hairy figure, naked except for a bearskin kilt or over-one-shoulder tunic, clutching a lumpy wooden club in one hand as he trudges barefoot through the wilderness or huddles with his fellows around a fire in a cave decorated with crude drawings. Look in the latest books on prehistoric times and, if they have illustrations, you can count on finding the same image repeated endlessly. This image dominates today's concepts of the prehistoric past.

It's a remarkable image, and far and away the most remarkable thing about it is that it's a fantasy without a shred of fact behind it.[1]

Just to begin with, the ubiquitous wooden club is a complete invention. Archaeologists have found traces of many wooden implements from the ice age, and many more are depicted in cave art, but never a trace or an image of a club. There's good reason for this: a club is probably the least useful thing an intelligent, tool-using creature can make out of wood. Millions of years before the first *Homo sapiens* hunted and gathered on the plains of Africa, hominids learned to control fire and put a sharp edge on stone tools, and with fire and sharp tools, wood can be transformed into countless useful things. Long straight sticks with one sharp end hardened in the fire provided early humans with spears for hunting and protection against predators; shorter, sturdier pieces of wood became digging sticks, yielding access to edible roots; throwing sticks took down small game; wooden fire-sticks allowed flame to be kindled.

Wood, though, was only one of dozens of materials the people of prehistory had at their disposal. They made nearly a hundred different kinds of stone tools, ranging from sturdy axes to delicate knives that hold an edge sharper than steel, and it takes only a few minutes of experience working with a sharp flint knife to prove that such tools are anything but clumsy. The stone used for these tools was carefully heat-treated to make it stronger and easier to work, and finished tools were set into elegantly carved hafts of wood or bone. In places where good stone could not be found on the sur-

---

1 Moser 1998 documents this in detail. See Moser 1998, Rudgley 1999, Settegast 1990, and Tudge 1998 for the following paragraphs.

face, ice age people traded for it—sometimes across thousands of miles—or mined it underground, using antler picks and shovels crafted from animal shoulder blades.[2]

The stonesmiths of the ice age produced, among many other elegant and useful things, razor-sharp spearheads that provided the business end for the primary weapon system of the time. To judge by cave art, ice age spears were fletched like modern arrows, and they were launched with *atlatls*, or spear throwers, ingenious devices that used the principle of leverage to more than triple a spear's effective range.[3] An atlatl-thrown spear has shorter range but much more impact than an arrow shot from a bow, and against the big game of the last ice age it was a good deal more effective.

Stone provided strength and sharp cutting edges, but ice age craftspeople turned to bone for more delicate work. Hair combs, fishhooks, flutes, and statues of exquisite workmanship and design came from the hands of ice age bonecrafters, but another product of their craftsmanship gives the lie to the bearskin kilt of the modern "caveman" fantasy. The tailors of the LGM had fine bone needles of the same design as modern ones, and they used them to sew clothing from leather. They had plenty of leather to work with, too, because animals made up a large portion of their diet and, like most tribal peoples today, they seem to have wasted almost nothing of the animals they killed.

We don't know what their clothes looked like, since leather and natural fibers don't last long enough to come into the hands of archaeologists, but they certainly didn't have to settle for bearskin kilts to keep out the freezing ice age winds. Native American buckskins or the warm sealskin garments of the Inuit, for example, would have been easy to make with ice age technology. Hide tents like the tipis of Native Americans on the Great Plains would be equally well within reach, and many other kinds of housing as well.

---

2 Rudgley 1999, 168–75.
3 Comstock 1999.

↑ ▥ ⊞ ‖ ◍ ‖‖ Ⴙ ♭ Ᵽ Ɛ ↳
Ᵽ ˈↄ | ⸸ ⵉ ⸌ⵍ ⵕ Ⴟ ⵞ

Paleolithic Writing?

*These are among the most common abstract signs found in the painted
caves of France and Spain. Their resemblance to writing is one of the many
mysteries of the ice age. (After Settegast 1990 and Rudgley 1999)*

In warmer regions of the world, such as the Middle East, archaeologists have turned up the remains of thriving ice age villages con-
sisting of comfortable huts with wood frames and thatched roofs.
Caves, far from being the standard living spaces of our ice age
ancestors, seem to have been primarily religious shrines and pil-
grimage sites. Certainly this is how archaeologists today interpret
the vast painted caves of Paleolithic France and Spain, with their
brilliantly executed fresco paintings and their enigmatic traces of
ritual activity.

Those same caves contain another feature that shakes the myth
of progress to its core. Along with the stunningly lifelike images of
wild animals and the oddly sticklike figures of human beings, many
of the painted caves have simple abstract signs that look for all the
world like writing. The figure above shows a selection of the most
common signs. If these appeared in an archaeological site at any
point more recent than 3000 BCE, archaeologists would simply assume that they represented a writing system. Since they date from
the Paleolithic, on the other hand, nearly all the archaeologists who
have even considered the possibility that these signs might be writing have rejected it with spluttering indignation. As Allan Forbes
and Thomas Crowder, two maverick archaeologists who have raised
the issue in their own writings, comment:

> The proposition that Ice Age reindeer hunters invented writing
> fifteen thousand years ago or more is utterly inadmissible and
> unthinkable. . . . If Franco-Cantabrians [the ice age peoples of
> southern France and northern Spain] invented writing thou-

sands of years before civilization arose in the Middle East, then our most cherished beliefs about the nature of society and the course of human development would be demolished.[4]

Still, if those cherished beliefs stand in the way of an honest assessment of our ancestors—and the evidence suggests that they do—then demolished they must be.

Just as startling is the solid evidence that people far back in the ice age mastered the trick of building boats and crossing the open ocean. This particular skill dates back before our own species. Fossil skeletons of a dwarf hominid descended from *Homo erectus*, the first *Homo* species to break out of Africa and spread throughout the Old World, made headlines a few years ago when they were found on the island of Flores in Indonesia, halfway between Java and the northeast coast of Australia. Part of a chain of volcanic islands rising from deep water, Flores was not part of the nearest mainland, the huge peninsula of Sundaland, even in the depths of the last ice age. Sometime before 93,000 BCE, the approximate date of the oldest stone tools on Flores, *Homo erectus* reached the island by boat.

Our own species arrived the same way around 50,000 BCE, about the same time that the ancestors of today's New Guinean peoples and the Australian aborigines reached their homelands across many miles of deep water, and by 28,000 BCE human beings sailed across four hundred miles of open ocean to reach the Solomon Islands from New Guinea.[5] People who can build deepwater boats and sail them across the sea reliably enough to get a stable breeding population established on a distant continent are clearly not the grunting savages of modern imagination.

The "caveman" image we all carry around in our heads, in other words, has nothing to do with the realities of prehistoric life. Where did it come from, then? In a brilliant 1998 study, *Ancestral Images:*

4 Cited in Rudgley 1999, 75.
5 Fagan 2004, 51.

The Iconography of Human Origins, archaeologist Stephanie Moser showed that it was invented long before modern archaeology itself. The lumpy club and rough skin garment came from the Greek hero Hercules, who carried a large club and wore nothing but a lion skin. In the late Renaissance, when the modern myth of progress was being invented, artists borrowed the old image of Hercules to portray what they thought primitive human beings must have looked like. The lion skin was replaced by bearskin in the nineteenth century, when fossils of cave bears caught the imagination of the Victorian media. Since then, despite mountains of evidence that flatly disprove it, that image has been glued into place in the modern imagination.

What gives the image its staying power? The myth of progress, once again, is the factor behind this extraordinary illusion. History shows that civilizations fall just as often as they rise. In order to convince themselves that human history is a one-way trip up from primitive savagery, as the myth claims, believers in progress thus have to project their own fantasies of primitive savagery back on the distant past and claim that, however improbably, human beings just like us sat around in abject squalor for hundreds of thousands of years before suddenly leaping up and creating our civilization in a mere five millennia. Though all known civilizations of the past have collapsed and taken most of their knowledge and cultural attainments with them, the image of the "primitive caveman" reassures believers in the myth that at least we've never stooped as low as our allegedly savage and ignorant ancestors.

The evidence shows that they were neither savage nor ignorant, but to face up to that evidence—to admit that humanity from its very beginnings had rich and complex cultures well adapted to the opportunities of their environments—challenges the logic of industrial society right down to its foundations. If our civilization is not the wave of the future, but just one more human culture following the same patterns of rise and fall as all the others that came before it, what justifies the arrogant way we've maltreated the rest of the world's human cultures and the living earth itself?

Pleistocene Permaculture

To understand the world of our ice age ancestors, then, getting rid of the fantasy image of "primitive cavemen" is the first requirement. To judge by the elegance and effectiveness of their tools and the beauty of their cave paintings and sculpture, the people of the last ice age had rich cultures and a technology roughly on the level of Native American peoples before European contact. Like these latter, the people of the LGM did not have metal tools or wheeled vehicles, and the enigmatic pictographs of the French and Spanish caves seem to have been their closest approach to writing. None of these limitations kept Native Americans from creating societies as complex as the Iroquois Confederacy or the Aztec Empire, and it's only prejudice driven by the mythology of progress that leads modern people to insist that people could not have created societies of the same complexity in ice age times.

The people of the last ice age did not practice agriculture, and this has sometimes been used as an excuse to label them primitive and ignorant. Recent studies have shown, though, that their food-producing methods were *more* sophisticated than agriculture, not less. Beginning as early as 40,000 BCE, they learned to manage entire ecosystems for food production.[6] Even on the bleak tundras of ice age Europe, people planted hazel bushes in sheltered areas to ensure a supply of edible nuts,[7] and in more temperate areas dozens of plants were propagated in this way. Instead of tearing out existing ecosystems to put in fields of a single crop and then fighting nature every step of the way from planting to harvest, they wove a wide range of food crops into the local ecology and benefited from natural cycles instead of struggling against them.

In 1978, Australian ecologists Bill Mollison and David Holmgren began creating a visionary system of ecological food and raw material production they called "permaculture," the art of crafting entire

6 Tudge 1999.
7 Eriksen 1996, 109.

ecosystems to meet human needs as well as those of other living things. It took decades before anyone realized that the new permaculture movement was unknowingly following a very ancient path. Long before the end of the last ice age, forgotten cultures all over the world had mastered the permaculture approach, and the test of time has shown that over the long term their approach works very well. Areas such as the New Guinea highlands, where this sort of prehistoric permaculture has been practiced for more than ten thousand years, are still fertile and productive today and produce abundant crops of food and raw materials.

Animals also played an important role in the resource base of ice age peoples. Since the beginning of modern archaeology, the wealth of animal bones found at ice age dwelling sites have been interpreted as the work of hunters, but recent studies cast doubt on this easy assumption. The people of the tundras of southern France, dwelling amid many different species of prey, lived almost entirely on reindeer.[8] This makes no sense at all if they were hunters—all the world's hunting cultures make use of a wide range of prey animals—but all the sense in the world if they had a lifestyle like the Sami of modern Lapland, who manage herds of half-tame reindeer, protecting them from wild predators while using them as a food source. Evidence suggests that ice age peoples in western Asia may have done the same thing with antelope, and their contemporaries in North Africa seem to have done it with Barbary sheep.[9] In the same way, people living on islands near New Guinea during the ice age brought food animals from the mainland to their island homes to provide a stable protein supply.[10]

Did ice age peoples take animal management the next step, to domestication? Dogs certainly lived in the company of human beings by the end of the last ice age, though ferocious arguments still rage in the archaeological literature about just how domesticated

---

8 Straus 1996, 90–92.

9 Settegast 1990, 3.

10 Allen and Kershaw 1996, 186.

they were.[11] Far more controversial are pieces of evidence suggesting that ice age peoples in Europe domesticated horses. Horses are the most common animals in the ice age art of southern France, and a significant number of Paleolithic carvings of horses show unmistakable halters and bridles on the animals' heads.[12] A leading group of British paleoecologists has pointed out that the evidence for horse domestication in Paleolithic France is strong enough that those who insist horses were simply a food item now bear the burden of proof.[13] No one has yet presented a valid argument for why this evidence should be ignored, but ignored it has been.

The evidence for Pleistocene permaculture is crucial to our theme, because one of the arguments constantly leveled against the Atlantis legend by debunkers is the claim that, since agriculture had not yet been invented in 9600 BCE, a settled urban society like the one Plato describes could not possibly have existed. The evidence simply doesn't support this claim. It is true that the sort of Paleolithic permaculture outlined in this chapter likely produced fewer cities than the agriculture that replaced it, for the simple reason that grain crops are much easier to store and transport than the mixed produce of a managed ecosystem and communities in an agricultural society thus can draw food supplies from a larger area. Historic and present-day societies using permaculture tend to live in villages rather than larger towns, and cities emerge only where particularly favorable conditions or important trade connections allow them.

Still, in historic times, human societies that practiced no agriculture at all created towns, erected public art, developed trade and cultural networks covering thousands of miles, and developed an extraordinarily rich material culture. The Native American peoples of the Pacific Northwest, among many others, did all these things without agriculture—and the tools they used to craft their cedar longhouses, heraldic totem poles, oceangoing canoes, and suits of

---

11 Eriksen 1996, 119–20.
12 Several examples are shown in Settegast 1990, 27.
13 Jarman et al. 1984.

armor were no more technologically advanced than the ones used by people in the last ice age.[14]

If Pleistocene permaculture was as efficient and productive as it appears to have been, what happened to it? The answer has been made clear by the same recent studies of prehistoric climate change that shattered the uniformitarian belief in gradual warming after the ice age. While they have many strengths, systems that depend on tending existing ecosystems also have one crucial weakness: they can break down completely in times of drastic environmental change. The more complex a permaculture system becomes, the more vulnerable it is to changes in climate that make one or more critical species no longer viable. As temperatures soared worldwide through the Boreal phase, sending the global climate into turmoil, ancient systems of subsistence dependent on familiar ice age ecological conditions came unraveled across much of the world.

Under these crisis conditions, the transition from permaculture to agriculture offered the one hope of survival. By focusing efforts on a few hardy dryland grasses with edible seeds—the ancestors of today's wheat, barley, and other grains—and a few food-producing animals that could be brought entirely into the human ecosystem—cows, sheep, goats, and a few others—the people of the Boreal phase evolved a system that could keep on producing food despite the ecological chaos around them. By the time ecosystems reached a new stability thousands of years later, the skills and knowledge needed to manage the old Paleolithic permacultures had been lost, and farming was the new reality. Only in a few ecologically stable areas such as New Guinea and certain parts of the Americas did the old way of doing things survive.

This also casts a new light on one of the most puzzling details of the transition from nonagricultural to agricultural lifeways in the ancient world. Studies of skeletons from before and after the rise of agriculture have consistently shown that people in early ag-

---

14 See Rohner and Rohner 1986 for a discussion of the technology of the
  Kwakiutl, a typical Northwest Coast native culture.

ricultural societies in the Old World had poorer health and worse nutrition than their ancestors in nonagricultural times. This has been explained in various ways, and some recent writers have suggested that the invention of agriculture was all a colossal mistake.

The evidence for a collapse in health and nutrition, however, makes perfect sense when mapped onto the ecological crisis of the Boreal phase. With the rich nutritional resources of the old permaculture consigned to the past by drastic climate change, the survivors of the crisis had to eke out a living from the handful of grain crops and domestic animals they could keep alive through the crisis, and hunger must have been the rule rather than the exception. Still, farming was an effect of the crisis, not its cause, and the people of that time could not have gone back to the old ways no matter how much they may have wished to.

The World of 9600 BCE

At the beginning of the Atlantis window, then, the earth and its human population were both in the middle of an age of massive, disruptive change. Research into many details of that transformation is still ongoing, and much of what scientists think they know today will likely be overturned by new discoveries tomorrow. Still, the basic outlines of the world of 9600 BCE are clear enough.

The differences between that world and today's world stand out first. To begin with, huge ice sheets still blanketed much of the Northern Hemisphere. In North America, the western Cordilleran Ice Sheet had retreated into its core territory around the Canadian Rockies, but the much larger eastern Laurentide Ice Sheet still covered two-thirds of Canada and sprawled south as far as today's Great Lakes, with immense proglacial lakes filling most of the space between them. In Europe, the Scandinavian Ice Sheet had retreated from Britain and Germany but still blanketed all of Norway, Sweden, Finland, and the western parts of Russia. Huge inland seas of meltwater covered thousands of square miles of land on both continents, but the oceans were hundreds of feet lower than they are today. Britain was still part of Europe, and the Thames flowed into the Rhine in the midst of a vast and thickly inhabited coastal plain now far below the waves of the North Sea. On the other side of the Atlantic, dozens of now-drowned islands, some of them respectably large, rose above the waters along the eastern coastline from the Caribbean north to Canada's Atlantic provinces.[15]

The animals and plants that inhabited this world were a mixture of the familiar and the strange. The arctic tundras of the deep ice age had retreated into the north, but birch forests, muskeg swamp, and open water covered much of the land abandoned by the ice. In North America, caribou, bison, and wolves shared space with now-extinct camels, giant ground sloths, and sabertooth cats. In Europe, the local wildlife included the giant cave bear, the woolly rhinoceros, and the European bison as well as most of the species found there today.

Both continents also had elephants. The two species of elephant alive today, the African and the Indian, are survivors of a much larger group that flourished until just after the end of the last ice age.[16] In the North America of 9600 BCE, woolly mammoths lived on the northern tundra while the huge Columbian mammoth grazed the western plains, and the American mastodon thrived in woodland all over the continent. South America had three kinds of gomphotheres, primitive elephants long extinct everywhere else, while the Old World had more than a dozen species of elephants, mammoths, and mastodons, which spread from Spain to Java and from South Africa to northern Siberia. They also reached islands many miles away from land, for elephants of all kinds are strong swimmers and can cross open water with ease. Fishermen today working the Grand Banks off the shores of eastern Canada routinely bring up mammoth bones in their nets, relics of a time when the Grand Banks were islands in the Atlantic and mammoths thrived there.

---

15 I have used Fagan 2004, Mithen 2003, and Pielou 1991 as a basis for this
   reconstruction.

16 See the discussion of prehistoric elephants in Haynes 1991.

Like elephants, human beings flourished on both sides of the Atlantic by 9600 BCE. In the Old World, settled villages and towns practicing the Paleolithic permaculture described earlier in this chapter were the norm wherever the climate permitted. The ancestors of several later civilizations may well have dwelt in cities by this time. Records from Mesopotamia and India alike, for example, describe cities that existed "before the great flood," and both these regions in 9600 BCE included great swaths of fertile land that now lie deep underwater.[17]

On the eastern shores of the Mediterranean, the Natufian culture flourished, building plastered stone houses and crafting elegant tools and jewelry of bone, horn, and stone. Not long after 9600 BCE, in the wake of the vast ecological changes at the beginning of the Boreal phase, the Natufians created the oldest surviving city in the world at Jericho, guarded by stone fortifications that would not have looked out of place in a medieval castle.[18] Farther west in Europe, where the ice was closer and the climate much more harsh, settlements were smaller, and the Magdalenian culture, the creators of the greatest masterpieces of cave art, was giving way to the less artistically inclined Azilian.

The New World is a more complicated matter. Racism is an ugly word, but it's almost impossible to discuss the sorry history of American archaeology without it. Since colonial times, European colonists and their descendants have tried to insist that the Americas were wilderness—and thus free for the taking—when the *Mayflower* arrived. Of course, they were nothing of the kind, since tens of millions of Native Americans had lived there for many thousands of years before that time, but the rhetoric remains. The emotional need to excuse the invasion and conquest of two continents and the extermination of up to 95 percent of their inhabitants has been a major factor, though usually an unmentionable one, in American intellectual life for more than three centuries now.

17 See Hancock 2002.
18 Settegast 1990, 42–54.

Since the beginning of American archaeology, as a result, most of its practitioners have done their best to minimize the richness, complexity, and time span of native cultures in the Americas.[19] In the nineteenth century, American archaeologists focused most of their efforts on trying to prove that the native cultures of the Americas must have come from the Old World—that is, that they were just another group of immigrants with no more right to the land than the ones who came after them. The rise of scientific archaeology at the beginning of the 1920s made such theories impossible to sustain, but the viewpoint that replaced it insisted that Native Americans must have arrived on the continent very recently, no earlier than 3000 BCE. For more than a generation, any American archaeologist who dared to suggest otherwise—even on the basis of the abundant evidence of an ice age human presence in the Americas—put his career in jeopardy.[20]

When widely publicized finds of stone spear points in the bones of extinct ice age bison at Folsom, New Mexico, and elsewhere finally blew a mammoth-sized hole in this theory, the archaeologists quickly regrouped. From the 1930s until the end of the twentieth century, the standard account of the peopling of the Americas asserted that the first human beings to arrive in the New World must have come around 9,500 BCE, when a distinctive type of spear point—the famous Clovis point—spread over much of North America. This became known as the Clovis-first theory and quickly hardened into an orthodoxy as harshly defended as the one that died among the bison bones at Folsom.

In 1937, the archaeologist Ernst Antevs proposed that the appearance of the first Clovis points marked the opening of a gap between the two great ice sheets that blanketed North America in the last ice age—the Cordilleran Ice Sheet, centered on the Rockies, and the Laurentide Ice Sheet, centered over Hudson Bay—allowing

---

19 The issues surrounding the peopling of the Americas are covered capably for nonspecialists by Dewar 2002 and Thomas 2000, and in more technical detail by Crawford 1998.

20 Thomas 2000, 136–38.

wandering tribes to cross from the Bering Land Bridge into North America. Though Antev's claim was merely a speculation—he had precisely zero evidence to support it—the theory of a gap between the ice sheets quickly became a central part of the Clovis-first theory. If you attended schools in the United States or Canada at any point in the last sixty years, you almost certainly learned that this was how the ancestors of the American Indians reached North America.

This orthodoxy has stayed fixed in place even though every detail has been disproved since Antev wrote it. To begin with, neither Clovis points nor any other element of Paleo-Indian technology has been found in Siberia or Alaska, and the tools found at sites in these two places have nothing in common with their supposed North American descendants. Meanwhile, a completely different kind of spear point, called the Sandia point, has been found in American sites dating from well before the Clovis point's first appearance.

Genetic and linguistic analysis put two more nails in the coffin of the Clovis-first theory. The DNA in mitochondria, tiny centers found in all human cells that process sugars into energy, mutates at predictable rates, and measuring how far the mitochondrial DNA in a given group of people has drifted from the DNA in related peoples gives a good estimate for the amount of time since the group in question separated from its relatives. In the case of Native Americans, the shortest amount of time that would account for the divergence in mitochondrial DNA is twenty-five thousand years.[21] Linguists who have tried to account for the extraordinary richness and diversity of Native American languages have come up with even older dates, on the order of thirty-five thousand years.[22]

Then there are the radiocarbon dates. Most of these come from Latin America, where the Clovis-first orthodoxy never really got firmly established and archaeologists have been willing to keep

---

21 Dewar 2002, 121.
22 Nichols 1990.

digging past the levels where North American archaeologists usually stop. One famous site, Monte Verde in Chile, has produced abundant artifacts dating from 10,500 BCE—a thousand years too early for Clovis, and on the other end of the Americas to boot—and another series of finds solidly carbon-dated to 31,000 BCE.[23] More than a dozen other well-documented sites have turned up dates between these two figures, along with a few going back as far as fifty thousand years, a respectable figure even by Old World standards.

The final problem with the Clovis-first hypothesis is that recent geological research has shown that the ice-free corridor between the Cordilleran and Laurentide ice sheets, the keystone of the entire theory, did not exist in 9500 BCE, or for many centuries after that time. When it did finally open, it was filled to the brim for centuries more by yet another huge proglacial lake, Lake McConnell. Not until 8000 BCE—long after the appearance of Clovis points south of the ice—was there an open route from the Bering Land Bridge to the rest of North America.[24]

Where did the Clovis points come from, then? For that matter, where did the ancestors of today's Native Americans come from? Some First Nations probably did come overland from Siberia after the gap opened between the glaciers. Others were here long before, and the evidence suggests that their ancestors came by boat. The same maritime technologies that allowed the ancestors of today's Australian aborigines and native New Guineans to reach their homelands before 40,000 BCE would have been quite sufficient to bring others along the cold but ecologically rich North Pacific coasts to the Pacific coast of the Americas. The way would have been easy to take, since ice-free pockets of shoreline—*refugia*, as ecologists call them—existed all along the western edges of the ice sheet.[25] Once south of the ice, these voyagers could readily have begun to expand across the continents.

---

23 See Dillehay 1989 and 1997, and the overview in Dewar 2002.

24 Dewar 2002, 470–85, and Lemmen et al. 1994.

25 Pielou 1991, 130–38.

The Clovis point, however, seems to have had a different origin. It has nothing in common with Asian spear points of the same period, and it has never been found on the west coast of North America. The majority of Clovis point sites, in fact, are in the southeastern corner of the United States. This is an odd place to find a technology that supposedly originated among immigrants from Asia. What clinches the question is that the nearest equivalents to the Clovis point anywhere on earth are found in the Solutrean stone technology from western Europe.[26]

Is it possible that peoples of the late Paleolithic crossed the Atlantic as well as the Pacific? The crossing is considerably more difficult, since the North Pacific route can be followed without ever leaving sight of the shore, while any Atlantic crossing would have involved many days sailing on the open ocean. Still, the fact that people were crossing open ocean by 50,000 BCE—as the peopling of Australia and New Guinea at that time proves—suggests that the possibility can't be dismissed.

Furthermore, another piece of hard evidence points to the same conclusion. The same mitochondrial DNA research that put a minimum date of twenty-five thousand years on human arrival in the New World also showed that one genetic marker found in some Native American populations is shared with peoples in Europe and western Asia—and only with them.[27] Nor is it necessary that such voyages only went in one direction, since by 9600 BCE the native cultures of the Caribbean and eastern North America had more than twenty thousand years of New World cultural development behind them, and the technologies from these regions that have been found by archaeologists are in no way inferior to the ones used in western Europe at the same time.

The world of 9600 BCE, in other words, was not inhabited by the slack-jawed savages fantasized by today's mythology of progress. Its peoples had technologies equivalent to those of historical

26 Dewar 2002, 133 and throughout.
27 Ibid., 121–26.

Native American cultures, including many thousands of years of experience with seafaring and sophisticated methods of food production equal to those that supported complex cultures in later times. While many of the specific details of Plato's narrative come out of the cultural habits of his own time and what his age remembered of the Bronze Age cultures preceding it, the basic picture of a fertile and thickly populated island with some sort of urban center at its heart, possessing a settled, elegant culture and an efficient maritime technology, was by no means out of reach in that age. Given this, is it possible to take the final step and locate a likely site for Plato's island kingdom?

Finding Atlantis

Plato's narrative clearly describes a sunken island somewhere in the western Atlantic ocean, located within easy reach of the shores of the New World and probably within twenty degrees or so of Gibraltar's latitude, so that it might reasonably be called "in front of the Pillars of Hercules." Since a sunken landmass in the Atlantic the size of North Africa and Asia Minor combined can't be squared with known geological facts but a smaller island can be, we can assume that the island was a little larger than the *Critias* measurements of 340 by 230 miles, though the catastrophe that submerged it and eleven thousand years of currents and tides since then may have altered those measurements somewhat. Since it was submerged sometime between 9400 BCE, the last date Plato gives, and the late ninth millennium—the Mayan date of 8238 BCE, the end of the Fire Sun, is as likely an endpoint as any other—it lies no more than two hundred feet underwater today. Since Plato reports that it was drowned in "a day and a night" by earthquakes and floods, it probably lies close to a continental shelf where methane blowouts could have occurred in the Boreal phase, an active tectonic region capable of creating massive tsunamis, or both.

Such a place actually exists. It's called Great Bahama Bank, and it lies under the ocean just southeast of the southern tip of Florida

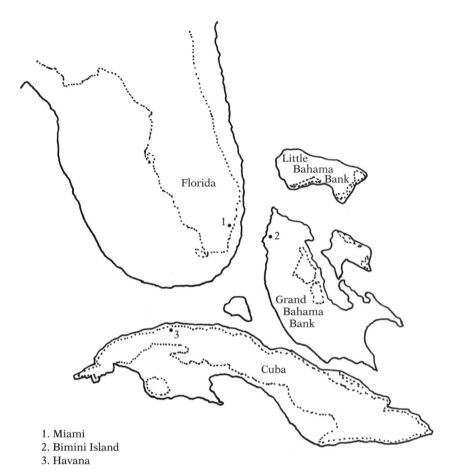

1. Miami
2. Bimini Island
3. Havana

Atlantis Found?

During the ice age, Grand Bahama Bank was a large island surrounded by hills, its dimensions corresponding closely to those Plato gave for the central plain of Atlantis.

and northeast of Cuba. Today it's a region of shallow water about 370 miles long and 225 miles wide, with dozens of small islands scattered around its edges and one large one, Andros Island, near its middle. Bimini, where the famous "Bimini Road" was found on the sea bottom in 1968, is on Great Bahama Bank, near its northern end. A little more than two hundred miles to the southeast of the bank lies the western end of a subduction zone, where the floor of the Atlantic ocean plunges into the mantle beneath the Caribbean tectonic plate, causing violent earthquakes as far back as records go.[28]

In 9600 BCE, at the beginning of the Atlantis window, most of Great Bahama Bank was well above water, and what are now islands around its edges were hills around the borders of a roughly rectangular central plain. A dozen smaller islands spread southeast and north from the main island, connecting it to the other island chains of the Antilles and to the mainland. Level and fertile, it would have been covered with semitropical forest, and the narrow strait separating it from Florida would have been no barrier to mastodons or dozens of other animal species—or, for that matter, humans.

By 9600 BCE, many thousands of years had passed since the ancestors of today's Native Americans reached the shores of the Gulf of Mexico and entered the rich maritime environments of the Gulf and Caribbean islands. As cultures emerged and blended in the rich ecologies of the islands, trade between different regions would have driven the emergence of an effective maritime technology linking the region together. Could such a technology have faced the challenge of crossing the Atlantic to Europe and North Africa, as Plato's legend requires? The exploits of the Polynesians, who crossed much greater distances of open ocean with the same Stone Age toolkit available to ancient Native Americans, shows that this possibility can't be discarded out of hand.

Yet the island cultures were perched on the edge of ecological catastrophe. As glacial meltwater flooded into the oceans and sea levels rose swiftly in the Boreal phase, Great Bahama Bank and its companion islands gradually slipped beneath the waves. As the waters rose and tectonic stresses built, a large earthquake in the subduction zone close by could easily have sent a tsunami right over Great Bahama Bank, sweeping away everything in its path

---

28 See Dolan and Mann 1998 for details on the very active Caribbean Plate subduction zone.

and leaving few traces behind. Equally, an underwater landslide amplified by unstable methane hydrates could have given way nearby and caused a tsunami, or one of the vast meltwater floods from Lake Agassiz that poured down the Mississippi Valley may have finished the process of drowning the bank. In any case, the result would have been a catastrophe like the one in the legend.

If Great Bahama Bank was the Atlantis of Plato's story, what realities could have given rise to the details of the legend? Lacking solid evidence, the only answers that can be offered are speculative. The easiest way to present them is to borrow one of Plato's own habits and tell a story of how the culture he called Atlantis might have risen, flourished, and collapsed.

A Hypothetical History

The story of the land that would one day be called Atlantis began far away on the cold shores of northeastern Asia sometime well before 50,000 BCE, as tribal peoples began moving north and east in skin-covered canoes, heading into territory no human beings had yet settled. The rich maritime ecosystems of the region gave them plenty of food and raw materials, and like later immigrants, they readily learned the skills of survival in the harsh but rewarding environment of the North Pacific. There's no reason to think that they had any desire to move into new lands or any idea of the unexplored continents that awaited their descendants. All they knew was that each move farther along the coast brought them into open territory where new villages could be founded and their prey had not yet learned to be wary of human beings.

A few centuries of slow expansion brought their descendants to the icebound coast of what is now southern Alaska and was then part of the Bering Land Bridge. Pockets of ice-free land at the edge of the sea allowed the gradual migration to continue eastward and then south, until finally a canoe full of people who had spent their lives on the edges of the ice rounded a cape off today's Pacific

Northwest coast and cried out in wonder at the sight of green forests stretching away into the interior.

For all that, most of the migrants who followed that first canoe stayed near the coast, close to the sea that was their livelihood, though they traded skin-covered craft for sturdier dugout canoes and learned to add wild game and woodland food plants to their larders. More centuries of slow expansion brought their descendants south to the shores of Central America, where a hunter chasing a wounded deer crossed a ridge and stopped short, looking out with wide eyes on a second sea reaching out before him to the eastern horizon.

Thus began the settlement of the vast inland sea between North and South America. Dotted with countless islands and far richer ecologically than the Pacific coast, the Caribbean Sea and the Gulf of Mexico offered extraordinary opportunities to peoples who had mastered watercraft many millennia before. The islands varied wildly in geology, climate, and ecology, and thus had different resources; not every island had stone that would make good tools, for example, but almost all had something that the people who had good stone would take in trade. Over thousands of years, as the first scattered settlements grew into thriving villages and towns, trade networks sprang up, and the slender dugouts that first ventured onto Caribbean waters gave way to larger canoes that could carry cargoes from island to island.[29]

By the time the last ice age began to recede, around 14,000 BCE, the inhabitants of the thriving island cultures of the Caribbean and the Gulf of Mexico knew little about the ice sheets that had been so familiar to their distant ancestors. What they knew for certain was that the seas began to rise. Sometimes shorelines would remain the same for a generation or more, sometimes a few paces of shelving beach would be lost in a year or so, and now and then

---

29 Dugout canoes in the Caribbean in Columbus's time commonly reached lengths of eighty feet, and archaeological evidence shows that for more than four thousand years before then, similar craft maintained trade connections that reached from the Carolinas to Colombia and Brazil; see Benson 1977.

a great flood would come rushing down the Mississippi Valley and drowned entire islands beneath a wall of water. Traveler's tales from the cold lands of North America told of huge new inland seas in the shadow of the ice and sudden floods that left entire regions desolate, while refugees following the old route around the North Pacific told a harrowing tale of drowned lands we now call Sundaland submerged below the floods of Global Meltwater Pulse 1A. The rising waters posed serious new challenges to human societies around the world, and the people of the inland sea bore the brunt of widespread flooding. Out of their response to that challenge came the culture of Atlantis.

Yet it took the lucky accident of a summer storm to launch that culture on its way. That storm caught a large trading craft on its way north to Bermuda and blew it far to the east, across the unknown waters of the Atlantic, to islands that would one day be called the Azores. By this time, the trading canoes had evolved into something close to ships: sixty to eighty feet long, crafted from big trees harvested in the coastal forests of the mainlands to either side of the sea, fitted with planks along the sides for extra freeboard, reed-mat sails on a simple mast harnessing the wind, and outriggers for stability and extra cargo space. Like the craft that plied the waters of the western Pacific a few thousand years later, they were fast, nimble, and extremely seaworthy.

That first ship to reach the Azores made its way home weeks after it and its crew had been given up for lost, bringing word of new islands far out in the sea. Daring voyagers repeated the journey and then pushed farther east, reaching the shores of Africa and Spain. There they met people, belonging to ancient cultures of their own, who had goods to trade that no one in the western lands had ever seen before. Within a few years, a regular trade route linked the continents, following winds and currents that would be used again thousands of years later. The voyagers brought back many things, among them an old stone spear-point technology that was quickly refined and reworked by island craftspeople for the use of their own warriors. The Clovis point had arrived in the New World.

The diseases that would make contact with the Old World disastrous for the New in that future age had not yet found their way into human hosts, and the peoples on both sides of the ocean subsisted on the plants and animals of their own local ecosystems, so the biological consequences of later transatlantic contact did not follow in the wake of these earlier voyages of discovery. Still, the opening of the Atlantic trade route changed the balance of power in the inland sea, shifting influence away from the coastal lands of the gulf and the central islands toward islands farther east, closest to the newly discovered lands.

One island in particular, the island that a philosopher more than nine thousand years later would call Atlantis, came to dominate the main trade route to the eastern lands. Low, fertile, and edged with hills, it lay just east of the strategic passage between Florida and Cuba and formed the best starting place for voyages east following the Atlantic currents and winds. Well before 10,000 BCE, the people of Atlantis had parlayed their economic strength into political power, and the chiefs of the island received tribute from a dozen neighboring islands. By 9600 BCE, the chiefs' descendants were kings whose power extended over most of the islands in the inland sea and large portions of the coastal mainlands to the north, south, and west, and its central town became one of the first great cities in human history.

Compared to later cities, it was modest enough, a sprawling mass of thatched houses, dirt-paved streets, and shallow canals close to the sea, with the great house of the kings of Atlantis at its center and a bustling open-air marketplace near the shelving beach where watercraft from all corners of the Atlantic world landed to buy and sell. Another great house, the dwelling of the island's hereditary shamans, stood just outside the city, surrounded by tall wooden posts carved with sacred emblems only the shamans themselves could interpret. As Atlantis flourished, nuggets of native gold brought from Central America were hammered into sheets with stone hammers and used to cover the roof of the kings' house and the pillars of the city's gateways, so that poets many centuries later described Atlantis's capital as the City of the Golden Gates.

Even as Atlantis rose to power, though, the forces that would destroy it gathered strength. Chief among these was global temperature. Not long after the founding of the Atlantean kingship, the world's climate spiked suddenly upward, possibly driven by one or more large methane releases from under the sea; the Boreal phase had arrived. On the North American mainland, as elsewhere in the world, the ecological impact of the sudden heat wave pushed many ice age animals down the road to extinction, and the sudden die-off of cold-adapted food plants and the increased pace of meltwater flooding sent human societies reeling as well.

The ecological crisis on the mainland played into the hands of the Atlantean kings by weakening potential rivals, making the mainlanders ever more dependent on trade with the islands and providing a steady supply of strong young men from the northern lands for whom service in an Atlantean war band was the only alternative to starvation. Atlantis itself was shielded from the worst impacts of climate change by the sea, which kept local temperatures more moderate and provided food sources less vulnerable to sudden temperature change. Far to the north, however, meltwater poured off the shrinking ice sheets and filled the vast proglacial lakes brimful, setting the stage for catastrophe.

The centuries that followed the great warming of the early Boreal phase saw Atlantis at its zenith, the bustling hub of a network of trade and influence that stretched from the upper Mississippi Valley to the mouth of the Rio Plata and from the Pacific coast of Central America to busy Atlantean trading posts along the shores of Europe and North Africa. Atlantean navigators explored all along the shores of the Atlantic Ocean and even sailed south into the cold Antarctic seas, skirting Antarctica at a time when most of its shores were free of ice. At home, the wealth of a hundred cultures flowed through Atlantean markets and made Atlantis the envy of the Boreal world. In a pattern that would repeat throughout history, though, possession of great wealth and power only fed the desire for more, and the lure of wealth from across the Atlantic drove the kings of Atlantis to pursue the dream of an Old World empire.

For a time, that dream seemed within reach. At the high point of the Atlantean empire, around 9400 BCE, its viceroys exercised some level of control, and received some form of tribute, from most of the cultures of the western Mediterranean. Yet the costs of empire proved crippling to Atlantis, as more and more of the empire's resources had to be diverted from productive uses to maintain and extend its control over distant lands across the sea. Finally and inevitably, the Atlantean empire fell victim to its own imperial overstretch as fierce hill tribes from a region that would one day be called Greece overwhelmed an Atlantean expeditionary force, sparking a general revolt that broke the Atlantean grip over the whole Mediterranean basin.

On top of the economic costs of the lost empire, the loss of tribute and trade revenue from the Mediterranean colonies was a blow Atlantis could ill afford, and others followed. Not many years after the Mediterranean revolt, one of the vast proglacial lakes far to the north burst its banks, spilling more than two thousand cubic miles of water down the Mississippi Valley into the Gulf of Mexico. The surging waters drowned dozens of low-lying islands and countless villages throughout the inland sea, killing many thousands and leaving what was left of the empire's economy in tatters.

As troubling to the Atlanteans, though, was the flood's impact on Atlantis itself. For the first time in the island's history, the flood topped the ring of hills that surrounded it and poured into the fertile central lowlands. Once the flood receded, the people of Atlantis struggled to rebuild, but a shallow bay filled the center of the island thereafter. The kings and their courtiers drew up grand plans to build levees and drain the salt water back into the sea, but the economic impact of a lost war and the disastrous flood put harsh limits on what could be done. Worse still, the seas kept rising, and it slowly became apparent to many people throughout the Atlantean empire that all their efforts would only delay the inevitable.

The years that followed were a time of decline for Atlantis and its empire, as coastlands around the Atlantic world shrank before the rising seas. Still, nobody was prepared for the final disaster when it struck. One unseasonably hot day a few centuries after the great Mediterranean revolt, a mighty undersea earthquake shook the eastern end of the inland sea, toppling trees and wrecking houses on a hundred islands. Minutes after the ground stopped shaking, horrified watchers on the southeast coast of Atlantis saw the sea draw back more than two miles from the shore. As conch trumpets sounded a warning inland, the waters returned in force. A huge wave crashed into what was left of Atlantis and rushed over it from end to end, sweeping away nearly everything on the island and dragging most of its people down to a watery grave.

The few bedraggled survivors, those who clung to flotsam or scrambled above the few boats not wrecked by the wave, found themselves in a changed world once the waters poured away. The wave had stripped away most of the island's soil and vegetation as well as nearly all of its homes and buildings, leaving only bare rock, mud, and debris. Desperate efforts by the few who had boats and canoes saved many survivors from death by exposure and thirst, but most of the island would never be habitable again, and over the following weeks, the remaining people of Atlantis sought new homes on the mainland, far from the rising waters.

In the years that followed, several of the islands and mainland regions less affected by the flooding tried to fill the void left by the destruction of Atlantis, but conflict broke out among them, and raids and reprisals shredded the trade networks that had once formed the foundation of Atlantean ascendancy. Meanwhile, the seas continued to rise all around the world, flooding villages and towns, drowning fertile land, and wrecking ancient cultures. More earthquakes shook the eastern end of the inland sea, while others set in motion by the melting of the European ice sheets shook the Mediterranean; one of the latter caused a catastrophic landslide in the country that would later be called Greece, giving birth to a legend of an army swallowed up by the earth. The transatlantic routes flickered out as long-distance trade became a luxury none of the surviving peoples could afford. A long and bitter dark age settled over the Atlantic world.

Long after the last of the great trading canoes made their final voyages and the final traces of the old empire flickered out, though, people still recalled something of the way things had been in the glory days of Atlantis. In the cold, rainy highlands of northwestern Europe that would someday become the islands of Britain and Ireland, tales described a land across the sea where winter never came—a land later cultures would call the Summer Country, Avalon, and Tir na nÓg. On the shores of northeastern Mexico, a people whose distant descendants would become the Aztecs remembered that their ancestors had come from a lost land they called Aztlan, the Place of Reeds. Inland from the eastern shores of the Mediterranean Sea, where the Natufian culture began building the walls of Jericho to protect themselves from raiders in the troubled times after Atlantis fell, merchants and scholar-priests gathered scraps of Atlantean geographical knowledge and passed them down through the generations to the Babylonians and Greeks, who included them in maps that still puzzle researchers today.

On the western shores of North Africa, finally, some survivor of the floods put together an epic poem about the fall of Atlantis, and it spread across North Africa to the Nile Valley through the green years of the late Boreal phase, when the Sahara was a vast grassland full of game. In this poet's imagination, Atlantis became a paradise, with the hills around its coasts turned into mountains and the City of the Golden Gates a grander metropolis than it had ever been; refugees with their minds full of nostalgic memories do such things. Sometime during Egypt's Middle Kingdom, perhaps, when storytellers in the western Nile Delta still remembered the old tale, some Egyptian scribe copied down a brief version on papyrus, and twelve centuries later an elderly priest who had read the story repeated it to a foreign traveler named Solon.

Testing the Hypothesis

The point of this highly speculative story is not to reveal "the truth about Atlantis," if a phenomenon of so many levels and dimensions can be said to have a single core of truth, but simply to suggest one way Plato's account of Atlantis could have worked out in terms of the geological and archaeological realities of 9600 BCE. The rise and fall of Atlantean civilization might have happened in a different way, of course, and it's also possible that it never happened at all. Showing that something is possible is not the same thing as proving that it happened—a point of logic far too often lost sight of in Atlantology—and the story just recounted is simply an attempt to show that Plato's narrative can't be dismissed out of hand as a scientific impossibility.

To go further requires evidence. The question of evidence, however, has been one of the most vexed issues in the entire Atlantis controversy since Ignatius Donnelly's time. Donnelly himself filled the pages of *Atlantis: The Antediluvian World* with details he thought proved the existence of an ancient continent in the middle of the Atlantic, but nearly all of them either have many possible explanations or turned out not to be true in the light of later research. Pointing out similarities between Old World and New World cultures, to cite one of Donnelly's main themes, doesn't prove the existence of Atlantis, because other factors—the possibility of transatlantic contacts more recent than 9600 BCE, for instance—could explain those similarities equally well. In the same way, quoting nineteenth-century oceanographers who thought the Mid-Atlantic Ridge might have been above water in the distant past proves nothing, since we now know those oceanographers were quite simply wrong.

Still, the debunkers who insist that Atlantis can't have existed since no obvious evidence for it has yet been found are just as illogical as the true believers who keep on citing outdated science to support their beliefs. If Atlantis existed, it vanished around 11,500 years ago in a part of the world where most artifacts don't last long. Like other cultures of its time, it likely relied for building and other goods on wood, plant fibers, and other organic materials that decay fast. Stone buildings were rare in the world of 9600 BCE, and metal was at most what it was to some Native American peoples: a rare material hammered into prestige items from native nuggets and surrounded by many taboos.[30]

Furthermore, sea levels were between two hundred and three hundred feet lower than they are today, and nearly all ancient peoples in maritime environments lived close to the water that provided them with food and transport, so nearly all the potential archaeological sites lie deep underwater, with eleven millennia of sand and mud on top of them for good measure—to say nothing of the likely results of floods, earthquakes, and tsunamis during and after the end of the last ice age. Under the circumstances, evidence of Atlantis is necessarily sparse and difficult to find. Still, some options certainly exist.

Genetic analysis offers one avenue for exploration that is only just beginning to open. If something like the Atlantis described in this chapter existed, further research should show the traces of a small but significant mingling of New World and Old World populations around the time of the Atlantis window. Populations can move quite a bit in 11,600 years, of course, but on average those traces should be most common in southeastern North America, northeastern South America, and the Caribbean islands in the New World, and in the Iberian Peninsula, southern France, and the western end of North Africa in the Old World—the areas most closely in contact during the age of Atlantis.

Linguistic analysis offers a second useful test. If a prehistoric maritime culture in the West Indies crossed the Atlantic and established enough of a bridgehead on the far side to fight wars with the cultures of the Mediterranean, loanwords and other scraps of language would have gone with them. Only a handful of languages on either side of the ocean are even remotely descended from the ones spoken there during the age of Atlantis, but those would be good

---

30 This was the role of native copper, for example, in the Northwest Coast tribes of North America, who used it purely for ceremonial objects.

candidates to search for potential borrowings. In the Old World, Basque and Berber are good candidates, and so is Old Irish, which likely absorbed many words from the pre-Celtic language of Ireland. In the New World, the native languages of southeastern North America, the Caribbean, the Yucatán, and the northern coast of South America are all worth checking. This work, it's worth noting, needs to be done by qualified professional linguists—wildly inaccurate efforts by amateur linguists have bedeviled the question of Atlantis since before Donnelly's time, producing much more confusion than clarity.

A more speculative but potentially more powerful approach relies on scientific methods that locate the exact place where the raw material for a stone tool was taken from the earth. This has already had an impact on our image of the past, revealing that fine stone from certain places traveled thousands of miles along well-defined trade routes long before the beginning of history. If the Atlantis theory is correct, trade goods—including high-quality stone—would have traveled both ways across the Atlantic, and stone tools found in sites on either side of the ocean should be checked for the possibility of a transatlantic source. The same is true for other materials that can be tracked back to their source. Since current methods also allow archaeologists to figure out the date of artifacts to a fair level of precision, it would take only a few definite finds from the right period to put the Atlantis theory on a solid footing.

The most conclusive approach, though, would have to rely on sea floor sampling. If a tsunami or meltwater flood finished the work of the rising oceans and drowned Grand Bahama Bank as quickly as Plato claimed, a thick layer of topsoil, vegetation, and other material washed away by the waters would remain in deep water where the flood left it. Material deposited all at once by a flood, a tsunami, or some other sudden event forms what oceanographers call a *turbidity layer*, a thick layer of mud and debris without the internal layering found in ordinary sea-floor mud. A turbidity layer can be identified from core samples of the ocean floor, and organic material in the core samples can be dated by the radiocarbon method.

The exact location of the turbidity layer is hard to guess in advance. A tsunami from the Caribbean Plate subduction zone would have come from the southeast, a meltwater flood from the Mississippi would have come from the west, and a tsunami caused by a methane blowout and underwater landslide could have come from any direction at all. Any of these three options could have left debris in any direction, furthermore, depending on how the waters drained from the island. Deepwater currents and similar factors would also have had an influence on where debris came to rest, and all of it would now be under another eleven millennia of seafloor mud, not to mention the turbidity flows from any later tsunamis in the region. Careful study of the undersea geography of the Bahamas, followed by systematic core sampling, would be needed to find the traces of the flood that drowned Atlantis.

If the hypothesis presented in this chapter is correct, then, the wreckage of Atlantis is buried deep and will be difficult to reach except by the scattershot method of drilling sediment cores into the sea floor. The elegant drowned city shown off by Captain Nemo must unfortunately be left to the realm of fiction. Still, if funding can be found to search the sea floor for likely areas and drill sediment cores, it's intriguing to think about what might be found. Topsoil and the remains of trees and other vegetation carbon-dated to the right time would be enough to prove that something like the end of Atlantis had happened to Great Bahama Bank, but if an artifact happened to turn up—a carved piece of mastodon ivory, say, or a scrap of worked stone that came from an Old World source—the case for Atlantis would become difficult to refute.

Some valuable Atlantis research has already been done on one part of Great Bahama Bank. The Association for Research and Enlightenment (ARE), the organization founded by Edgar Cayce, has sponsored several expeditions to the island of Bimini, on the northern end of the bank. A 1968 ARE expedition led by Robert Ferro

The "Bimini Road"

and Michael Grumley found a long row of flat, rectangular rocks, looking for all the world like an ancient stone road, in shallow water near Bimini, and the three Poseidia Expeditions sponsored by ARE and led by expert scuba diver David Zink in 1975, 1976, and 1977 took detailed photographs and measurements of the "Bimini Road."[31] Because an extensive underwater archaeological dig is well beyond ARE's financial resources and no mainstream archaeologist will risk his reputation on such a project, no one is yet sure whether the "road" is a natural formation or an ancient artifact—a point that has not stopped geologists who should know better from stating their opinions as definite fact. If the other tests proposed here are carried out and turn up evidence for Atlantis, serious underwater exploration in the area of the "road" would be a likely next step.

Assessing the Legends

The material in the first three chapters of this book—the body of legend, legominism, and speculation that has grown up around Plato's story of Atlantis—and that in the following two chapters— the geology and archaeology that may put a foundation under the Atlantis legend—approach the old riddle of Atlantis in very different ways. At this point, however, it's worth bringing them together,

---

31 See Ferro and Grumley 1970 and Zink 1978 for accounts of these expeditions.

by putting the Atlantis theories side by side with what scientific evidence shows about the world as it existed during the Atlantis window. Whether or not my hypothesis about the location of Atlantis is correct, enough is known about the time of Atlantis to check how well the various approaches measure up to the facts of geology and archaeology.

The man who launched the Atlantis legend on its long career, Plato himself, stands up to such an examination well. Some of the details of his account are borrowed from the city-states of his own time, but a surprising number of his claims fit the world of 9600 BCE very closely. From the sheer fact that this was probably the most drastic period of sea level rise in the history of our species, to little details like the elephants that thrive on his Atlantis and its likely equivalents, enough of his story matches the realities of the end of the ice age to make it probable that he had some source of information, however fragmentary, about the distant past.

Several other early Atlantis writers also do tolerably well when compared to the facts we've explored in the last two chapters. The Atlantis-in-America theory proposed by Francesco Lopez de Gomara, John Swan, and so many others in the sixteenth and seventeenth centuries makes good sense of the data, especially since there were many large islands off the shores of the Americas that drowned when sea levels rose just after the age of Atlantis. Swan's thoughtful conjecture that "if America joyned not to the west part of [Atlantis], yet surely it could not be farre distant" is one of the few theories that makes the Atlantis legend work in the context of geology.

The Atlantis of the rejected-knowledge movement is much more of a mixed bag. Many of these writers parrot the inaccurate science of an earlier time or build soaring conjectures that lack any real foundation in evidence. The shadow of Ignatius Donnelly still dominates the field, though Donnelly himself would probably be the first to discard his old theories and build new ones based on today's science if he had the chance. Other writers in the rejected-knowledge movement, however, have raised important questions about the shape of prehistory, pointing out impressive evidence for lost cities and civilizations scattered all over the world.

These discoveries are at least as important for our understanding of our world as any rediscovery of Atlantis could be. What they show, boiled down to the simplest possible terms, is that the modern faith in progress is founded on empty air. Instead of a single upward movement from primitive cave dwellers to modern technological societies, they suggest, human societies have risen and collapsed countless times in the past, and the unpredictable changes of an unstable planet make civilization a very risky project over the long term.

Toward the less successful side of the rejected-knowledge movement's version of Atlantis, on the other hand, are the claims that Atlantean civilization evolved technologies similar to the ones that modern industrial societies wield today. Here the problem is as simple as it is unanswerable: no trace of any such technologies has been found anywhere in the world in geological strata dating to the age of Atlantis. The people of the Atlantic basin during the early Boreal phase either definitely had or could easily have developed the technologies described in the imaginary history outlined in this chapter, but the same thing simply isn't true of the aircraft, explosives, and other high-tech devices described in many recent speculations about Atlantis. Only if John Michell is right, and the ancient technology was so different from ours that today's archaeologists do not even recognize it as a technology, could this claim be supported, and any attempt to prove that would require something more than the vague claims floated in recent literature. It remains a possibility, but an unproven one.

The occult Atlantis, finally, includes some unnervingly accurate details along with a great many others that have no foundation at all in prehistory. Many of the latter were admittedly never meant to do so. The Atlantis that had so central a role in Blavatsky's great legominism—a huge continent filling much of the Atlantic Ocean—

never existed outside of the symbolic universe created by *The Secret Doctrine*, and there's good reason to think that it was never meant to be anything but a vehicle for communicating occult truths to the general public. The occult societies that have kept the legominism in circulation for so long had a role to play, and they played it well, but contributing to accurate knowledge of prehistory was not part of their mission.

Still, tucked away among the symbolism and the untested visions were insights that, if nothing else, count as astonishingly good guesswork. Blavatsky and her fellow occultists were absolutely right to claim that the age of Atlantis ended in a series of floods, not a single disaster, and the three destructions occult lore assigns to Atlantis have a curious similarity to the three great warming periods—Bölling, Alleröd, and Boreal—that sent sea levels surging upward in the waning years of the ice age. If the theory in this book turns out to be correct, the old occult claim that the Atlanteans belonged to the "red race"—that is, that they were closely related to Native Americans—will also be shown to be correct. The odd way that Mu and Lemuria gradually drifted loose from their original moorings, finally settling as a single continent right where today's scientists put the huge drowned landmass of Sundaland, also suggests that the occultists might have been on to something.

The visionary end of the occult movement was particularly good in its aim. At a time when mainstream Atlantology insisted that Atlantis was a continent in the middle of the Atlantic Ocean, the Fraternity of the Inner Light identified it as a relatively small island and put it close to the coasts of the Americas, where the evidence suggests it might well have been. Even Edgar Cayce, whose visions included so much improbable material, was right to point out that Atlantis in its heyday had a much cooler climate than its present latitude would suggest, and he pointed straight to the Bahamas as the place where evidence for Atlantis might best be found. If the theory proposed in this book turns out to be correct, other details in the Cayce readings may be worth a second look.

Yet a very large part of occult Atlantis lore finds no reflection in prehistory at all. Such central themes as the conflict between the followers of the One Spirit and the Lords of the Dark Face, the Atlanteans' responsibility for the destruction of their continent, and the work of the seedbearers who brought Atlantean knowledge to the new cultures of the dawning age entered the Atlantis legend for the first time with Blavatsky's great legominism, but only the most forceful twisting allows any trace of these things to be found in the prehistoric evidence. It would be reasonable to dismiss these as purely symbolic elements meant to communicate occult teachings, except for one troubling fact: while these things have nothing in common with the realities of the prehistoric past, they have all too much relevance when put in the context of our own future.

SIX

The New Atlantis

Among the strangest things about Atlantis is the way its legend leapt out of obscurity in the last decades of the nineteenth century to become one of the most powerful cultural themes of the modern age. Even if every word Plato wrote about the subject is literally true, after all, Atlantis is just one more civilization that rose, flourished, and collapsed during our species' long history, older than those currently accepted by mainstream historians but not exceptional in any other way. There was no shortage of lost cities and vanished cultures in the history books of the 1870s and 1880s, and many more have been found since then. Why should an odd story tucked away in the writings of a Greek philosopher, of all things, have turned into a cause célèbre in the busy world of the late nineteenth century—and why should it still be the focus of so much obsessive interest more than a century later?

Part of the reason, certainly, lies in the way the Atlantis legend challenges the mythology of progress. Most of the lost civilizations known to the late nineteenth century left some legacy, however fragmentary, to future generations. This enabled believers in progress to fit them into the comforting story of humanity's journey from the caves to the stars, since each of these dead civilizations could be seen as stepping stones on the way, contributing something to a

189

bigger and brighter future before falling by the wayside. The idea that a civilization of the past might have collapsed completely—so completely that only the faintest traces of its existence survive to the present—is hard to square with the story of progress.

The other vanished civilizations uncovered by the rejected-knowledge movement make this point with even greater force. If Atlantis is not alone, and many other civilizations before and after it rose and fell without leaving anything to the future, the dream of progress gives way to a hard awakening, and the people of the industrial world have to face the daunting possibility that our hopes for a Promethean future among the stars may be daydreams or even delusions. In this case, the purblind thinking that leads people to pollute and strip-mine the earth and let the future deal with the consequences may be damaging the only planetary home we will ever have. Still, the Romans, the Mayans, and many other once-great civilizations of the past already serve as a harsh reminder that history is not a one-way street. Why should Atlantis, more than anything else in the modern imagination, become a lightning rod for such fears?

The answer may be as close as today's headlines. The Atlantis obsession of the modern industrial world makes an uncomfortable amount of sense in the light of current events, because a growing body of evidence suggests that our own civilization is heading straight toward the fate that legend assigns to Atlantis.

The Heat Is On

As I type these words, newspapers worldwide are headlining the release of a new study by the Intergovernmental Panel on Climate Change (IPCC), a huge scientific task force supported by governments worldwide and charged with working out the reality behind the global warming "controversy." That last word belongs in quotes because there hasn't actually been a serious scientific controversy on the subject for most of a decade. All ten of the ten hottest years in recorded history have happened since 1990. More than a dozen different lines of evidence show that our planet is heating up, that it has already reached global average temperatures never before recorded in history, that the warming trend is speeding up year by year, and that global temperatures have risen in lockstep with the amount of carbon dioxide (CO_2) dumped into the atmosphere by the smokestacks and tailpipes of our industrial society.[1] While the oil industry, their hired think tanks, and a dwindling band of right-wing pundits with no scientific training continue to insist that nothing is happening, the only controversy among the vast majority of climatologists at this point is how bad it will get—and how soon.

The science behind global warming has been well understood for more than a century. Carbon dioxide and several other gases, including methane, trap heat in the earth's atmosphere via the so-called "greenhouse effect." The more CO_2 is in the atmosphere, the more heat is trapped and the hotter the earth gets. Burning coal, oil, natural gas, and other fossil fuels puts CO_2 into the atmosphere. Since the beginning of the industrial revolution around 1750, the total amount of CO_2 in the air has more than doubled, driving global temperatures upward. Today, the rate at which CO_2 pours into the atmosphere is climbing steeply as people around the world pursue a lifestyle that demands ever more cars, conveniences, and consumer goods and burn more fossil fuels to provide these things. At the present rate of increase, the amount of CO_2 in the atmosphere will double again in only thirty years.

This would be bad enough if CO_2 pollution drove climate warming in a simple, linear way. One of the core principles of the environmental sciences, however, is that little changes have big impacts. Our planet's climate is maintained by a delicate balancing act among dozens of different factors, and any change in one factor can drive wide swings in others. It takes only a slight shift in the relationship between the earth and the sun, for example, to launch an ice age or end one, because these little changes trigger complicated climate feedback loops that do the rest of the work,

---

1 See, for example, Alley 2000, Hunter 2003, and McCaffrey 2006.

amplifying that initial bit of heating or cooling until it changes the face of the world. Two feedback loops that are already beginning to amplify the effects of CO_2 pollution have already been identified by worried scientists, and every climatologist knows there may be others we haven't discovered yet.[2]

The first feedback loop is driven by *albedo*, the reflectiveness of the earth's surface. Ice and snow have a much higher albedo than liquid water—that is, ice sheets reflect most of the sun's heat back out into space, but open water reflects a lot less. Thus, as long as sea ice covers the North Pole, most of the sunlight that falls there during the long polar summer bounces right back out again, keeping the Arctic Ocean cold. Once the ice cap melts and open water appears, though, the water soaks up more of the sun's heat, warming the Arctic Ocean and speeding up the collapse of the remaining ice. This feedback loop is already hard at work right now. In the summers of 2005 and 2006, polar surveys found open water at the North Pole for the first time in more than a million years, and the real possibility that the Arctic Ocean may be ice-free year round within this century is being discussed by oceanographers today. If that happens, a major factor that keeps the earth at its present temperature will be gone.

The second and even more dangerous feedback loop involves methane (CH_4), the likely cause of the worldwide temperature spike at the beginning of the Boreal phase. Methane is around twenty times as effective as carbon dioxide at holding heat in the atmosphere. It's produced by rotting organic matter, and there are huge amounts of it locked up in two places. The first is permafrost, ground that has been frozen solid since the beginning of the last ice age, 120,000 years ago. There's a lot of methane there, since permafrost currently makes up around 25 percent of the land area of the Northern Hemisphere, including most of Siberia and Canada. The second, even larger amount is hidden under the oceans in methane hydrates like the ones discussed in chapter 4. No one

---

2 See McCaffrey 2006, 92–95, for the data cited in the next three paragraphs.

knows how much methane is in these two places, but current estimates put the figure at well over 12 trillion tons, or more than a hundred times the total amount of carbon dioxide now in the earth's atmosphere.

What makes this so dangerous is that the permafrost and methane hydrates holding all this methane imprisoned are temperature sensitive. Warm permafrost above freezing, and the methane in it begins to bubble out. Raise sea temperatures even a few degrees, and methane hydrates start fizzing, releasing bubbles of methane that rise through the water and burst on the surface. The result in either case is more methane escaping into the atmosphere. The more methane that gets into the atmosphere, the more heat is trapped, sending land and sea temperatures higher still and potentially releasing yet more methane in a vicious cycle. A steady rise in methane levels in the atmosphere appears in Greenland ice cores right around the time of the beginning of the Boreal phase—one piece of evidence that this particular feedback loop helped drive catastrophic warming then.[3]

Climatologists today worry that large-scale methane releases could once again send temperatures worldwide soaring thirteen to fifteen degrees Fahrenheit. in a decade or less, as happened around 9600 BCE. Mark Maslin, whose research into undersea mudslides was discussed in chapter 4, cautions that the same sort of catastrophic methane blowout can happen today due to global warming, especially if ice sheets collapse and put stress on nearby faults.[4]

The potential for methane to add to global warming isn't simply an abstract scientific theory at this point, either. Methane is already beginning to enter the atmosphere from permafrost and methane hydrates alike. News reports from Siberia describe swamps in melting permafrost where methane can be seen visibly bubbling up through standing water. In 2002, similarly, the crew of an oceanographic research ship witnessed a sudden, explosive blowout of methane from

---

3 Alley 2000, 114–15.
4 Maslin 2004, 56.

deep waters near Santa Barbara, California. Scuba divers in the water at the time of the blowout said that it sounded like an freight train going by under the sea, and careful tracking of the column of methane bubbles showed that some 98 percent of the methane released from the sea floor reached the atmosphere.[5]

With these feedback loops in place, along with the potential risks from others we don't yet know about, global warming is serious business. Two of the world's remaining three continental ice sheets, the West Antarctic Ice Sheet and the Greenland Ice Sheet, are already showing clear warning signs of impending collapse. Two huge ice shelves connected to the West Antarctic Ice Sheet have already collapsed—the larger of the two, Larsen Ice Shelf B, was the size of Rhode Island before it broke apart—and recent satellite surveys of the West Antarctic found huge rivers of meltwater flowing under the ice sheet, draining into the sea, and potentially setting the stage for a catastrophic collapse. Meanwhile, cutting-edge research in Greenland shows that the ice sheet there is melting ten times faster than it was only a few years ago, and meltwater rivers beneath the ice like the ones in West Antarctica have been detected in Greenland as well.[6]

Can Global Warming Be Stopped?

Most of the talk about global warming nowadays focuses on finding some way to stop it without giving up the technological comforts and conveniences of modern life. The problem is that stopping CO_2 emissions into the atmosphere would require shutting down most of modern technology. Everything that burns gasoline, diesel oil, or any other petroleum product dumps extra CO_2 into the atmosphere, and so does everything that burns coal or natural gas. Drive a car, and CO_2 pours out of the tailpipe; go shopping, even on foot, and the goods for sale in every store you visit came

5 The methane release is documented in Leifer et al. 2006.
6 See *BBC News* 2002, Connor 2007, Pearce 2004, and Shukman 2004.

on trucks, trains, ships, or planes that churned out even more CO_2; flip a switch to turn on the lights or boot up a computer, and odds are the power plant at the other end is dumping still more CO_2 into the air, since more than 70 percent of America's electricity is produced by burning natural gas or coal.

Imminent changes in the availability of fossil fuels make this situation significantly more dangerous than it already is. For most of the last century, petroleum has been the largest single energy source in the developed world, but petroleum reserves worldwide are starting to run short. The sheer volume of petroleum used by the global economy—85 million barrels every single day—draws down reserves at a phenomenal pace, and new discoveries of oil are falling short of production year after year. The result is the widely discussed Peak Oil problem, the approach of the day when oil production reaches its all-time peak and begins an inexorable decline.[7] Exactly how long we have until this happens is a topic of fierce debate among experts right now, but even the most optimistic estimates give us less than twenty-five years.

Natural gas faces similar problems, with soaring production and shrinking reserves, made worse by the fact that many natural gas producers are starting to convert natural gas to liquid fuel to make up for depleting petroleum supplies. Meanwhile, many countries in the Third World, China above all, have begun rapid industrial growth and are buying up oil and other energy resources in an effort to catch up to the Western industrial nations and claim a larger role in the international order. The result is a squeeze on oil and natural gas supplies that will only get worse as reserves continue to dwindle.

That leaves coal, the most abundant fossil fuel—and the dirtiest. In the last few years, hundreds of new coal-fired electrical plants have come online around the world, with many more under

---

7 Peak Oil itself poses major potential challenges to the survival of industrial civilization, for reasons too complex to explore here. Among the large recent literature on the Peak Oil situation, the best general overview remains Heinberg 2002.

construction as you read these words. Each of these plants can be expected to dump millions of tons of CO_2 into the atmosphere in its working life. Methods for pulling CO_2 out of power plants' smokestacks and storing it somewhere else have been discussed at great length, and a few small pilot projects have been funded, but talk and pilot projects do nothing to stop the torrents of CO_2 pouring into the atmosphere from these plants right now.

Talk and small pilot projects are also the only steps being taken so far to replace fossil fuels with energy sources that don't generate CO_2. Modest amounts of wind power and solar power plants are being built today, but these amount to a small fraction of the investment going into coal-burning plants. A few new nuclear power plants have been planned, but nuclear power has serious drawbacks of its own, and fissionable uranium—the fuel for today's reactors—also faces the same squeeze between rising demand and dwindling reserves.

Converting from a fossil fuel economy to any of these alternatives would take trillions of dollars of new investment and decades of rebuilding. Think of what it would cost and how long it would take, to name only one example, just to replace every gas station in America with a hydrogen filling station! Meanwhile, next to nothing has been done to start the changeover yet, which means that all that money has to come out of tomorrow's budgets, and CO_2 will keep on pouring into the atmosphere for decades to come even if the transition process starts today.

Like so many of the environmental problems looming before our society, the global-warming crisis is hard to solve, because it combines short-term benefits with long-term costs. Burning fossil fuels provides obvious, immediate benefits—fast transportation, comfortable homes, plentiful consumer products, and much more. The downside comes years or decades later, as the CO_2 dumped into the atmosphere in the course of providing those benefits sends the earth's climate spinning out of control. When it comes to giving up short-term benefits in order to avoid long-term costs, our species has a notoriously bad track record, especially so in a case like this one, where the short-term benefits include nearly everything people in the industrial world consider a normal lifestyle.

The late John Kenneth Galbraith, one of the most brilliant minds in modern economics, discussed the resulting mindset in his mordant 1984 book *The Culture of Contentment*. Like the aristocracy of France in the decades before the French Revolution broke out, most people today realize at some level that the current course of our society is unsustainable and will end in disaster. The costs of doing anything about it are so high, however, and impact everyday life so directly that nearly everybody does their best to ignore the problem and hope that it will go away by itself. That attitude led most of the French aristocracy straight to the guillotine when the French Revolution finally came. So far, modern industrial civilization has shown very few signs of breaking away from its equally dysfunctional attitude, and the stakes are much higher.

The implications of all this will not sit well with all those people whose response to the crisis is to hope that it will go away, that somebody else will deal with it, or that they can make the necessary changes happen in the course of business as usual. With every day that passes, many tons of CO_2 pour into the atmosphere, pushing the earth's climate closer to the point where feedback loops take over and drastic climate change begins—a point that scientists today cannot predict, and will probably recognize for certain only after we cross over it and start suffering the consequences.

Far from dealing with the problem, governments and business interests either treat it as a publicity issue to be met with ineffective sound bites or actively make matters worse by pursuing short-term economic growth at all costs without any regard to the catastrophic environmental consequences. The halfhearted and hopelessly inadequate Kyoto treaty, which merely tried to slow down the rate at which CO_2 gets dumped into the atmosphere, has been flatly rejected by the countries responsible for most of the world's CO_2 pollution—

and even most of the countries that signed it failed to cut their emissions enough to meet its requirements.[8]

While politicians drag their heels and corporations pursue business as usual, time is running short. In February 2007, scientists in the IPCC reported that even if all human-caused CO_2 emissions stopped at once, there was a 50 percent chance that enough had already been dumped into the atmosphere to cause the collapse of the Greenland and West Antarctic ice sheets and set off radical changes in the world's climate that will last thousands of years into the future.[9] Each day that passes without serious action whittles away at our remaining chance of stopping the global-warming juggernaut. Meanwhile, governments and ordinary people alike show no signs of finding the wisdom or the political will to embrace the hard choices and drastic actions needed to stop CO_2 pollution before it passes the critical tipping point and global climate spins out of control. It's understandable that people of good will still hope to stop global warming, but it may be time to face up to the hard realities of the situation and start preparing to survive its consequences instead.

What Global Warming Means

As we have seen, even very modest changes in the earth's temperature have drastic consequences in terms of climate and sea level. In the past, shifts in global temperature of one or two degrees Fahrenheit drove climate changes that made harvests fail, deserts spread, and civilizations crumble. Larger changes like the ones that ushered in the Alleröd and Boreal phases, five to fifteen degrees, caused continental ice sheets to collapse and drowned tens of thousands of square miles of dry land under rising seas. Average global temperature has already climbed more than two degrees since 1860, more than enough to kick off severe climate changes worldwide, and re-

8 See Gattuso 2006 and Pearce 2006.
9 See Adam 2007.

alistic current estimates predict that global temperatures will climb another three to ten degrees before 2100, well up into the range that has made ice sheets collapse in the past.[10] This estimate leaves out the possible effects of methane escaping from permafrost and undersea hydrates, the wild card in the global-warming deck, because no one yet knows how fast this might happen or how much methane might surge up into the atmosphere, so the figures just quoted should be considered minimums.

The consequences of a global temperature increase of three to ten degrees are drastic enough all by themselves. As the world heats up, sea surface temperatures in the tropics shoot upward, shifting hurricanes and tropical storms into overdrive and redefining rainfall patterns worldwide. Drought belts and monsoons shift to new places, and changes in average temperature allow tropical diseases like malaria and yellow fever to spread into what are now temperate climates.

The most serious risks, though, lie far from the tropics, in the Greenland and West Antarctic ice sheets. Both of these continental glaciers have already begun to show signs of breaking up under the pressure of rising temperatures, and scientists warn that the rivers of meltwater flowing under the ice today could allow huge amounts of ice to slide off into the sea in a very short time. If either one collapses, sea levels worldwide will surge upward twenty to thirty feet, drowning hundreds of coastal cities, including New York, Miami, Los Angeles, and Washington, D.C. If both of them collapse, a fifty-foot rise in sea level would put most of Florida and large sections of two dozen other states underwater, turning nearly half of the U.S. population into refugees from the rising waters. The impact of a Greenland Ice Sheet collapse on the tectonics of the Atlantic basin is likely to be drastic in the extreme, and coastal regions of North America and Europe already at risk from flooding will likely also face massive earthquakes and tsunamis as the

---

10 These figures are from the authoritative IPCC Third Assessment, which is considered conservative by many climatologists. See Hunter 2003, 135–41.

earth's crust responds to the loss of trillions of tons of ice in a geologically short period of time.

The ultimate threat of global warming lies in the vast East Antarctic Ice Sheet, the single largest accumulation of ice on earth today. About the size of the Laurentide Ice Sheet, which blanketed the northeastern quarter of North America during the last ice age, the East Antarctic sheet holds enough water to raise sea levels by around 250 feet worldwide. Scientists have not yet detected signs of instability in this immense continental glacier, but the best current science suggests that a global temperature rise of fifteen degrees Fahrenheit—a figure that could easily be reached by 2150 at current rates of CO_2 emission, or much sooner if methane begins venting into the atmosphere in a big way—would be enough to tip it irreversibly toward collapse.[11] In the aftermath of an East Antarctic Ice Sheet meltdown, huge areas that are now dry land— most of northern Europe, more than half of Russia, the Mississippi and Amazon valleys, and all of the British Isles except for Wales and the Scottish highlands, just to start with—would slip beneath the waves. As the earth's atmospheric and ocean circulation systems shift into overdrive and pump heat toward the poles, most of the world's land areas would become tropical jungles bordering shallow seas. This is what the world looked like 100 million years ago, when dinosaurs ruled the planet, and it could be what the world looks like again within a few centuries.

It's important to be clear about the consequences of the time of troubles we are unleashing on ourselves via global warming. Our planet, to begin with, is in no danger. The earth's biosphere has shrugged off drastic climate shifts many hundreds of times before now and can easily handle another one. The changes set in motion by our addiction to fossil fuels are no more extreme than the ones caused by the end of the last ice age; they simply shift our planet from one familiar set of climate conditions to another, warmer one. Many species will go extinct, but extinction is business as usual on

---

11 McCaffrey 2006, 92.

our unstable planet, and new life forms will quickly evolve to fill niches in the new environments of the future.

Human beings likewise will most likely endure. Our species evolved in a time of drastic climate change and, even without high technology, has been able to adapt to every environment on the planet except the continental ice sheets themselves. In the hothouse world of the future we are making for ourselves, people will find ways to survive, and within a dozen generations or so the humid jungles and vast shallow seas of the future earth will seem as familiar to our descendants as the more temperate world we know today does to us.

What is unlikely to survive the approaching change to a jungle planet is modern industrial civilization. The complicated networks of production, distribution, energy, and communications that hold industrial societies together were designed and built in an age of stable climate, and the steady depletion of the fossil fuels that drive our civilization today promises to leave little for societies in the future to use to cope with the consequences of an age of severe climate change. Hit by catastrophic coastal flooding, drastic changes in rainfall patterns and climate belts, the spread of tropical diseases into temperate regions, and many other impacts of global warming, we face the dawning of an age of decline in which infrastructure collapses, population declines, and the survivors return to much simpler ways of life amid the ruins of a vanished industrial civilization.

Dr. Richard Duncan, a retired professor of electrical engineering whose work on energy resources is widely respected among students of Peak Oil, has proposed a theory that makes uncomfortable sense of these possibilities.[12] The Olduvai Theory, named after the site in Kenya where some of the oldest human fossils have been found, predicts that industrial civilization will turn out to be what engineers call a *pulse waveform*, a single curve rising from

---

12 See Duncan 2001 and 2006 for good summaries of the Olduvai Theory, the basis of the next two paragraphs.

background noise to a peak and then returning to background levels. To measure the waveform of industrial society, Duncan uses the simple but useful figure of world energy per capita—the amount of energy that, on average, each person in the world has at his or her disposal. Since every aspect of industrial society demands large amounts of energy, this makes a fair measure of the level of industrialization worldwide.

Western industrial nations first began moving away from the "background level" of agricultural societies in the early eighteenth century, as steam engines came into general use, but until the late nineteenth century, world energy per capita changed little; steam power was expensive, and most work was still done by sun, wind, water, and muscle, as it had been for thousands of years. Not until 1930 did energy per capita reach 30 percent of its peak level, the point that engineers use to define the beginning of a pulse waveform. Thereafter, energy per capita soared, reaching its peak around 1970. Since then, however, it has bumped along a rough plateau, and many analyses—including Duncan's—suggest it will begin to decline in less than a decade as oil reserves dwindle and dirtier, less efficient coal has to be used to replace it. Factor in the other pressures coming to bear on industrial civilization, global warming among them, and that decline could be swift. Duncan's figures predict that world energy per capita could return to its 1930 levels as soon as 2030 and decline to the "background level" of agricultural society over the decades following.

Major shifts in climate all by themselves have pushed many civilizations of the past over the edge into decline or collapse.[13] The chaos left behind in New Orleans by Hurricane Katrina, a storm given strength by abnormally high sea surface temperatures that are one more product of global warming, offers a small foretaste of what the future holds in store for us in a world of rising waters and soaring temperatures. As seas rise, cities drown, crops fail, in-

---

13 Ponting 1992 offers a useful summary of the role of climate change and environmental collapse in the fall of historically documented civilizations.

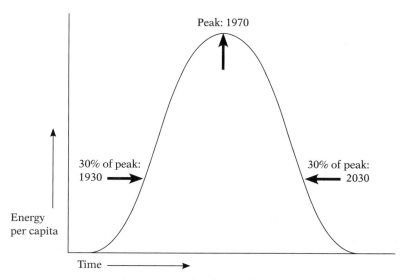

The Course of Industrial Society?

According to Dr. Richard Duncan's Olduvai Theory, the history of modern industrial society is following a pulse waveform, a single curve that does not repeat. His calculations suggest that the peak was reached around 1970 and the termination of the pulse waveform will happen sometime in the middle decades of the twenty-first century.

frastructure breaks down, hurricanes and tsunamis ravage coastal regions, and weather patterns spin out of control, the chance that the modern industrial system will hold together is small at best. If it breaks down, leaving more than six billion people to struggle for survival against long odds, our society will join the long list of past civilizations that thought they could ignore nature's limits and paid the price: Rome, Babylon, Nineveh, Tyre . . .

And Atlantis?

Atlantis Past, Atlantis Future

The sudden resurgence of Atlantis as a cultural theme in the 1870s and 1880s takes on an extraordinary significance when seen in the light of today's global-warming crisis and its likely consequences over the years to come. If it was a coincidence, it's one of the strangest on record. Nobody at the time of the Atlantean revival thought of the clouds of smoke pouring from factory smokestacks as any-thing but a minor nuisance—the first scientist to suggest that CO_2 emissions could cause global warming, the brilliant Swedish chem-ist Svante Arrhenius, published his first paper on the subject in the late 1890s. Only in the last few decades, as ice cores from Greenland sparked a revolution in climatology, has it been possible to predict that global warming could drive sudden changes in the earth's cli-mate, melt the great ice sheets, and flood coastal regions worldwide. Yet more than a century before then, just at the time when CO_2 pol-lution first reached significant levels in the earth's atmosphere and set the industrial world on a trajectory toward catastrophic global warming, a nearly forgotten story about a lost civilization drowned beneath the seas leapt out of obscurity to become one of the most potent narratives of the age.

There is a profound irony in this process, because the name of Atlantis was invoked by a man who played a crucial part in launch-ing modern society on its present course, the great Elizabethan philosopher Francis Bacon. In his Utopian work *The New Atlan-tis*, he envisioned a society devoted to the pursuit of scientific and industrial progress, centered on a great "think tank"—the House of Salomon—where scientists and scholars sought to dominate na-ture for human benefit. Bacon's new Atlantis remained safely above water, at least in the world of his imagination. Still, the occultists who brought Atlantis back onto center stage in the Western world's collective imagination may well have appreciated the unintentional prophecy in Bacon's choice of a name for his project.

Certainly the driving forces behind the rediscovery of Atlantis had little if anything to do with coincidence. As suggested earlier in this book, Helena Petrovna Blavatsky and the circle of occult-ists who supported her mission appear to have seeded the idea of Atlantis into the collective imagination of the Western world de-liberately as part of a calculated campaign meant to change the worldview of their time. Blavatsky's first great book, *Isis Unveiled*, invoked Atlantis as one of many themes that allowed her to present occult traditions as a valid alternative to dogmatic religion and materialist science. When Ignatius Donnelly's book raised the stakes by making Atlantis intellectually respectable and sparking the birth of the rejected-knowledge movement, and the initial gambit represented by *Isis Unveiled* fell short of her hopes, Blavatsky seized the opportunity by putting the lost continent at the heart of her sprawling legominism *The Secret Doctrine*.

In the process, though, she redefined the Atlantis legend from top to bottom. Nowhere in his account of Atlantis does Plato say that some Atlanteans opposed their country's quest for empire, or suggest that the Atlanteans brought their fate on themselves, or even hint that Atlantis might have had something to offer the future, much less that the Atlanteans took steps to pass on their legacy. None of these themes appear anywhere in Atlantology before Blavatsky. They belong to her legominism, part of her grand attempt to get certain key ideas moving through the crawlspaces of the Western world's collective imagination. There's no reason to think they have anything to do with whatever ancient history might lie behind Plato's story. They speak to Blavatsky's own time—and to ours.

None of the evidence for sudden climate change and the collapse of the glacial ice sheets after 9600 BCE, to begin with, points to human action as the cause. If human beings in the Atlantic basin or elsewhere dumped enough CO_2 into the ice age atmosphere to cause the great glaciers to melt, that fact could be read clearly in the Greenland ice cores, and the telltale signs aren't there. The end of the last ice age, like its beginning, unfolded from natural cycles—a useful reminder that nature can bring about cataclysmic change all by itself, without any need for human intervention. If the great harbor cities and coastal lowlands of the modern industrial world end up three hundred feet under water, though, we will have brought that disaster on ourselves by our own actions, just as the Atlanteans of Blavatsky's story did.

From the second half of the nineteenth century on, equally, the cultures of the industrial world have split along the same fault lines as Blavatsky's Atlantis. On one side of the balance stands a minority that still reveres the spiritual dimensions of reality, preserves old traditions of inner development, and recognizes that the living earth is not a commodity we own but a community to which we belong. On the other stands the great majority of today's humanity, who consider material wealth, power, comfort, and convenience to be the only reasonable goals for human life and see the earth purely as a source of raw materials for our use and a dumping ground for our waste. It's not hard to see, in this great division, Blavatsky's vision of struggle between worshippers of the One Spirit of Nature and worshippers of the demons of matter, or for that matter Edgar Cayce's schism between the Children of the Law of One and the Children of Belial.

Cayce's visions are of particular importance in this context. Historians and biographers who have studied every scrap of evidence about Cayce's life have yet to turn up any evidence linking him to the network of occultists who stood behind Blavatsky and supported her mission. A gifted but untrained seer, Cayce knew none of the techniques that scryers in occult lodges use to sort out the different layers of meaning in their visions. All he knew was that his trance communications routinely brought through bits of information about a technologically advanced civilization that had doomed itself to destruction by its mishandling of the secret powers of nature. The communications spoke of aircraft, worldwide communications networks, and many other things of the same kind, and they associated all of this with the name of Atlantis.

Cayce came to the conclusion that his trance work was bringing through information about the lost continent he read about in the occult literature of his time. Given his knowledge base and his circumstances, it was a reasonable conclusion, even an unavoidable one—but in the light of today's knowledge, another possibility seems more likely. What if the information Cayce's trance states brought through came not from a lost civilization of the distant past, but from our own future?

This implies, of course, that the methods used by occult lodges and the trances of visionaries can actually obtain accurate information about the future. Few ideas have been as roundly denounced by the propagandists of today's materialist worldview, but the possibility remains open. We simply don't know enough about the subtle connections between mind and matter or the nature of time to rule it out. Since long before the people of Mesopotamia first looked to the skies to trace portents of times to come, human beings have sought to understand the future before it happens, developing intricate systems of divination and prophecy that guided most societies before our own.

The myth of progress insists that all these systems are simple superstitious folly. Like the imaginary savages of the Stone Age, however, this insistence says more about our own need to ignore our ancestors' achievements in order to glorify our own than it does about anything else. Yet one of the messages that global warming brings us is that the entire mythology of progress is false right down to its core. In the light of the future we are making for ourselves, the story of human existence takes on a very different shape from the one the myth of progress portrays, and the conclusions our culture has built on the foundation of that myth rest on empty air.

Before the beginning of the industrial revolution three centuries ago, after all, human life followed patterns that had changed very little in millennia. All things considered, the life of a peasant, a soldier, or a priest in the Egypt of the Old Kingdom pharaohs was not significantly different from the life of their equivalents in the France of Louis XIV four thousand years later; both societies even had a Sun King. Factor in the change from Paleolithic permaculture to the less sophisticated but more resilient technology of agriculture, and patterns not that different reach back many millennia into prehistory. Tools changed slowly over that time, the most important raw materials shifted gradually from stone to bronze to iron, and human cultures rang a thousand changes on common themes, but technological progress played a very minor role in human life. Rather than a story of progress, the history of the world through all those thousands of years was a story of waveform pulses like the one in Duncan's Olduvai Theory, as a series of unique human cultures emerged, flourished, and then crumbled beneath the burdens of their own mistakes or the sudden blows of some natural catastrophe.

That only changed in the early eighteenth century, when the cultures in one small corner of the world figured out the trick of extracting energy from fossil fuels and built a society like no other in history. It was not a better society than its predecessors, just vastly more powerful, and it used its powers to exploit and harm at least as often as it used them to help and heal. Intoxicated with the power that fossil fuels gave them, however, many people in that society came to believe that they were the darlings of creation, the fulfillment of the whole sweep of human history, and reassured themselves that the expansion of their power would go on and on endlessly into the future. Yet the very fossil fuels that made their society possible have also brought it to the edge of self-destruction, as the greenhouse effect shifts the world's climate from an age of stability to a time of chaos. In the aftermath of the industrial age, will the peoples of the future hothouse earth look at the rusting ruins of our skyscrapers and see just one more civilization that rose and fell like so many before it?

The first echoes of this awareness may be the hidden driving force behind the transformation of Atlantis from a half-forgotten story in Plato's writings to a potent cultural theme in the modern world. That transformation was catalyzed by Blavatsky and the occultists who supported her mission, and it was given additional force by the members of occult lodges who took up her legominism and spread it around the world. Still, the legominism—and especially the Atlantean legend that formed its core—may well have drawn much of its power from the slowly dawning awareness, unconscious in most people but present all the same, that the Atlantis legend as Blavatsky and the occultists presented it mirrored the approaching fate of the industrial world itself.

The Time of the Seedbearers

If the fate of legendary Atlantis is also the destiny industrial civilization has made for itself, the third new theme that Blavatsky added to the Atlantis legend may prove to be the most important of all. In her vision of world history, the legacy of Atlantis was carried to the four corners of the earth by small groups of initiates who became the seedbearers of the coming age. Whether or not anything of the sort happened in the Atlantic basin in the years just after 9400 BCE—and neither Plato nor any other writer before Blavatsky's time suggests anything of the kind—such a project makes a great deal of sense today.

The decline and fall of other civilizations in the past has brought about the loss of vast amounts of every kind of knowledge. Of the science, philosophy, and literature of ancient Greece and Rome, for instance, maybe 5 percent survived the collapse of the Roman Empire and reached modern times intact. The writings of many of the most famous poets and philosophers of antiquity have been completely lost or survive only in scrappy quotes preserved in works by other authors. Other aspects of culture suffered even more drastic fates; out of the rich musical heritage of ancient Rome, for example, all that survives is a single scrap of one melody lasting less than 25 seconds.[14]

The heritage of our civilization faces the same fate if industrial society breaks down. The losses may be even more drastic, since we store our knowledge in forms that might as well have been designed to make them as inaccessible as possible to future generations. Our books are written on high-acid paper that breaks down in a century or so, unlike the parchment that preserved Roman literature straight through the Dark Ages or the low-acid paper used until the early nineteenth century, and recent shifts toward electronic data

---

14 This passage is preserved in the tenth-century Codex Victorianus Laurentianus and has been recorded by Gregorio Paniagua and the Atrium Musicale de Madrid in their *Musique de la Grèce Antique* (Arles, France: Harmonia Mundi, 1979).

storage put even more information at risk. Lacking the high technology needed to maintain the Internet or read CD-ROMs, for example, the information resources they contain will become as unreachable to the future as Atlantis is to us.

Blavatsky and her supporters had never heard of the Internet, of course, and nothing in her writings suggests that she was even aware that the books of her time were more fragile than the ones her occultist great-grandfather collected in the late eighteenth century. Still, lost knowledge forms a constant theme in *Isis Unveiled* and other works of the same time, and many of the occult lodges that followed her lead and worked with her legominism were deeply aware of the fragility of human knowledge. Blavatsky herself spent many years in Egypt, where the ruined temples and tombs of the pharaohs provided a constant reminder that civilizations fall, taking much of their cultural and intellectual legacy with them.

The central focus of Blavatsky's legominism, as well as her creation of the Theosophical Society itself, takes on an intriguing new appearance in this light. In the late nineteenth century, the spiritual traditions of a hundred cultures of past and present lay neglected, and much of what survived existed mostly in a handful of secret organizations vulnerable, like any secret tradition, to the disruptions brought by the collapse of a civilization. Like most of the cultural avant-garde of the late nineteenth century, as we have seen, occultists at that time felt deeply that industrial society had taken a wrong turning and was heading down the road to self-destruction. That awareness played a powerful role in shaping Blavatsky's legominism, as it shaped the many variations on her theme taken up by other occult societies at that time. Did it also drive the extraordinary decision on the part of Blavatsky and her backers to open the doors of the mysteries to all comers and publish the secret teachings of occultism for anyone to read, in the hope that more of the occult tradition would survive an approaching collapse?

If this was Blavatsky's plan, it succeeded to an extent she can hardly have imagined. Today, the secrets of the ages are secret no longer. Teachings that were once the closely guarded inheritance of occult initiates can be found lining the shelves in bookstores and public libraries around the world, open to anyone willing to take the time to read them. The results have been mixed, to be sure; there are more serious occultists today than ever before in history, but the number of hucksters, charlatans, and lunatics in the occult scene is also at an all-time high. Still, the goal of the operation—if that is what it was—has been accomplished. If sheer availability is enough to preserve occult traditions through the rising waters and catastrophic climate change that will likely mark the twilight of industrial civilization, preserved they will be.

Yet Blavatsky's legominism implies another phase to the plan. The most original and evocative part of her narrative of Atlantis tells of the seedbearers sent out from the doomed continent to Atlantean colonies around the world, carrying the ancient mysteries of the Spirit of Nature to be preserved for the initiates of future ages. Of all her contributions to the Atlantis legend, this theme has had the strongest impact on later writers. When the initiates of the Fraternity of the Inner Light tried to assemble their visions about Atlantis into a coherent narrative, for instance, the Atlantean initiates who brought the secrets of the Sun Temple and Sea Temple to ancient Britain played a central role. Outside the closed doors of occult societies, the vision of the seedbearers put roots just as deep into the popular imagination; even Donovan's pop-music version of the Atlantis legend centered on the seedbearer theme.

It's impossible to tell who Blavatsky and her backers had in mind for the seedbearers of the age that will follow industrial civilization. She may well have intended the Theosophical Society itself for that role or, later on, the society's Esoteric Section, the inner circle where she taught authentic occultism after the rest of the society followed her calculated lead and focused its attention on the legominism of *The Secret Doctrine*. While it's possible that one or more of the surviving fragments of the society might rise to the occasion even today, it seems more likely at this point that if anyone embraces the hard task of preserving the legacy of spiritual traditions for the future, it will be groups and individuals from the wider community of people interested in occultism and alternative spirituality.

The tasks faced by today's seedbearers will differ from those of their legendary models in many ways. Instead of the drowning of a single island or continent, the rising spiral of crises facing industrial civilization promises an extended series of environmental, political, and social disasters in which drastic changes in climate, rising sea levels, depletion of fossil fuels and other resources, and unexpected environmental changes driven by feedback loops we don't yet know about will all play a part. Instead of simply sailing to another land, the seedbearers of the near future will need to choose places of safety with care, plan for time scales many centuries in length, and change strategies as the situation shifts around them. Instead of being handed some set of teachings ready-made by the priests of an Atlantean temple, finally, those people who aspire to be seedbearers today must sort through competing spiritual systems and occult traditions to find the things that they consider most worth saving, and they will also have to consider what other legacies of the past and present—literary, artistic, cultural, scientific, and practical—also need to be kept for the future.

It's a challenging job. A few people in the occult community have already taken it up in one way or another, but many more are needed if the extraordinary richness of the world's spiritual and occult teachings are to be preserved through the time of troubles the modern industrial world is busily bringing on itself. A recruiting pitch would be a waste of time here—either you feel called to this immense task, or you don't. Even in Atlantis, according to occult tradition, only certain members of the priesthood sailed overseas as the seedbearers of the coming age, while others had other duties and remained on their doomed homeland until the waves came rushing in.

For those who feel the call, though, plenty of work needs to be done, and it must be started soon. The decline and fall of modern industrial civilization will likely be a slow process, but Hurricane Katrina serves as a recent reminder that some parts of that process can happen abruptly, with very little warning. If the City of the Golden Gates ever existed outside the realms of vision and prophecy, its people doubtless heard and ignored just as many warnings of the approaching danger as we have done in our own time, but the waves of change that shatter our comfortable dreams of perpetual progress may yet come on us as suddenly as the rushing waters that sent the Atlantis of legend to the bottom of the sea.

Piercing the Veil of Time

There must be very few people nowadays who haven't dreamed of time travel. The thought of slipping free of time's clutches—going back in time to some extraordinary event in the past or forward into the unknown world of the future—haunts the modern imagination, and with good reason. Our age, as historian John Lukacs has pointed out,[1] is unique in the intensity of its awareness of historical change. No other culture in recorded history has ever been quite so fascinated with the differences that separate it from its own past. The same spirit that leads people today to read historical novels, visit places where famous events happen, and join reenactment groups to experience the lifestyles of another age tempts us with the thought that we might be able to experience the past more directly.

Science-fiction writer H. G. Wells seems to have invented the concept of a vehicle that could travel through time in his 1895 novel *The Time Machine,* and since then quite a number of researchers have tried to turn fiction into fact and build a working model. So far, at least, none of them have succeeded, or at least none of them have gone public with solid evidence of a successful trip into the

---

1 See especially Lukacs 1968.

past or the future, which is of course not quite the same thing. Current theories of physics suggest that a black hole—a kind of collapsed star that creates gravitational fields strong enough to twist the fabric of space and time—could be used under certain very specific conditions as a gateway into the past or the future. A very large cylinder of solid material spinning at more than half the speed of light could do the same thing.[2] The nearest suspected black hole to the earth—none have been discovered for certain—is around 3,200 light years away, though, and the spinning cylinder is not much easier to manage, since we can't yet make anything faster than a subatomic particle move more than a few percent of the speed of light. Today's time travelers will have to look elsewhere.

Physicist Paul Nahin, in his 1993 book *Time Machines*, argues that there's at least one good piece of evidence that none of them has succeeded, or ever will. Once working time machines were invented, he argues, people from every later time would go back to historically important events, where their presence could not have been missed. "From the moment after the first time machine was constructed through the rest of civilization," Nahin proposes, "there would be numerous historians (to say nothing of weekend sightseers) who would want to visit every important historical event in recorded history. They might each come from a different future, but all would arrive at destinations crowded with temporal colleagues—crowds for which there is no historical evidence!"[3]

This argument is less strong than it looks at first glance, because its logic depends on the mythology of progress. Nahin assumes that once time machine technology is discovered, it will remain available for "the rest of civilization." The possibility that an exotic and expensive technology could be lost in the course of history's ups and downs—and never recovered afterward—seems not to have occurred to him. (To be fair, it doesn't seem to occur to most other writers about the future, either.) Just as the Apollo moon landings

2 See Parker 1991 for a readable account of these theories.
3 Quoted in Childress 1999, 62.

turned out to be not the beginning of a golden age of manned space exploration, but the high-water mark of a hugely expensive project that cost too much to push any further, time machines might prove too costly in terms of resources, energy, and the future equivalent of money to use more than a few times. Still, none of this brings a time machine any closer to us here and now.

If it takes a working time machine to solve the mystery of Atlantis, in other words, we may be out of luck. This notion assumes, though, that advanced technology is the only valid way to pierce the veil of time. What if this assumption turns out to be incorrect? What if the key to time travel is as close as our own minds?

Time and the Mind

In one of his letters, Albert Einstein wrote, "People like us, who believe in physics, know that the distinction between past, present and future is only a stubborn, persistent illusion."[4] If he is correct—and very few people ever understood more about the twists and turns of time than Einstein did—the barrier dividing the past from the present is a mental barrier, and thus a product of certain states of human consciousness. Since what exists in consciousness can be changed by consciousness, this suggests that the mind potentially holds the key to time travel.

This same argument has been made by quantum physicist Fred Alan Wolf in his intriguing book *The Yoga of Time Travel* (2004). Like many other cutting-edge thinkers in today's sciences, Wolf has explored the close parallels between the latest discoveries in physics and the ancient teachings of mystics from around the world. Einstein's comment about the unreality of past, present, and future has many equivalents in mystical and occult literature. As Wolf points out, mystics consider the illusion of time to be part of a larger illusion, the belief in an enduring personal identity separate from the rest of the universe. Whenever this larger illusion slips

---

4 Quoted in Parker 1991, v.

aside, according to these teachings, past, present, and future meld, and the mind can grasp information from elsewhere in time and penetrate the secrets of the past—or the future.

An interesting body of evidence suggests that under the right circumstances, such methods can actually be effective sources of verifiable data. A discipline known as psychic archaeology has evolved over the last century or so, and it has had remarkable success in uncovering the pattern of the past, using nothing but the hidden powers of the human mind.

In 1907, for example, Frederick Bligh Bond, an architect and antiquary hired to superintend excavations at the ruins of Glastonbury Abbey in England, began working with a psychic, John Allen Bartlett. They hoped to locate several lost buildings on the abbey grounds, including the once-famous Edgar Chapel.[5] The method they chose was automatic writing, a practice in which a psychically sensitive person puts a pen in his or her hand and a piece of paper under the pen and then allows the pen to move spontaneously. In people with the necessary talent, the pen begins to write out words and sentences containing information the writer does not consciously know. It is then possible to hold a dialogue: another person asks questions while the automatic writer allows the pen to spell out the answers.

Using this improbable method, Bond and Bartlett received details of the abbey's ground plan and construction, including a sketch map of the site of the Edgar Chapel and precise details of its dimensions. Bond began excavating where the automatic writing directed, and before long he uncovered the Edgar Chapel's foundations. The lost chapel turned out to have the exact location and measurements given by the automatic writing.

Bond received a great deal of additional information through Bartlett and other psychics, including Dion Fortune herself, who worked with him for some time early on in her occult career. One

---

5 Benham 1993 has a good account of Bond's work. See also Bond 1920 for Bond's own account of his researches.

theme of the later messages was the location of an underground treasure chamber on the abbey grounds. When word of Bond's psychic activities leaked out, though, the church authorities who owned the abbey site removed him from his position and permitted no further excavations. The treasure chamber, which according to local legend contains nothing less than the Holy Grail itself, remains unopened.

Equally striking results came from a five-year effort in Alexandria, Egypt, headed by veteran psychic archaeologist Stephan A. Schwartz.[6] The Alexandria Project, as it was called, brought psychics and archaeologists together in an attempt to locate some of the most important sites in one of the classical world's greatest cities. The project's greatest success, the discovery of the lost palace of the Ptolemies, was only one of many identifications of archaeological sites that were described in detail by the project's psychics and then excavated by archaeologists. Schwartz himself has headed or been involved in more than a dozen similar projects, and in most of them, the psychics succeeded in guiding archaeologists to important finds and gave detailed and accurate descriptions of buried sites before the first shovelful of earth was removed.[7]

The very first words received via automatic writing by Frederick Bligh Bond and John Bartlett offer a key to the way this process works. They read, "All knowledge is eternal and is available to mental sympathy."[8] In the occult terminology of the day, *mental sympathy* meant the same thing in the workings of the mind that *frequency* means in radio or broadcast television. If your radio is tuned to the right frequency, you can pick up any station within range of your antenna; in the same way, if your mind is tuned to the right mental pattern, you can pick up the thoughts and experiences of other people tuned to the same pattern, whether or not those people exist in the material world at the same time you do.

---

6 The Alexandria Project is documented in Schwartz 1983.

7 See Schwartz 1978.

8 Benham 1993, 197.

According to occult tradition, as explained back in chapter 2, the medium for these patterns is the astral light, the subtle substance of consciousness that fills the universe and weaves it together.

Books on popular occultism from the beginning of the twentieth century onward claim that the astral light, or, as it is also called, the *akasha*, contains a reflection of every event that has ever happened in the universe. The sum total of these reflections make up the "akashic record," which can be perceived and interpreted by those with the necessary psychic gift. Like so much popular occult lore, though, this isn't quite what older and more detailed occult traditions teach.

In magical philosophy, the astral light belongs to the world of consciousness, not the world of matter, and what it reflects is every *mental* event in the universe. In other words, it doesn't contain objective images of Pearl Harbor, the drafting of the American Constitution, or the sinking of Atlantis. What it contains is reflections of the experiences of every living being who saw bombs falling on Pearl Harbor, the members of the Constitutional Convention hard at work, or waters rising over the City of the Golden Gates.

This sounds promising enough, but there's a catch. The astral light also reflects the experiences of everyone who ever watched the movie *Atlantis: The Lost Continent*, with its styrofoam temples, crystal-powered death rays, and fish-shaped submarines, not to mention all the other movies about Atlantis, from the 1921 French silent film *L'Atlantide* to the latest animated Disney production. The experiences of everyone who has ever read Jules Verne's portrayal of sunken Atlantis in *Twenty Thousand Leagues Under The Sea* are there, along with those of readers of all the other novels, short stories, poems, plays, and comic books about Atlantis. So are the experiences of everyone who has ever read a nonfiction book on the subject, from Plato's *Timaeus* to the latest products of today's rejected-knowledge industry, and so are your experiences as you read the book in your hands right now. They are *all* in the astral light, along with every other experience of every being in the universe, and every one of them can be contacted and experienced by tuning the mind to the right "frequency" through mental sympathy.

This latter is the problem, of course, because a twenty-first-century American who is trying to "tune in" to lost Atlantis is much more likely to get into mental sympathy with images from George Pal's worst movie than with experiences of the actual destruction of Atlantis. The hundreds of thousands of people who sat through *Atlantis: The Lost Continent* when it premiered in 1961 or have watched it since then on TV or video are all part of modern industrial society. They share most of the assumptions and thought patterns of people trying to access the akashic record today, and the images of the sinking of Atlantis they saw on the screen correspond closely to the ideas that most people interested in Atlantis have in their minds today. The people who witnessed the sinking of Atlantis eleven millennia ago, if that event actually happened in physical space and time, belonged to forgotten cultures with values and thought patterns very different from ours, and the things they saw, heard, and felt as their homeland slipped beneath the waves probably don't have much in common with our current ideas of what the sinking of Atlantis must have been like.

These problems are greatly amplified by the clumsy and indiscriminate use of hypnosis. Hypnotic trance is another way of bringing the mind into contact with the astral light, but it's a passive way that leaves the experiencer few options for sorting out the results of that experience. When people are hypnotized and asked to recall something, what they get depends once again on mental sympathy, but the mental state of the hypnotist as well as that of the hypnotic subject affects the results. Courts throughout North America no longer accept testimony extracted by hypnotism, because much more often than not, the "memories" that result from hypnotic regression are a random mix of memory, fantasy, and whatever ideas and expectations the hypnotist had in his or her mind during the session.

Many traditional occult orders, while they consider self-hypnosis to be a useful technique for personal transformation, strongly discourage their initiates from allowing anyone else to hypnotize them.[9] Distortions of this kind are one of the reasons why. Fortunately, there are proven ways to get in contact with the images of the astral light and screen out sources of misperception. The best of the methods for accessing the astral light is a technique called *scrying in the spirit vision*, or, more simply, *scrying*. For sorting out the results, the methods of meditation taught in traditional occult societies remain the best option.

Learning to Scry

The word *scry* is an old word meaning "see," and it still appears in old-fashioned English in the compound word *descry*, meaning "see at a distance." In magical parlance, though, scrying is the art of seeing what is not in front of the physical eyes, either because the target of scrying does not exist in the realm of matter or because it is distant from the scryer in space, time, or both. There are many different ways of doing this in the occult tradition, but the most common form of scrying uses the trained human imagination to perceive images in the astral light. Most people can learn it in a short time, and with systematic practice and patience, the art of scrying becomes a powerful and surprisingly accurate means of perceiving the hidden aspects of the cosmos.

The key to scrying, and to most other esoteric practices, is learning to enter a state of relaxed concentration. The word *relaxed* needs to be kept in mind here. Too often, what *concentration* suggests to modern people is a kind of inner struggle: teeth clenched, eyes narrowed, the whole body taut with useless tension. This is the opposite of the state you need to reach. Body, breath, and mind form the

---

9 In the Hermetic Order of the Golden Dawn, for example, initiates took an oath that barred them from being hypnotized by another person. See Regardie 1971, vol. 2, 27.

three dimensions of the work you need to do to pierce the veils of time, and excessive tension in any of them gets in the way.

To learn and practice scrying, you'll need a place that's quiet and not too brightly lit. It should be private—a room with a door you can shut is best, though if you can't arrange that, a quiet corner and a little forbearance on the part of your housemates will do the job. You'll need a chair with a straight back and a seat at a height that allows you to rest your feet flat on the floor while keeping your thighs level with the ground. A clock you can see without moving your head when you're seated on the chair is a useful addition, and a journal to write down the results of your work completes the toolkit. Once you're provided with your space, chair, clock, and journal, start working on the following exercises to prepare yourself for scrying.

Preliminary Exercise One

Sit on the chair with your feet and knees together or parallel, whichever is most comfortable for you. Your back should be straight but not stiff, your hands resting on your thighs, and your head rising gently upward as though a string fastened to the crown of your skull has been pulled upward. Your eyes may be open or closed, as you prefer; if they're open, they should look ahead of you but not focus on anything in particular. This is the standard position for meditation in Western magical traditions: comfortable, stable, balanced, and a good deal easier on the knees than some Eastern meditation postures.

Now spend ten minutes being aware of your physical body. Start at the crown of your head and work your way slowly downward to the soles of your feet. Take your time, and notice any tensions you feel. Don't try to force yourself to relax; simply be aware of each point of tension. Over time, this simple act of awareness will dissolve your body's habitual tensions by making them conscious and bringing up the rigid patterns of thought and emotion that form their foundations. Like so much in occult practice, though, this process has to unfold at its own pace.

While you're doing this exercise, let your body become as still as possible. You may find yourself wanting to fidget and shift, but resist the temptation. Whenever your body starts itching, cramping, or reacting against stillness in some other way, simply be aware of it without responding to it. These reactions often become very intrusive during the first month or so of practice, but bear with them. They show you that you're getting past the levels of ordinary awareness. The discomforts you're feeling are actually present in your body all the time; you've simply learned not to notice them. Now that you can perceive them again, you can relax into them and let them go.

Preliminary Exercise Two

Do the first exercise ten minutes daily for at least a week, or until the posture starts to feel comfortable and balanced. After that, it's time to bring in the dimension of breath.

Start by sitting down and going through the first exercise quickly as a way of "checking in" with your physical body and settling into a comfortable and stable position. Then turn your attention to your breath. Draw in a deep breath, and expel it in a series of short puffs through pursed lips, as though you were blowing out a candle.

When every last puff of air is out of your lungs, hold the breath out while counting slowly and steadily from one to four. Then breathe in through your nose, smoothly and evenly, counting from one to four. Hold your breath in, counting from one to four; hold the breath in by keeping the chest and belly expanded, not by closing your throat. Breathe out through your nose, smoothly and evenly, again counting from one to four. Continue breathing at the same slow, steady rhythm, counting in the same way, for ten minutes. The first "puffing" breath is called the *clearing breath*, and the rhythmic breath that follows it is called the *fourfold breath*. Together, they form a safe but effective set of breathing exercises used in many traditional magical orders.

While you're breathing, your thoughts will try to stray onto some topic or other. Don't let them. Keep your attention on the rhythm of the breathing, the feeling of the air moving into and out of your lungs. Whenever you notice that you're thinking about something else, bring your attention gently back to your breathing. If your thoughts slip away again, bring them back again. With practice, you'll find it increasingly easy to keep your mind centered on the simple process of breathing. At that point, you're ready to move onward to the art of scrying.

The Art of Scrying

Scrying itself builds directly on the foundations just given. Take the posture described above, move your awareness through your physical body from the soles of your feet to the top of your head, and then clear your mind and the energy channels of your body with five minutes or so of the fourfold breath. Next, imagine yourself facing a door. Spend some time making the image of the door as clear as possible. Don't limit yourself to an abstract image or purely visual imagery. See every detail of the door in your mind's eye, sense its weight and texture, and see it marked with a symbol, word, or number that represents the object of your scrying. For journeys into the past, the best thing to put on the door is a written place and date, such as PEARL HARBOR, DECEMBER 7, 1941, or CONSTITUTION HALL, PHILADELPHIA, 1791—or, of course, ATLANTIS, 9600 BCE.

Once the door and the words on it have been built up clearly in your mind's eye, picture the door slowly swinging open. Beyond it is a landscape of some sort. Let it take whatever form it wishes, and spend a minute or more letting it take shape in your imagination before going on. Then, slowly and clearly, imagine yourself rising from your chair, walking to the doorway, and passing through it. The door remains open behind you, and if you look back you can see your physical body sitting in the chair. Imagine yourself looking around at the realm beyond the door, and allow yourself to notice as many details as you can.

It's traditional, and useful as well, to make an invocation or prayer to a deity or other spiritual power at this point, asking to be guided and protected as you explore this part of the imaginal realm. Depending on your personal beliefs, you can simply call on the same power no matter what you're scrying, or you can invoke a god, goddess, angel, or divine aspect appropriate to what you're scrying. For work on Atlantis itself, Pagans will find that the Greek sea god Poseidon, his Roman equivalent Neptune, the Irish sea god Manannan, or the equivalent sea deity from another pantheon are good choices, while Christians, Jews, and Hermetic mages will find the Archangel Gabriel, the angelic ruler of water, an appropriate power to invoke.

If you wish, you can ask the power you invoke for a guide. If you choose to do this, wait after finishing the invocation for the guide to appear. It may take human, animal, or some other form. Whatever its form, ask it whether it comes in the name of the spiritual power you've invoked, and ask it to repeat the power's name. Once you're comfortable accepting guidance from the guide, ask it to show you some of the secrets of whatever you're scrying.

Your guide may take you on a journey and show you things, or it may instruct you directly. Ask it any questions that seem relevant, and pay close attention to its answers. When the journey or the instruction comes to an end, ask your guide to bring you back to your starting point, thank it for its guidance, and bless it in the name of the deity you invoked earlier. It may seem strange at first to treat an "imaginary" being as though it has a real, objective existence outside your head, but regular practice with scrying will teach you that this approach has value. In magical philosophy, the realm of imagination, taken on its own terms, is as real as a rock, and it's a common experience of scryers that you can get accurate information from the beings and objects of that realm.

Whether or not you wish to call for a guide, pay close attention to the scene you encounter on the other side of the door. Every detail of the imaginary landscape around you and every word spoken to you has something to teach. Treat the things you encounter as though they were real for the duration of the scrying. When you have learned what you can from the scene and whatever entities you have encountered there, go back to your starting point.

Then return through the doorway, imagine yourself sitting back in the chair where your physical body has been all the while, and slowly and carefully imagine the door closing. As it closes, concentrate on the thought that no unwanted energies or beings can come into your daily life from the realm in which you've been scrying. Use a few cycles of the fourfold breath to clear your mind, and then use the clearing breath to close the scrying. Write up the experience in a journal as soon as possible, while the details are still fresh in your mind.

You may find yourself a little disoriented at first after scrying, especially the first few times you do it. If so, eating some food will close your visionary senses down and bring you solidly back into your body. Routine activities such as washing the dishes can also help reorient your awareness back to the realm of ordinary experience. It's almost always a good idea to wait for several days after a scrying before trying again, to give yourself time to refocus on your own place and time in the material world. Too many scryings in too little time can make it hard for you to function in the everyday world and, in extreme cases, can lead to mental illness. If you ever find that imagery from your scryings is starting to intrude into your thoughts whether you want it to or not, it's a good idea to take a long vacation from this form of work. The regular practice of meditation, using the method presented later in this appendix, will usually forestall such problems and keep you grounded in ordinary reality.

Journeying to Atlantis

The technique of scrying can be used for many different purposes, of course, and piercing the veil of time to view lost Atlantis is only one of them. Since this book is about Atlantis rather than scrying in general, though, we'll concentrate on the art of scrying through time, or as it's sometimes called, *transtemporal clairvoyance*. If you decide that another application of scrying interests you more, the principles covered here can be applied to any other form of scrying, and you can also find detailed discussions of the art in published works on magical practice.[10]

The most important advice you can receive in this work can be summed up in three words: *take your time!* The art of scrying has to be learned and mastered before it can be used effectively to travel more than a hundred centuries into the past, which is what you're trying to do here. Just as novice musicians start on scales and simple tunes before trying anything more demanding, novice scryers need to start with brief journeys into well-documented historical periods before venturing into the shadows of prehistory.

Once you've completed the preliminary exercises, start your scrying work by trying to experience the place that you live as it was one hundred years ago. When you visualize the door, see a date exactly a century earlier written on it. Concentrate on the idea that what's on the other side of the door is the place you're sitting precisely one century in the past. When the door opens, pass through and see what you see. After you return, write down the results in as much detail as possible in your journal.

The next step is the one most beginners avoid for as long as possible, but it needs to be faced, and the sooner the better. Go to your local public library or historical society and find out as much as you can about what the place where you lived looked like exactly one hundred years ago, and compare that to the results of your scrying. Note where your vision was accurate and where it wasn't,

---

10 See, for example, Regardie 1971, vol. 4, 11–48.

and see if you can figure out where the inaccurate material came from. Was it something from a movie or a TV show? Was it a child-hood memory about some other place, or imagery from a dream? All of these can show up in scryings, especially when you're first learning the art.

After you've checked out as many details of the scrying as you can, try again, choosing a different date or going to a different place—say, the center of your hometown as it existed seventy-five years ago. Af-ter you've done this, look up the results and compare your visions to the facts. Repeat the process, using different targets in space and time.

As you do this, two things will start to happen. First of all, your accuracy will begin to improve. Some people have a burst of "be-ginner's luck" when they first start scrying, then get poor results for a time and gradually improve; others start at the bottom of the learning curve and slowly but steadily get better results. Either way, practice makes perfect. Second, you'll start learning how to filter out inaccurate material in advance, recognizing what came from an old movie or a dream even before you start checking your visions against known historical information. Both of these are important, since you need to be able to scry as accurately as pos-sible before you venture beyond recorded history.

As you continue your experiments with scrying, move steadily farther away from your own location in space and time. Once you can get good results reliably, it's useful to choose a place and time about which you know absolutely nothing—say, the Hittite Empire in 1400 BCE, if you don't happen to have a good background in the cultures of the ancient Near East—and use that as the goal of sev-eral scryings. Afterward, go to the library and learn as much as you can about the ancient Hittites (or whatever ancient culture you've chosen) and see how well you did. Then do the same thing with some other ancient society you know nothing about—the Etrus-cans, say, or the Tocharians. When you can reliably get accurate details on an ancient culture thousands of years in the past by scrying, you're ready to try for Atlantis itself.

To begin with, aim for a point on the shores of the Atlantic Ocean or the Mediterranean Sea around 9600 BCE, and see what you find. Before you begin, do your best to forget the theories about Atlantis presented in this book or any other. Approach the experience with an open mind, learn as much as you can, keep detailed notes, and decide on your next target for scrying based on your results. You're venturing into the unknown at this point, and any other advice would be a waste of time.

The Art of Meditation

The results of scrying are often challenging to interpret, and another standard practice taught in occult lodges is worth bringing in to help with this phase of the work. This is the art of meditation. For the last hundred years or so, most people in the Western world have thought of meditation as something exotic and Oriental, as though the West had no meditation systems of its own. The word *meditation* itself, however, comes from the Latin *meditatio*, and as far back as the early Middle Ages that word already stood for powerful methods of inner practice that can stand comparison with any meditation tradition in the world.

An important difference, however, separates most Western methods of meditation from their Asian equivalents and from recent systems created in the West but based on Eastern models. Although there are exceptions, most Eastern methods of meditation seek to stop the normal flow of thought through the meditator's mind. By fixing the attention on a mantra, a mandala, a breathing pattern, or bare attention itself, these methods empty the mind of content so that consciousness can return to its sources in the unknown.

Western traditions of meditation, by contrast, seek the same goal in a different way. Rather than abolishing thoughts, the Western approach turns the thinking process itself into a vehicle for deeper levels of consciousness. By focusing the mind intently on a chosen theme and allowing it to follow that theme through a chain of linked ideas while keeping it from straying, the Western meditator transforms thinking from half-random mental chatter into a powerful and focused way of understanding. At the same time, the knowledge and insight unfolded by this form of meditation often has great value on its own terms.

Before you can use this form of meditation effectively, you'll have to practice the two preliminary exercises given at the beginning of the scrying section until you can do them both easily. Once you've reached this point, you're ready to begin meditating.

Start by selecting a small portion of one of your scrying—a single image or idea. This becomes the focus or, as it's called, *theme* of the meditation. One of the common mistakes that beginners make is choosing a theme that's too large and then floundering about in meditation, missing most of what could have been gained by close attention to the little details. Choose the very first image you saw in your vision, or the first nonvisual perception you had if that was the nature of your experience, and extract everything you can from it before moving on. This often means that you'll spend a week or two meditating for every session you spend scrying, but that's not a drawback—quite the contrary. The slower and more systematically you go, the more you can expect to learn and the clearer and more accurate your scryings will become.

When you've chosen your theme for a session of meditation, sit down in the meditation posture and spend a minute or two going through the first preliminary exercise, being aware of your body and its tensions. Then begin the fourfold breath and continue it for several minutes. During these first stages, don't think about the theme, or for that matter anything else. Simply be aware, first of your body and its tensions, then of the rhythm and pattern of your breathing, and allow your mind to enter into clarity and stillness. If thoughts arise, release them and return to stillness.

After five minutes, change from the fourfold breath to ordinary, slow breathing. Bring the theme to mind. If it's an image, picture the theme in your mind's eye, as though it stood hovering in the air in front of you. If it's something else, bring it before your mind as clearly as you can. Pay attention to it for a time, and then begin thinking about what it means. Recall as much about that element of your vision as you can, and think about it in a general way. Then, out of the various thoughts that come to mind as you consider the theme, choose one and follow it out step by step, thinking about its meaning and implications, taking it as far as you can.

Unless you have quite a bit of experience in meditation, your thoughts will likely wander from the theme again and again. Instead of simply bringing them back in a jump, follow them back through the chain of wandering thoughts until you reach the point where they left the theme. If you're meditating on the image of a temple beneath blue water, for example, and suddenly notice that you're thinking about your aunt Alice instead, don't simply go back to the temple and start again. Work your way back. What got you thinking about Aunt Alice? Memories of her living room when you were a child. What called up that memory? Recalling the taste of the salted nuts she used to put out for guests. Where did that come from? Thinking about squirrels. Why squirrels? Because you heard the scuttling noise of a squirrel running across the roof, and it distracted you from thinking about the temple.

Whenever your mind strays from the theme, bring it back up the track of wandering thoughts in this same way. This approach has two advantages. First of all, it has much to teach about the way your mind works, the flow of its thoughts, and the sort of associative leaps it habitually makes. Second, it develops the habit of returning to the theme, and with practice you'll find that your thoughts run back to the theme of your meditations just as enthusiastically as they run away from it. Time and regular practice will shorten the number of side trips until eventually your mind will learn to run straight ahead along the meanings and implications of a theme without veering from it at all.

In your first sessions, spend ten minutes meditating in this way; when this is easy, go up to fifteen minutes, and if you can spare the time, add five more minutes whenever the period you've set yourself seems too easy. When you're done, repeat the cleansing breath once to close the meditation. Write up the experience in your journal as soon as possible afterward. Be sure to note the images and ideas that came up in the meditation, and keep track of anything that shows up repeatedly. It's often in this way that key insights will surface.

Meditation, Symbolism, and Meaning

This form of meditation is called *discursive meditation*, because it often takes the form of an inner discourse or dialogue. For the last century or so, since the Theosophical Society first popularized Eastern meditative techniques in the West, it's received very little attention outside of a few Western occult schools, where it forms a central technique of training. Initiates of traditional occult lodges are shown complicated symbolic images during their initiations and then expected to use discursive meditation on those images to extract the information packed into them. Tarot decks crafted by the heads of magical orders, for example, usually contain a wealth of magical instruction ready to be decoded and read by discursive meditation.

The famous Rider-Waite deck, designed by Golden Dawn initiate Arthur Edward Waite and illustrated by his fellow initiate Pamela Colman Smith, is bursting at the seams with a wealth of Qabalistic and Hermetic magical lore hardly noticed by tens of thousands of ordinary tarot readers who simply recognize it as one of the best divination decks around. Alchemy offers the spectacle of an entire esoteric science taught by symbols, emblems, and allegories that make no sense at all to a casual glance but can be interpreted readily once the key of discursive meditation is applied.

This makes traditional occult symbolism sound like nothing more than a code meant to keep knowledge out of unauthorized hands.

The reality is more complex. The secrets of occult philosophy and practice aren't secret because somebody decided to hide them, they're secret because they can't be understood and used until the person trying to understand and use them has had certain inner experiences and learned to look at the world in a particular way. Occult symbols such as tarot cards and the emblems of alchemy are designed to lead toward those experiences and point to that way of looking at the world. When explored and "unpacked" through discursive meditation, they provide keys and insights that allow the occult student to become an initiate in the full sense of the word.

The same sort of "unpacking" process should also be used on the results of your scryings into the past. What comes to you from the astral light, even if you're good at filtering out the kinds of distorting material discussed earlier in this appendix, is likely to include a mix of different things. Some of it can be taken literally, but not all, and even the images and ideas that can be taken literally often have a secondary, symbolic meaning. Like the events in dreams, the results of scrying need to be interpreted before they can be fully understood, and meditation is the best way to learn how to interpret them.

A failure to recognize this has done much to give today's popular occultism its dubious reputation. Back in the 1980s, for example, several channelers in the New Age scene passed on messages from disembodied beings claiming that Jesus of Nazareth, after his crucifixion and resurrection, went to Ireland and married a Druid princess. As a statement about history, this is pretty fair nonsense; there's not a bit of evidence to support it, and plenty of reasons to doubt it. Treat it as a symbolic message, though, and it suddenly takes on much more meaning and relevance. To suggest that Christianity needs to embrace the feminine and the nature-centered dimensions of spirituality—all the things the phrase "Druid princess" communicates as a symbol—is to say something meaningful and potentially very important.

The same thing is true of many other things obtained by scrying and other visionary practices. As we saw back in chapter 2, historian K. Paul Johnson has shown that many of Edgar Cayce's apparently inaccurate statements about the past and the future make sense, and have valuable messages to communicate, if they're understood as spiritual teachings expressed in symbolic form. For that matter, some of them turn into highly perceptive prophecies of the future when read symbolically. Atlantis may not have physically risen to the surface of the Atlantic Ocean in 1968 or 1969, as Cayce predicted, but it certainly emerged out of the waters of the Western world's collective imagination during the cultural ferment of those years. In prophecy as elsewhere, in other words, literal meanings are not the only game in town.

Glossary

albedo: a measure of how much light a surface will reflect

Alleröd phase: the second main warming phase during the end of the last ice age, from 11,800 to 10,800 BCE

Atlantic phase: the first cool phase of the Holocene epoch, from 6200 to 3500 BCE

Atlantis: according to Plato, a large island in the western Atlantic Ocean, destroyed by floods and earthquakes sometime after 9400 BCE

Atlantology: the branch of the rejected-knowledge movement devoted to theories about Atlantis

BCE: "before the Common Era," modern nonsectarian equivalent of BC ("before Christ")

Bölling phase: the first major warming phase during the end of the last ice age, from 12,700 to 12,400 BCE

Boreal phase: the warm phase that followed the end of the last ice age, from 9600 to 6200 BCE; the drowning of Atlantis probably took place during the early Boreal

catastrophism: the scientific theory that some of the earth's landforms were shaped by major catastrophes, such as very large floods, in the distant past

CE: "Common Era," modern nonsectarian equivalent of AD (*"Anno Domini,"* Latin for "year of the Lord")

channeled scablands: region of the Pacific Northwest devastated by glacial floods at the end of the last ice age

Chicxulub impact: the collision of the earth with a six-mile-wide meteor 65 million years ago, which caused the extinction of the last dinosaurs

discursive meditation: the traditional Western approach to meditation, which uses the thinking mind to explore symbols and visionary experiences

epoch: in geology, a period of time lasting several million years, marked by distinctive fossils and rock formations; the present epoch is the Holocene

euhemerism: the theory that mythology is a distorted reflection of ancient historical events; named after the Greek philosopher Euhemerus, who first proposed it

greenhouse effect: the process by which carbon dioxide and other gases, including methane, trap heat in the earth's atmosphere

Holocene: the current geological epoch, which began at the start of the Boreal phase, around 9600 BCE

isostatic rebound: the process by which continental areas pressed down into the earth's mantle by the weight of ice sheets rise up gradually after the ice sheets melt

Last Glacial Maximum: the time when the most recent ice age reached its furthest extent, approximately 20,000 to 14,000 BCE; abbreviated LGM

legominism: in occult traditions, a method by which wisdom traditions are transmitted in a form that appears to be intended for an entirely different purpose; the Atlantis legend in nineteenth- and twentieth-century occultism is a classic legominism

Lemuria: hypothetical lost continent in the Indian Ocean suggested by nineteenth-century geologists; the name was borrowed by occultists in the late nineteenth and twentieth centuries and used for visionary material related to Sundaland

LGM: see **Last Glacial Maximum**

methane: CH_4, a carbon compound produced by rotting organic matter; it is twenty times more effective as a greenhouse gas than carbon dioxide

methane hydrates: compounds of frozen water and methane found in cold-water regions of the world's oceans, containing huge amounts of methane that could be released into the atmosphere by global warming

Mu: fictional lost continent of the Pacific, invented by James Churchward in the early twentieth century and identified with Lemuria by later writers

native metals: metals such as copper and gold that are found in pure metallic form in nature and thus can be worked by hammering in societies that have not yet learned how to smelt metallic ores

occultism: a system of traditions, teachings, and practices that interpret material reality as a reflection of spiritual levels of being and provide tools by which individuals can directly experience and work with spiritual forces

Older Dryas phase: the second cool phase during the end of the last ice age, from 12,400 to 11,800 BCE

Oldest Dryas phase: the first cool phase during the end of the last ice age, from 14,000 to 12,700 BCE

permafrost: permanently frozen soil, which contains large quantities of trapped methane; around 25 percent of the land area in the Northern Hemisphere is permafrost

Pleistocene: the geological epoch containing the most recent ice ages, beginning around 1.2 million years ago and ending at the start of the Boreal phase, around 9600 BCE

Preboreal phase: the transition from the cold Younger Dryas phase to the warm Boreal phase, from 10,200 to 9600 BCE

proglacial lakes: lakes of meltwater that formed at the edge of the retreating ice sheets during the end of the most recent ice age; the source of catastrophic flooding

rejected-knowledge movement: a cultural movement of late-nineteenth-, twentieth-, and twenty-first-century industrial societies that opposed the worldview of contemporary materialist science and proposed a variety of alternative worldviews to replace it

scrying: the art of using the trained imagination to access visionary experiences from the imaginal realm

subduction zone: a region where one of the earth's crustal plates is being driven underneath another plate

Sundaland: the name given by modern geologists to a landmass off what is now Southeast Asia that was flooded at the end of the last ice age; visionary material relating to Sundaland may have helped shape occult traditions about Lemuria

tectonic: related to the interaction of the slowly moving plates that make up the earth's crust

trireme: in ancient Greece and Plato's account of Atlantis, a warship propelled by three tiers of oarsmen

tsunami: a large and destructive wave caused by an undersea earthquake or landslide; also known as a "tidal wave"

turbidity layer: a layer of debris laid down underwater by a flood, tsunami, or other sudden event, easily distinguished from more ordinary layers of sea-floor mud

uniformitarianism: the scientific theory that all the earth's landforms were shaped by the same slow processes of change at work in today's world and that major catastrophes had no role in geological history

Younger Dryas phase: the third and most extreme of the cool phases during the end of the last ice age, from 10,800 to 10,200 BCE

Bibliography

Adam, David. 2007. "Climate Change: Scientists Warn It May Be Too Late to Save the Ice Caps." *Guardian*, February 19. http://environment.guardian.co.uk/climatechange/story/0,,2016243,00.html.

Ager, D. V. 1993. *The New Catastrophism*. Cambridge: Cambridge University Press.

Allen, Jim, and Peter Kershaw. 1996. "The Pleistocene-Holocene Transition in Greater Australia." In Straus et al. 1996, 175–99.

Alley, Richard B. 2000. *The Two-Mile Time Machine*. Princeton, NJ: Princeton University Press.

Alvarez, Walter. 1997. *T. Rex and the Crater of Doom*. Princeton, NJ: Princeton University Press.

Andrews, Shirley. 1997. *Atlantis*. St. Paul, MN: Llewellyn.

———. 2004. *Lemuria and Atlantis*. St. Paul, MN: Llewellyn.

Ashe, Geoffrey. 1990. *Mythology of the British Isles*. London: Methuen.

Baker, Scott. 1999. "Thong-thrown Arrows and Spears." In Wescott 1999, 192–94.

Baker, V. R., ed. 1981. *Catastrophic Flooding: The Origin of the Channeled Scabland*. Stroudsburg, PA: Dowden, Hutchinson & Ross.

Ballard, Arthur C. 1999. *Mythology of Southern Puget Sound.* North Bend, WA: Snoqualmie Valley Historical Museum.

Barbour, Julian B. 2000. *The End of Time: The Next Revolution in Physics.* Oxford: Oxford University Press.

BBC News. 2002. "Antarctic Ice Shelf Breaks Apart." March 19. http://news.bbc.co.uk/2/hi/science/nature/1880566.stm.

Bellamy, H. S. 1936. *Moons, Myths, and Men: A Reinterpretation.* London: Faber & Faber.

Benham, Patrick. 1993. *The Avalonians.* Glastonbury, Somerset: Gothic Image.

Benson, Elizabeth P., ed. 1977. *The Sea in the Pre-Columbian World.* Washington, DC: Dumbarton Oaks.

Berlitz, Charles. 1994. *Atlantis: The Eighth Continent.* New York: Ballantine.

Blakeslee, Sandra. 2006. "Ancient Crash, Epic Wave." *New York Times*, November 14. http://www.nytimes.com.

Blavatsky, Helena Petrovna. 1972. *Isis Unveiled.* 2 vols. Pasadena, CA: Theosophical University Press.

Bond, Frederick Bligh. 1920. *The Gate of Remembrance.* Oxford: Blackwell.

Burl, Aubrey. 1985. *Megalithic Brittany.* London: Thames and Hudson.

Calvin, William H. 2002. *A Brain for All Seasons.* Chicago: University of Chicago Press.

Campion, Nicholas. 1994. *The Great Year.* London: Arcana.

Castleden, Rodney. 1998. *Atlantis Destroyed.* London: Routledge.

Cayce, Edgar Evans. 1968. *Edgar Cayce on Atlantis.* New York: Warner.

Cervé, Wishar Spenle [Harvey Spencer Lewis]. 1923. *Lemuria: The Lost Continent of the Pacific.* San Jose, CA: AMORC.

Childress, David Hatcher. 1996. *Lost Cities of Atlantis, Ancient Europe and the Mediterranean.* Kempton, IL: Adventures Unlimited Press.

———. 1999. *The Time Travel Handbook.* Kempton, IL: Adventures Unlimited Press.

Childress, David Hatcher, and Richard Shaver. 1999. *Lost Continents and the Hollow Earth.* Kempton, IL: Adventures Unlimited.

Churchward, James. 1925. *The Lost Continent of Mu.* London: Washburn.

Collins, Andrew. 2000. *Gateway to Atlantis.* London: Headline.

Comstock, Paul. 1999. "Throwing Darts with the Baton de Commandement." In Wescott 1999.

Connor, Steve. 2007. "Scientists Sound Alarm over Melting Antarctic Ice Sheets." *Independent*, February 16. http://environment.independent.co.uk/climate_change/article2274481.ece.

Cooper, George H. 1936. *The Druid Bible.* San Jose, CA: Victor Hillis.

Coughlan, Sean. 2007. "Lost World Warning from North Sea." *BBC News*, April 23. http://news.bbc.co.uk/2/hi/uk_news/education/6584011.stm.

Crawford, Michael H. 1998. *The Origins of Native Americans.* Cambridge: Cambridge University Press.

Crowley, Aleister. 1976. *Magick in Theory and Practice.* New York: Dover.

Davies, Paul. 1995. *About Time: Einstein's Unfinished Revolution.* New York: Simon & Schuster.

De Camp, L. Sprague. 1970. *Lost Continents: The Atlantis Theme in History, Science, and Literature.* New York: Dover.

De Santillana, Giorgio, and Hertha von Dechend. 1977. *Hamlet's Mill.* Boston: David R. Godine.

Dewar, Elaine. 2002. *Bones: Discovering the First Americans.* New York: Carroll & Graf.

Diamond, Jared. 2005. *Collapse.* New York: Penguin.

Dillehay, Tom D. 1989. *Monte Verde: A Late Pleistocene Settlement in Chile*, vol. 1. Washington, DC: Smithsonian Institution.

———. 1997. *Monte Verde: A Late Pleistocene Settlement in Chile*, vol. 2. Washington, DC: Smithsonian Institution.

Dobbs, Betty Jo Teeter. 1975. *The Foundations of Newton's Alchemy.* Cambridge: Cambridge University Press.

Dolan, James F., and Paul Mann, eds. 1998. *Active Strike-Slip and Collisional Tectonics of the Northern Caribbean Plate Boundary Zone.* Boulder, CO: Geological Society of America.

Donnelly, Ignatius. 1976. *Atlantis: The Antediluvian World.* Repr., New York: Dover. (Orig. pub. 1882.)

Donnelly, Jeffrey P., et al. 2005. "Catastrophic Meltwater Discharge Down the Hudson Valley." *Geology* 33, no. 2 (February): 89–92.

Doreal, Maurice. 1939. *The Emerald Tablets of Thoth the Atlantean.* Sedalia, CO: Brotherhood of the White Temple.

Dunbavin, Paul. 1995. *The Atlantis Researches.* Nottingham: Third Millennium Publishing.

———. 2003. *Atlantis of the West.* New York: Carroll and Graf.

Duncan, Richard C. 2001. "World Energy Production, Population Growth, and the Road to the Olduvai Gorge." *Population and Environment* 22, no. 5 (May): 503–22.

———. 2006. "The Olduvai Theory: Energy, Population, and Industrial Civilization." *The Social Contract* 16, no. 2 (Winter): 134–44.

Edmundson, Munro S. 1988. *The Book of the Year: Middle American Calendrical Systems.* Provo: University of Utah Press.

Ellis, Richard. 1998. *Imagining Atlantis.* New York: Alfred A. Knopf.

Eriksen, Berit Valentin. 1996. "Resource Exploitation, Subsistence Strategies, and Adaptiveness in Late Pleistocene–Early Holocene Northwest Europe." In Straus et al. 1996, 101–28.

Fagan, Brian. 2004. *The Long Summer.* New York: Basic Books.

Ferro, Robert, and Michael Grumley. 1970. *Atlantis: The Autobiography of a Search.* New York: Bell.

Flem-Ath, Rand, and Rose Flem-Ath. 1995. *When the Sky Fell: In Search of Atlantis.* Toronto: Stoddart.

Flem-Ath, Rand, and Colin Wilson. 2000. *The Atlantis Blueprint.* New York: Little, Brown and Co.

Fortune, Dion [Violet Firth]. 1989. *Glastonbury: Avalon of the Heart.* Wellingborough, Northants.: Aquarian.

Frejer, B. Ernest. 1995. *The Edgar Cayce Companion.* Virginia Beach, VA: ARE Press.

Galanopoulos, A. G., and Edward Bacon. 1969. *Atlantis: The Truth Behind the Legend.* London: Nelson.

Galbraith, John Kenneth. 1992. *The Culture of Contentment.* Boston: Houghton Mifflin.

Gamble, C., and O. Soffer, eds. 1990. *The World at 18,000 BP: High Latitudes.* London: Unwin Hyman.

Gattuso, Dana Joel. 2006. "Kyoto's Anniversary: Little Reason to Celebrate." *National Policy Analysis* 537 (February). http://www.nationalcenter.org/NPA537EuropeKyoto206.html.

Godwin, Joscelyn. 1993. *Arktos: The Polar Myth in Science, Synmbolism, and Nazi Survival.* Grand Rapids, MI: Phanes.

———. 1994. *The Theosophical Enlightenment.* Albany, NY: State University of New York Press.

Godwin, Joscelyn, Christian Chanel, and John P. Deveney. 1995. *The Hermetic Brotherhood of Luxor.* York Beach, ME: Weiser.

Goodrick-Clarke, Nicholas. 1992. *The Occult Roots of Nazism: Secret Aryan Cults and Their Influence on Nazi Ideology.* New York: New York University Press.

———. 2002. *Black Sun: Aryan Cults, Esoteric Nazism and the Politics of Identity.* New York: New York University Press.

Greer, John Michael. 1998. *Inside a Magical Lodge.* St. Paul, MN: Llewellyn.

Haines, Tim, and Paul Chambers. 2006. *The Complete Guide to Prehistoric Life.* Buffalo, NY: Firefly.

Hallam, Tony. 2004. *Catastrophes and Lesser Calamities.* Oxford: Oxford University Press.

Hancock, Graham. 1995. *Fingerprints of the Gods.* New York: Crown.

———. 2002. *Underworld: The Mysterious Origins of Civilization.* London: Crown.

Hapgood, Charles. 1969. *Maps of the Ancient Sea Kings.* New York: Dutton.

Haynes, Gary. 1991. *Mammoths, Mastodonts, and Elephants: Biology, Behavior, and the Fossil Record.* Cambridge: Cambridge University Press.

Heinberg, Richard. 2002. *The Party's Over: Oil, War, and the Fate of Industrial Civilizations.* Burnaby, BC: New Society.

Heindel, Max [Carl Grashof]. 1909. *The Rosicrucian Cosmo-Conception.* Oceanside, CA: Rosicrucian Fellowship.

Hope, Murry. 1992. *Atlantis: Myth or Reality?* London: Arkana.

Huggett, Richard J. 1989. *Cataclysms and Earth History: The Development of Diluvialism.* Oxford: Clarendon Press.

Hunter, Robert. 2003. *Thermageddon.* New York: Arcade.

Jacobs, Margaret. 1988. *The Cultural Meaning of the Scientific Revolution.* Philadelphia: University of Pennsylvania Press.

Jarman, M. R., G. N. Bailey, and H. N. Jarman, eds. 1984. *Early European Agriculture.* Cambridge: Cambridge University Press.

Johnson, K. Paul. 1994. *The Masters Revealed: Madame Blavatsky and the Myth of the Great White Lodge.* Albany, NY: State University of New York Press.

———. 1998. *Edgar Cayce in Context.* Albany, NY: State University of New York Press.

Jowett, Benjamin. 1892. See Plato 1892.

Kafton-Minkel, Walter. 1989. *Underground Worlds.* Port Townsend, WA: Loompanics.

Kennett, J. P., K. G. Cannariato, I. L. Hendy, and R. J. Beh. 2002. *Methane Hydrates in Quaternary Climate Change: The Clathrate Gun Hypothesis.* Washington, DC: American Geophysical Union.

Khei, X° [George Winslow Plummer]. 1920. *Rosicrucian Fundamentals.* New York, NY: Flame Press.

King, David. 2005. *Finding Atlantis.* New York: Harmony Books.

Kingsley, Peter. 1989. *Ancient Philosophy, Mysticism and Magic.* Oxford: Oxford University Press.

Knight, Gareth. 2000. *Dion Fortune and the Inner Light.* Loughborough, Leics.: Thoth.

Leifer, I., B. Luyendyk, J. Boles, and J. Clark. 2006. "Natural Marine Seepage Blowout: Contribution to Atmospheric Methane." *Global Biogeochemical Cycles* 20 (3): GB3008.

Lemmen, Donald S., et al. 1994. "Later Glacial Drainage Systems along the Northwestern Margin of the Laurentide Ice Sheet." *Quaternary Science Review* 13: 805–28.

Lévi, Eliphas. 1972. *Transcendental Magic.* Trans. Arthur Edward Waite. York Beach, ME: Weiser.

Lewis, C. S. 1996. *That Hideous Strength.* New York: Scribners.

Lilly, William. 1647. *The World's Catastrophe.* London: John Partridge and Humphrey Blunden.

Lukacs, John. 1968. *Historical Consciousness.* New York: Harper & Row.

Lynas, Mark. 2004. *High Tide: The Truth About Our Climate Crisis.* New York: Picador.

Macdougall, Doug. 2004. *Frozen Earth: The Once and Future Story of Ice Ages.* Berkeley: University of California Press.

Mainzer, Klaus. 2002. *The Little Book of Time.* New York: Springer-Verlag.

Maslin, Mark, M. Owen, S. Day, and D. Long. 2004. "Linking Continental-Slope Failures and Climate Change: Testing the Clathrate Gun Hypothesis." *Geology* 32:53–56.

Mathers, S. L. MacGregor, et al. 1987. *Astral Projection, Ritual Magic, and Alchemy.* Rochester, VT: Destiny.

McCaffrey, Paul, ed. 2006. *Global Climate Change.* New York: H. W. Wilson.

McGuire, Bill. 2002. *A Guide to the End of the World.* Oxford: Oxford University Press.

Mertz, Henriette. 1976. *Atlantis: Dwelling Place of the Gods.* Chicago: Swallow Press.

Michell, John. 1969. *The View Over Atlantis.* New York: Ballantine.

Mithen, Steven. 2003. *After the Ice: A Global Human History, 20,000-5,000 BC.* Cambridge, MA: Harvard University Press.

Moser, Stephanie. 1998. *Ancestral Images: The Iconography of Human Origins.* Ithaca, NY: Cornell University Press.

Mowat, Farley. 1998. *The Farfarers.* South Royalton, VT: Steerforth.

Muck, Otto. 1978. *The Secret of Atlantis.* Trans. Fred Bradley. New York: Time Books.

Nahin, Paul. 1993. *Time Machines.* New York: Springer Verlag.

Nichols, Johanna. 1990. "Linguistic Diversity and the First Settlement of the New World." *Language* 66, no. 3 (Fall): 475–521.

Olsen, Christina. 1994. "Carta da Trionfi: The Development of Tarot in Fifteenth-Century Italy." PhD diss., University of Pennsylvania.

Oppenheimer, Stephen. 1998. *Eden in the East.* London: Weidenfeld and Nicolson.

Oreskes, Naomi. 1999. *The Rejection of Continental Drift.* Oxford: Oxford University Press.

Palmer, Trevor. 2003. *Perilous Planet Earth.* Cambridge: Cambridge University Press.

Parker, Barry R. 1991. *Cosmic Time Travel.* New York: Plenum.

Pearce, Fred. 2004. "Greenland Ice Cap 'Doomed to Meltdown.'" *New Scientist*, April 7. http://www.newscientist.com/article.ns?id=dn4864.

———. 2006. "Kyoto Promises Are Nothing but Hot Air." *New Scientist* 22 (June): 10.

Pielou, E. C. 1991. *After the Ice Age: The Return of Life to Glaciated North America.* Chicago: University of Chicago Press.

Plato. 1892. *The Dialogues of Plato.* Trans. Benjamin Jowett. Oxford: Clarendon Press.

Ponting, Clive. 1992. *A Green History of the World: The Environment and the Collapse of Great Civilizations.* New York: St. Martin's.

Ramage, Edwin S. 1978a. *Atlantis: Fact or Fiction?* Bloomington: Indiana University Press.

———. 1978b. "Perspectives Ancient and Modern." In Ramage 1978a, 3–48.

Ramaswamy, Sumathi. 2004. *The Lost Land of Lemuria: Fabulous Geographies, Catastrophic Histories.* Berkeley: University of California Press.

Ramsay, Raymond H. 1972. *No Longer on the Map.* New York: Viking Press.

Rao, S. R. 1999. *The Lost City of Dvaraka.* New Delhi: Aditya Prakashan.

Rather, L. J. 1979. *The Dream of Self-Destruction.* Baton Rouge: Louisiana State University Press.

Ravilious, Kate. 2005. "Skyscraper That May Cause Earthquakes." *Guardian*, December 2. http://www.guardian.co.uk/science/story/0,3605,1655977,00.html.

Regardie, Israel. 1971. *The Golden Dawn.* 4 vols. St. Paul, MN: Llewellyn.

Richardson, Alan. 1985. *Dancers to the Gods.* Wellingborough, Northants.: Aquarian.

Rohner, Ronald P., and Evelyn C. Rohner. 1986. *The Kwakiutl.* Prospect Heights, IL: Waveland.

Rudgley, Richard. 1999. *The Lost Civilizations of the Stone Age.* New York: Free Press.

Rue, Loyal D. 1989. *Amythia.* Tuscaloosa, AL: University of Alabama Press.

Russell, Jeffrey Burton. 1991. *Inventing the Flat Earth.* New York: Praeger.

Sarmast, Robert. 2006. *Discovery of Atlantis.* Los Angeles: First Source.

Schele, Linda, and David Freidel. 1993. *Maya Cosmos.* New York: Morrow.

Schwartz, Stephan A. 1978. *The Secret Vaults of Time.* New York: Grosset & Dunlap.

———. 1983. *The Alexandria Project.* New York: Delacorte.

Settegast, Mary. 1990. *Plato, Prehistorian.* Hudson, NY: Lindisfarne Press.

Severin, Tim. 2000. *The Brendan Voyage.* New York: Random House.

Shukman, David. 2004. "Greenland Ice Melt 'Speeding Up.'" *BBC News*, July 28. http://news.bbc.co.uk/2/hi/europe/3922579.stm.

Soffer, O., and C. Gamble, eds. 1990. *The World at 18,000 BP: Low Latitudes.* London: Unwin Hyman.

Spanuth, Jurgen. 1953. *Atlantis: The Mystery Unraveled.* New York: Citadel Press.

Spence, Lewis. 1968. *The History of Atlantis.* Repr., New York: University Books.

Straus, Lawrence Guy. 1996. "The Archaeology of the Pleistocene-Holocene Transition in Southwest Europe." In Straus et al. 1996, 83–99.

Straus, Lawrence Guy, Berit Valentin Eriksen, Jon M. Erlandsen, and David R. Yesner. 1996. *Humans at the End of the Ice Age: The Archaeology of the Pleistocene-Holocene Transition.* New York: Plenum Press.

Thomas, David Hurst. 2000. *Skull Wars.* New York: Basic Books.

Thompson, R. Campbell. 1900. *The Reports of the Magicians and Astrologers of Nineveh and Babylon in the British Museum.* 2 vols. London: n.p.

Thorndyke, Lynn. 1949. *The* Sphere of Sacrobosco *and Its Commentators.* Chicago: University of Chicago Press.

Timlett, Peter Valentine. 1974. *The Seedbearers.* New York: Bantam.

Tolkien, J. R. R. 1977. *The Silmarillion.* New York: Ballantine.

Trithemius, Johannes. 1647. "Of the Heavenly Intelligences" (English translation of *De Septem Secundeis* by William Lilly). In Lilly 1647, 42–56.

Tudge, Colin. 1998. *Neanderthals, Bandits and Farmers: The Origins of Agriculture.* New Haven, CT: Yale University Press.

Turner, Robert. 1998. *Ars Notoria.* Edmonds, WA: Holmes Publishing Group.

Verne, Jules. 1925. *Twenty Thousand Leagues Under the Sea.* New York: Charles Scribner's Sons.

Vitaliano, Dorothy. 1973. *Legends of the Earth: Their Geologic Origins.* Bloomington: Indiana University Press.

———. 1978. "Atlantis from the Geological Point of View." In Ramage 1978a, 137–60.

Waters, Frank. 1975. *Mexico Mystique.* Chicago: Swallow.

Wauchope, Robert. 1962. *Lost Tribes and Sunken Continents.* Chicago: University of Chicago Press.

Weaver, Andrew J., et al. 2003. "Meltwater Pulse 1A from Antarctica as a Trigger of the Alleröd-Bölling Warm Interval." *Science* 299, no. 5613 (March 14, 2003): 1709–13.

Webb, James. 1974. *The Occult Underground.* La Salle, IL: Open Court Press.

Wescott, David, ed. 1999. *Primitive Technology.* Layton, UT: Gibbs-Smith.

West, R. G. 1972. *Pleistocene Geology and Biology.* London: Longman.

Wolf, Fred Alan. 2004. *The Yoga of Time Travel.* Wheaton, IL: Quest.

Wright, Herbert J. 1978. "Glacial Fluctuations, Sea-level Changes, and Catastrophic Floods." In Ramage 1978a, 161–74.

Yates, Frances. 1969. *Theatre of the World*. Chicago: University of Chicago Press.

Yeats, William Butler. 1990. *A Vision and Related Writings*. London: Arena.

Zink, David. 1978. *The Stones of Atlantis*. New York: Prentice-Hall.

Index

adeptship, 36
Agharta, 85
akashic record, 220–21
albedo, 192, 237
Allen, Jim, 103
Alleröd phase, 134, 136, 138–39,
  143, 186, 198, 237
Amelius, 17, 22
America, as Atlantis, 33–34, 38, 45,
  184
Americas, settlement of, 166–67
Ammianus Marcellinus, 17
Ancient Mystical Order Rosae
  Crucis (AMORC), 59
Andrews, Shirley, 73
Andros Island, 169
Antarctica, 29, 31, 105, 112, 115,
  133, 135, 141, 150, 175, 194
Antilia, 29, 32–33, 90, 100
Aquarius, Age of, 20, 52
Ariosophy, 93–94
Aristocles, 8
Aristotle, 16, 18, 25
Arktogäa, 94
Ars Notoria, 63
Arrhenius, Svante, 204
Ashurbanipal, 19
Association for Research and
  Enlightenment (ARE), 182–83

astral light, 64, 220–222, 234
Atlantic phase, 135, 237
Atlantology, 73, 80, 88, 95–96, 98–
  99, 106, 111, 113, 116, 179, 186,
  205, 237
atlatl, 153
Avalon, 30, 178
Aztecs, 34–35, 157, 178

Bailly, Jean-Sylvain, 99
Bering Land Bridge, 87, 165–66,
  171
Berossus, 21–22, 34
Besant, Annie, 57
Bimini, 169–70, 182–83
Bimini Road, 169, 182–83
Blavatsky, Helena Petrovna, 41–51,
  53–58, 61–62, 64, 69, 71–75, 77,
  80, 83, 88–89, 93–94, 106, 111–
  12, 150, 185–87, 204–6, 208–11
Bölling phase, 134, 138, 140, 142,
  237
Bond, Frederick Bligh, 218–19
Boreal phase, 135–36, 142–43, 145,
  150, 160–61, 163, 168, 170, 175,
  178, 185, 192–93, 237–39
Brasseur de Bourbourg, Charles-
  Etienne, 94–95
Bretz, J. Harlan, 137–39

To Write to the Author

If you wish to contact the author or would like more information about this book, please write to the author in care of Llewellyn Worldwide and we will forward your request. Both the author and publisher appreciate hearing from you and learning of your enjoyment of this book and how it has helped you. Llewellyn Worldwide cannot guarantee that every letter written to the author can be answered, but all will be forwarded. Please write to:

John Michael Greer
℅ Llewellyn Worldwide
2143 Wooddale Drive, Dept. 978-0-7387-0978-9
Woodbury, MN 55125-2989, U.S.A.
Please enclose a self-addressed stamped envelope for reply,
or $1.00 to cover costs. If outside U.S.A., enclose
international postal reply coupon.

Many of Llewellyn's authors have websites with additional information and resources. For more information, please visit our website at:

www.llewellyn.com